MILDRED
ON THE MARNE

MILDRED ON THE MARNE

MILDRED ALDRICH
FRONT-LINE WITNESS 1914–1918

DAVID SLATTERY-CHRISTY

Informed by the letters, diaries, journals and memoirs of
Mildred Aldrich 1853–1928
Chevalier de la Légion d'Honneur Nationale
De la République Française

First published 2013 by
Spellmount, an imprint of

The History Press
The Mill, Brimscombe Port
Stroud, Gloucestershire, GL5 2QG
www.thehistorypress.co.uk

British Library Cataloguing in Publication Data.
A catalogue record for this book is available from the British
Library.

ISBN 978 0 7524 9768 6

Typesetting and origination by The History Press
Printed in Great Britain

CONTENTS

In memory of my grandfathers – who both fought in the Great War 1914–18 – my father and stepfather, and members of my extended family, who all shared their memories of two world wars with me. Their experiences and first-hand accounts of both world wars enabled me to understand the sacrifices they made willingly for future generations.

Joseph John Slattery (1886–1974), Irish Guards
Walter Edward Reginald Pratley (1896–1939), Royal Berkshire Regiment
Leslie John Slattery (1921–96), Royal Berkshire Regiment
Patrick Walter Slattery (1922–67), Royal Air Force
Alec Aveyard (1919–2012), Royal Engineers (REME)
Harold Greenwood (1887–1961), Gunner, Lancashire Fusiliers
Harry Greenwood (1917–2008), Transport Corps, Lancashire Fusiliers

For my friend Alan Bardsley, who was so enthusiastic and supportive of this project, and the proposed revival in 2014 of my stage play *Forever Nineteen*, based on Mildred's experiences, for which he had started constructing brilliant designs. Also Major James Houldsworth for his quiet determination, influence and friendship. Taken too soon, sadly missed.

We will remember them.

INTRODUCTION

A LONG JOURNEY

It is more than twenty years since I first discovered Mildred's remarkable story. In the early 1990s I was researching an idea for a stage play based on my paternal grandfather, Joseph John Slattery, and his experiences of the Great War. He joined the Irish Guards in 1914 and was from Clon Mel, Tipperary, Ireland. He was sent to Gallipoli and later to France and survived. It was whilst undertaking this research that a vague mention was made of an elderly American lady who retired to a hilltop overlooking the Marne Valley, France, from where she experienced the first major battle of the war, which stopped the Germans from taking Paris. I was hooked and had to know more about her.

Forever Nineteen, the play I created, was set in Mildred's house, La Creste, and told the story of how she stayed to help the British soldiers and how she coped when the Germans marched up her hill. The play went on to tour in the United Kingdom, where it played to packed houses at Manchester City of Drama and both the Buxton Festival and Edinburgh Festival. It even had a small production in New York. It received an award alongside *Les Misérables* in Manchester in 1993 – Mildred mentions Jean Valjean and Cossette, and Victor Hugo's book. The French connection continues and illuminates Mildred's foray into Edwardian theatre.

It always puzzled me why Mildred had been forgotten and so little was known about her. Perhaps the reason behind this was because she died in 1928, just before the great economic crash and depression, and then the rise of Hitler's Nazi Germany. The subsequent outbreak of the Second World War pushed her remarkable story into a darkened corner of the twentieth century's archive of history. It languished there for nearly a hundred years. It is time it was brought into the light, dusted off and appreciated once again.

My hope is that the publication of the story of this remarkable woman will bring her a new legion of admirers in the twenty-first century and, at the very least, will honour her with the respect her deeds in the Great War so justly deserve. Her letters, diary and journal, which outlined her intended autobiography (that was never actually published), along with her published books of letters from 1915 to 1919, have informed this biography. Her voice is strong and still shines through. She had great foresight and thought of us here in the future way back then.

You could say then that this book has been more than twenty years in the making – certainly so if you allow for all the years between *Forever Nineteen* and undertaking final research at the Schlesinger Library, Harvard University, which kindly gave me permission to use Mildred's papers, to produce this book in time for the hundredth anniversary of the start of the Great War in 2014. My admiration for her achievements and her courage knows no bounds. I hope she would have approved and consider I have done her justice.

David Slattery-Christy

ACKNOWLEDGEMENTS

Special thanks to:
Ellen Aveyard; Allan Bardsley; Beinecke Library, Yale University; Eric Bogle; Meryl Bruen; Nica Burns; Nicki Casey; Eve Flint; Richard Kenneth French; Bill Greenwood; Graham Greenwood; Harvard Student Agencies (Research); Michael Harvey; Major James Houldsworth; Sarah Hutcheon – Harvard University; Gareth Johnson Ltd; Michael Lawson; Jenny Le – Harvard University HSA; Lyn Macdonald; Frederic Marchal; Lynn Nortcliff; Olivier Richomme; Rosy Runciman; Ellen M. Shea – Schlesinger Library; Florence Emily Slattery; Robert Smith Literary Agency; Schlesinger Library, Harvard University; John Ulrich – Harvard University HSA; Lee Wosltenholme; Eva Wrightson – Beinecke Library; Office of the Légion d'Honneur, Paris

Thanks to all my family and friends for putting up with my constant discussions about Mildred and the Great War. Not forgetting my mother for patiently reading and commenting on all the draft chapters.

This book would not have been possible without the kind permission of the Schlesinger Library, Harvard University, which allowed me to freely use previously unpublished documents and memoirs relating to and created by Mildred Aldrich held in its archive. The library staff and research assistants there were beyond compare and I thank them for their patience and courteous, efficient help at all times. It would also be fair to say that Mildred herself, by creating collections of letters to friends, and publishing them during the Great War, has brought that time to life, and given me an invaluable source of letters and documents to influence her story.

Finally I would like to thank author and historian Lyn Macdonald and her book *1914*, which first brought Mildred to my attention many years ago. In a note to me she mentioned the differences a century on and the irony of another famous American moving close by – but with different consequences for those now living in the area:

> Miss Aldrich did indeed have an exciting war – her house is still there and the village and surroundings much as she described them despite the encroachment of Euro Disney a few miles away.
>
> Lyn Macdonald

1

DRUM BEATS AND DESTINY

Then suddenly one day the miracle happened – once again,
unannounced, the Giant Hands came out of the clouds,
and lifted me to a hilltop, and to my supreme adventure.

Mildred Aldrich

On a very cold, wintry but sunny November day in 1913, in northern France, a self-proclaimed 'aged' American lady stepped off the train at a small branch line at Esbly, near Voisons, a few miles outside of Paris. Mildred Aldrich was 60 on the sixteenth of that very month and she had come to view another potential retirement home, one that perhaps this time she could both like and afford – and more importantly one that would suit her needs, modest as she considered them to be.

Mildred had lived in Paris since 1898, where she had arrived from Boston, Massachusetts, with dreams and desires to continue to make a living as a journalist and writer. As a woman devoid of youth, unmarried and working in a world dominated by powerful men, her journey was far from easy and certainly not successful in any financial sense – although she did write as foreign correspondent for the *Boston Herald* and *The New York Times* for a period. However, this was a world where an unmarried career-driven woman was viewed with some suspicion. That a woman should want any kind of career apart from accepting a suitable husband and becoming respectably married was generally frowned on in the Victorian and Edwardian eras. Mildred let them all frown as much as they pleased; she was determined to march to the beat of her own drum.

Drums of another kind were also beating hard, following their allotted course and becoming more and more audible across the wider European continent in late 1913. The conflicts in the Balkans were getting out of control and the German Kaiser, Wilhelm II, was already planning his next move to take advantage of these ever-shifting and unstable political sands. The warning sound of those determined and ever-louder beating drums would very soon turn into the rattle of guns, bringing with them the stench of fear, turmoil and death, and changing the world forever.

A century later it is hard for us to imagine how age was perceived in 1913. Today, at the age of 60, Mildred would not be seen as an 'aged' woman at all, and certainly not someone who should be content to retire and feel her life was over because she seemingly had nothing useful left to offer or give to the world. Mildred herself stated that:

> In spite of everything I was still tremendously interested in life – it was still to me a great show. But I was weary, and no longer physically strong. I was nearing the age when women who are not already successful don't achieve much of importance. In my youth women of my world were usually grandmothers at sixty, and put on silk frocks and muslin fichus and lace caps, and sat at the fireside and knitted, with nothing to do but wait for the end.

There was to be no cosy fireside decline for Mildred. She was as yet oblivious to the fact that destiny was manoeuvring her to a particular place at the 'right' time, and that what she perceived as the beginning of the end of her life was in fact just the beginning of its most important phase, personally and creatively. Everything that happened before this was just a prelude for Mildred. Her most important role in history was about to unfold. Like the iceberg that had recently drifted towards the on-coming *Titanic*, Mildred drifted into the epicentre of what would arguably be the most catastrophic event in twentieth-century history. 'What I really wanted was peace and quiet. But I had not earned them,' declared Mildred in 1913. She was also only too aware of how desperate her financial situation had become – destitution was a real and worrying possibility:

It had been a stock joke among my friends who had known me longest that I should, of course, end up in the 'poor house', and they took great delight in telling me that I would be the 'star boarder' and 'hold a salon' and that they would all travel great distances to see me on my 'reception days'. I enjoyed the joke when I was younger, and laughed as heartily as any of them. But the time came when it ceased to be a pleasant joke, but the habit of laughing at it persisted.

Mildred had, during her time living in Paris, been associated with the great and good of the arts and literature, such as Thornton Wilder, Picasso, Mira Edgerly, the Irish novelist James Stephens and later a youthful Ernest Hemingway. Mildred was also a close friend to Gertrude Stein, her brother Leo, and Gertrude's partner Alice B. Toklas, and was thus a frequent visitor to their salons. It was these influential friends who turned out to be her financial saviours, enabling her to seek out that retirement home she secretly yearned for. Mildred's health problems arose partly through her love of cigarettes and especially the Egyptian black tobacco brand she favoured; her heart problems and breathlessness were a direct result of, or at the very least exacerbated by, this destructive habit. She was therefore very aware that she possessed no skills aside from her writing talent that would garner her any employment. She could no longer clean, cook or do anything domestic, or ever could beyond basic requirements. Besides, this work could be better done by other women, usually half her age, of which there were plenty looking for suitable *femme de menage* positions. If anything, and much to Mildred's annoyance, she would need the services of domestic help herself – a fact that irritated her fierce, independent spirit. Mildred was a feisty and determined woman who faced up to her physical problems; she would not give in to the vagaries of life, ever. 'My head was more than tired – my memory was failing – which was very serious,' declared Mildred in an attempt to face her fears head on. It would seem this was just what is accepted today as normal forgetfulness, but it was perceived by Mildred in her time as the creeping up of an 'aged' affliction that confirmed her inability to work or be useful to the world:

I remember things long past. Details of yesterday and today faded almost without any registering at all. That was disastrous. Then in the spring of 1912 a bad attack of bronchitis confined me to the house for weeks, and always after that it was difficult for me to climb my five flights of stairs and my doctor began to quietly insinuate into my mind the idea that I ought to be preparing to simplify my life – to find some way of living which would enable me to get more air and out-of-doors life than was possible to me living in a city, way up in the air, although I did have a balcony.

At first she derided and dismissed this implausible suggestion and, as was her way, heartily laughed it off as absurd. Besides, she had neither the means nor the inclination to leave Paris. It would, she mused privately, be nice to be able to have a garden, and more open space and fresh air in which to potter away her days, but she would not even consider returning to Boston and would always have to stay at least near Paris. How near or far seemed irrelevant because the financial situation put paid to any thoughts of a proper retirement.

In spite of her doubts and fears for the future, Mildred, to her credit, remained outwardly optimistic, as was her inclination when faced with life's unpleasant surprises. She had many times come to accept the slings and arrows of fate upon her life and had made the most of all the good, and learned – or tried to – from all the bad. She attempted at all times to see the positive wherever possible. Her instinct when faced with this well-intentioned doctor's advice was to rebel and throw caution to the wind, to take up her sturdy walking stick and march off into the French countryside, her favourite books in her satchel, and to live amidst nature under the stars as she walked and explored the endless beauty of that countryside. Her fantasy was quickly dashed aside when, on telling her doctor this delusional plan, he laughed uproariously and declared, 'You'd better keep to flat country. You can't climb hills, and how far do you think you would go before someone gave you a lift?'

'That reminded me,' reflected a dejected Mildred, 'of what Ellen Terry had said so many years before – that if she had her life to live over again, when things went wrong she would just lie down and scream – and that if one kicked hard enough, and screamed loud enough, one was sure to be picked up. But that was not at all what I wanted. I was ready to do almost anything except scream.'

Thankfully for us Mildred didn't scream. She began to find herself, and her sturdy determination once again prevailed. She decided to at least discuss the possibility and to start to look for somewhere she could live happily for her last years. She also began to write about and document this new phase of her life. Her diary and journal entries have brought her voice to life again and she can be heard clearly. Mildred's voice, through her writing, will thankfully contribute considerably to this account of her life – a life that would not have been that remarkable had she not found herself on that path with destiny where she would meet head on the Great War. It is what she would later recall, with some resigned amusement, a moment of unexpected salvation, when 'suddenly one day the miracle happened – once again, unannounced, the Giant Hands came out of the clouds, and lifted me to a hilltop, and to my supreme adventure'.

Before she arrived at that hilltop, for that adventure, Mildred spent time reflecting on her life and her years in Paris – she also admonished herself for not taking her doctor's advice seriously, at least initially. But it made her think and it made her start to appreciate the past and the life she had enjoyed thus far. Her love of Paris and the French was paramount to her:

I had had all that Paris had to give me. Nothing could ever take that from me. My memories were my sacred possessions. I was conscious of not having wasted my time in Paris. I had kept myself alive and interested in my hardest hours by walking the streets (in the twelve years that walking had been possible for me) with all the writers and artistes who had loved Paris and immortalised it. I knew the Paris of all the historical periods. I had hunted out every inch that remained of her old walls. I knew the Paris of Victor Hugo's Notre-Dame and all its errors. I knew the Paris of the romances of Dumas, and Balzac. I had wandered all over the left bank with Huysmans when I was reading Là-Bas and En Route, just as I had read La Cathédrale at Chartres. I had made all the day trips from Paris that were possible in every direction – not only the usual trips that every visitor to France knows, but Senlis, Étampes, Provins, Marly and Louveciennes, St. Leu, Ermonville and Montmorency, Pontoise and Montlery, and all the beautiful valley of Chevreuse from St. Rémy to the Abbaye of Cernay, and I had climbed on foot to the Hermitage St Sauveur, above Limay, across the river from Mantes. All this was in the days before automobiles opened up so many of these places to the traveller by road. My experience is that even now the ordinary tourist knows but little more about such places, than their names and sorts of food one can get. Getting from one place to another in a fixed length of time is altogether different from walking the road as we used to do in my day.

Mildred's passion and love of her adopted country shines through and her voice comes alive again when she recalls her many adventures in Paris and in those last days living in the city. She recalled with delight her meeting with the Irish novelist James Stephens. His novel, *The Crock of Gold*, had enchanted and enthralled her and she was quick to enthuse about his talents to her friends – and indeed anyone else who cared to listen. Mildred was overjoyed to be able eventually to call him a friend.

'I am never likely to forget my first reading of that whimsical book – so full of humour and fancy wisdom and charm,' wrote Mildred, going on to explain, 'I had a friend stopping with me at the time – and I remember how I could not resist sharing my delight of almost every page – and how I gloated over the Irish form of the phrases almost as much as I did over the humour of the book.'

Mildred had been introduced to Stephens by mutual friends from Dublin, who first wrote to her and told her that Stephens and his family were coming to Paris in the spring of 1913. They requested that she meet them and show them something of the city. Meeting and spending time with Stephens and his family was the happiest experience of what turned out to be the final months Mildred would live in Paris:

> He is not only a poet – he is a great soul, and sometimes, if the spirit moves him to tell the story of the road by which he came into his own, as he told it to me as we sat on the terrace of the Lilas one afternoon, it will be one of the most moving documents in the history of the marching on to destiny of a lonely and abandoned boy on whose brow Art, in most untoward circumstances, laid her royal accolade.

That Stephens had endured a poverty-stricken existence growing up in Ireland is fairly well documented, but Mildred finds a romance in these facts that at times borders on the sentimental and overshadows her real appreciation of Stephens as a writer of note. One suspects from her sometimes gushing praise that she was a little star-struck by him and easily seduced by his engaging 'Irishness', which Stephens was adept at exuding to suit his audience. It was a quality he possessed that she admired; one that perhaps reminded Mildred of those old-fashioned, paternalistic values she had experienced growing up in Boston several decades before. She was smitten and didn't care who knew about it:

> Those who saw him in America know something of what he is like – and that he is just like his books – more so than any other writer that I know. The same sort of burr of the pure Irish, which the form of his sentences and his use of words puts on his writing – and his English is exquisite – hangs on his spoken words and gives it its charm. He has not a Brogue, really – it is better than that – but oh, he is so Irish.

Mildred goes on to consider, rather dreamily, if anyone had ever 'remarked how strangely he suggested the Westall portrait of Byron – the same brow, the same line of chin, the same retreating of the curly hair on the temples – the one so beautiful – the other the reverse – but the resemblance is there'. Talented as Stephens undoubtedly was, Byron he was not, and this appraisal seems to mock his less than beautiful features and outward appearance. However, Stephens would meet Mildred again a few months later. This time he would visit her in the house she would find on the hill – just before the shadow and sound of the guns would stampede across the French countryside in the autumn of 1914.

Mildred, determined to be positive in the task, found herself exasperated whilst house hunting. She held out no great hope for the house she had been asked to look over at Huiry, overlooking the Marne Valley, less than 20 miles from Paris. As she climbed into the little *diligence* carriage, harnessed to a rather grumpy and weary-looking donkey, she started off on what she anticipated would be a rather jerky and uncomfortable journey to the top of the hill. Cold and somewhat miserable, she could only keep an open mind and count her blessings. Such as they were, she mused.

Gertrude Stein had told Mildred that a pension was possible, even for her. Mildred at first found the suggestion abhorrent lest it erode her firmly defended independence. Eventually though she found herself taking the offer a little more seriously. She had little choice in the matter, which irked her more if she chose to admit it. 'One day Gertrude asked me what I would do if I could do just what I wanted. She had a mania for trying to sort out the lives of other people, so

I answered her, after a bit of reflecting.' One can imagine that initially Mildred perhaps humoured Stein and did not reply with total sincerity – a fact that is borne out in her rather flighty reply:

> I should like nothing better, if it were possible – which it were not – than to retire from the world, and live out the rest of my life in some quiet place, where I should no longer have the need to keep up appearances – see no one except the few friends who cared enough to make a great effort – have no social duties – not feel any need to know what the prevailing shape of sleeves was – and, in finding rest, perhaps find peace – and in that peace – if I found it – who knew what might happen?

Mildred was then astounded to be told by Stein that all this was indeed possible. Mildred declared that, 'I was at an age when many people, who had chosen as I had the worst paid career [as a writer] in the world ... and that [after all] I could have a small pension.' She seemed genuinely startled and was, probably for the first time in her life, truly speechless. Stein seems to have enjoyed the role of fixer for her friend, but she still had to work at Mildred to make her see it as genuine and acceptable with no loss of pride or independence:

> Then I was reminded [by Stein] that that sort of aid had been extended to some very famous men and women just as proud as I was, to the everlasting honor [*sic*] of those, who by good luck or successful labor [*sic*], had a more than ordinary share of the world's goods. That argument was not sound to me. I saw no grounds on which I was entitled to it.

Her main worry was the thought of taking money from someone and being a burden to them – perhaps even feeling she would become their responsibility in time. That she didn't really grasp the concept of the pension at first suggestion is obvious. It also worried her that the benefactor was anonymous – this no doubt added an element of mystery and perhaps suspicion in her mind:

> I was told that [the benefactor's identity] was not my affair – if anyone able to do the pensioning chose to do it – that it was only the interest on a modest sum to be paid to me during my life, the principal to return

to the person [or persons] in question on my death – that therefore the sacrifice was only that of the interest on the investment during my life – that there was no obligation – that I need never know from whom it came – or know anyone in the matter except the bank, which would regularly send me the money every month.

Mildred spent time thinking about this offer and looking at it from all angles, finally making a decision. 'It was a long argument – and, at the end, it was the old law, – self preservation. I really did not know what else to do. It is difficult to make this part of my confession – but I did have a feeling that I must always thank God for the unexpected, especially when it meant escape from disaster.' Disaster it would certainly have been, because without the pension Mildred would have been destitute and homeless; there was no welfare system to step in and support her.

It was never made clear to Mildred that the pension was provided partly by Stein. It is also likely that Stein was the proposer of the idea and behind the scenes the investment that provided Mildred with a modest monthly pension was put together by an artist friend, Mira Edgerly, along with others, as a way of helping her without her feeling in any way obliged to them. Edgerly was a fellow American in Paris and had been herself encouraged by John Singer Sargent to continue painting – her speciality was portraiture on small ivory panels.

'Although I had achieved success as a miniature painter,' recalled Edgerly:

I became more and more impressed with its limitations, and I rebelled against the limitations of conventional thinking … True I had the inspiration of the superb breadth and dignity of Holbein's works and those small portraits of Cromwell by Cooper so justly called 'life sized and little', but the desire to include groups and full length likenesses brought me to go on and develop this entirely individual contribution in portrait-painting. Shortly after this came the comment of John Sargent, the turning point of my career … with renewed energy and confidence I attacked the resistance of conventions and the handicap of standardised miniature techniques.

Mildred had originally introduced Edgerly to Stein and encouraged her inclusion into the Paris salon set. Edgerly was lucky to be financially wealthy and could spend her time developing her talent without financial worries. That said, she remained a loyal friend. Mildred had no idea Edgerly and Stein were responsible for her pension.

It is also an indicator of the esteem in which Mildred was held amongst her friends at that time. Little did they realise they too were being drawn into and aiding the plans destiny had in store for Mildred. The peace and quiet she hoped for would be far removed from the reality of the situation she would find herself in. That was to come. She now had to focus on actually finding a suitable house. The search was well and truly on!

With suggestions from various friends she began to consider the possibilities. What became apparent early on was the cost and how she would have to widen her search to several miles beyond her beloved Paris. The rents, as with her current apartment, were far too high and would be impossible to meet when living expenses were added. There was no doubt that, generous as the pension was, it was meagre in terms of what it was able to provide. However, in spite of any setbacks, Mildred ploughed on with her search, honestly believing that out there somewhere was something suitable for her needs:

I had thought it had simply to be a house in the country – no matter where, provided it was not too far from the active world, and that the rent very cheap. But I had not been searching long before I was reminded that a leopard does not change its spots nor a woman her character. I wanted a place in the quiet and retirement of the country, but I did not want just any old place – I wanted a place that I could love at first sight. Also I was troubled by the fact that although I had been in Europe for sixteen years, I still reckoned values in dollars and cents ... Francs don't mean anything to me.

Fortunately Mildred had French friends who insisted on giving her a helping hand and also asked her to do nothing without them present – the French system where leases, rents and property matters generally are concerned tended to be complex and bewildering to the unfamiliar. The *Code Napoléon* was a minefield where family ownership rights were concerned, as she would soon find out.

'The first place I saw that I liked,' continued Mildred in her journal:

I found myself. I did not think it was far enough off [out of Paris] – but I loved it at first sight. It was a little house at Viroflay ... It was high up on the hill above the [river] Seine, with the heights of Meudon and St. Cloud on the other side. A winding country road wound up to it, and the long white house stretched along the narrow street. I saw the two-storey front with its eight windows filled with boxes of ivy geraniums trailing their pink blossoms. The front door on the street level opened onto the landing in the middle of the staircase and one half descended to the kitchen and dining room and the garden and the other mounted to the salon and bedrooms. The salon was a long room extending right through the whole depth of the house from the street to the garden and had two windows at either end – a lovely room of great possibilities.

Mildred seemed to connect with this house but the problem lay with its location and small garden – which allowed for little in the way of food growing and keeping chickens for eggs, although it was not completely devoid of potential. That said it had serious security issues for a woman intending to live alone:

> The garden was walled – in great disorder, but as inspiring with possibilities as was the salon – but on the other side of the wall ran the railway to Versailles – it was only twenty minutes' walk there by road. I thought I wanted it at once, but it was vetoed – first because it was too accessible – right on the road travelled by the tramps from Paris; second, because the rent – 900 francs (then the value of 180 dollars a year, 15 dollars a month) – was pronounced too much for my means. I abandoned the idea at once.

Her French friends no doubt had her safety in mind and would have advised against the house even if it had been financially viable, which clearly it wasn't. Mildred was unfazed by this initial disappointment and continued her search. However, her new found enthusiasm quickly waned.

> Then a place near Rambouillet – an hour from there through the forest by diligence [carriage] was suggested. It was part of the country which I did not know. It was a tiny house of three rooms, with a tinier garden. It had no outlook at all – but the rent of only 180 francs a year – the value then of 36 dollars a year – three dollars a month – 75 cents a week. I did not like it at all. It said nothing to me

except 'shelter'. Still if shelter was to be had at that figure I expected that it was my duty to take it.

Her obvious lack of enthusiasm casts a gloom over her recollection and one suspects that even Mildred, a slave to her limited resources, would have rather foregone shelter of any kind rather than compromise and accept that particular house – cheap as the rent may have been. Her saviour turned out to be the owners of the property recalled a rather relieved Mildred: 'I was willing, but the gods were not. The proprietor was anything but agreeable and it was impossible for us to come to an agreement regarding the long lease I wanted.'

So there ended yet another chapter in the search for a house. Mildred pondered these thoughts and wondered what awaited her at the top of this hill, as she was jolted along in the cart pulled by a grumpy donkey whose name she now knew was Ninette. Odd name for a donkey, she thought. As they trundled up the hill to Huiry, the surrounding land-scape began to reveal itself and suddenly the air and space became inviting and invigorating – as did the view.

Her artist friend, Mira Edgerly, had originally found the house on the hilltop at Huiry and discovered it was for sale. It was in a tiny hamlet on the left bank of the Marne, just a few miles from the cathedral town of Meaux. Mildred's reaction on first seeing the house, La Creste, was to agree with her friend that it did indeed have 'a picturesque jumble of roofs' and she described her first reaction on seeing the house thus:

I tumbled in adoration before the site and outlook – I always loved space and air … It stood – that jumble of six gable roofs – almost at the top of the hill. A little over a mile to the north flowed the Marne, and about the same distance to the south the Grand Morin hurried to flow into it. It was isolated, and it was not. It stood on a little road which ran across the fields from one river to the other – hardly more than a rough cart road for farm wagons. There was one house opposite. Above it half a dozen houses constituted the hamlet of Huiry, only two houses of which were visible, and a quarter of a mile down the hill was a street of houses which composed a little village calling itself at the east end, Voisins, at the west Joncheroy. It was isolated being the first or last house in the hamlet – according to the direction from which it was approached.

Mildred had an overwhelming sense of destiny that day, for reasons that baffled her and made no sense at all. Amidst the confusion in her mind she attempted to explain her feelings:

> There was no doubt in my mind the moment I stood on the spot. It was my house. If it had been made for me the place could not have suited me better. I felt that I had lived sixty years just to arrive there. The rent was 250 francs a year – the value of 50 dollars – less than a dollar a week. I felt that no one could find fault with that.

It transpired that Mildred's 'artist friend', whom she never named but it seems highly likely was Mira Edgerly, wanted to buy the house if Mildred liked it and let her have it on a lifetime lease at a small rent. She would then live in it herself once she retook possession, although Mildred declared that, 'with my [family's] tendency to long life she would be kept waiting!' No matter; Mildred agreed and she went ahead with the purchase.

Although ideal in most ways, Mildred, practical as ever, declared there was one drawback to the house:

> The house was not habitable. I did not think about that at once. I saw it first on a dry sunny day. The next time I saw it – it was a chilly rainy day. I knew then, that while it would do admirably for a summer retreat, and a picknicky life, it would do anything but well for an elderly woman, far from well, as an all-the-year-round residence – her only home. My common sense saw it as a risky venture. But risky or not, I was going to chance it.

Once these practical matters were addressed and the property purchased, Mildred faced the future with a newfound confidence and couldn't wait to start making La Creste her own:

> The house looked larger than it was. It consisted of but two rooms that were habitable – a living room – the once white-washed walls and rafters of which were smoked, stained and smeared with the damp and soot of many years – and up a walled staircase of plaster and rubble, the treads of which were worn away in the middle, a very small bedroom with still smaller room which could serve as a dressing room.

There was a dark double room opening from the west side of the living room, where I was told chickens and rabbits had once lived, and on the south side of the same room, extended under its own gable roof, what had once been the home of the cow, over the earth floor of which had been laid flooring of loose planks already well rotted.

There was no kitchen of any sort – the living room had been a real 'living room' for those who had occupied the house – they had cooked in it, and slept in it. It was in fact probably the only part of the house that had ever been lived in, except in summer. For that matter, so far as I could learn, the house had not been lived in for some years in winter.

All the rest of the picturesque jumble of buildings consisted of lofts (only reached from the outside by ladders and pulleys) and sheds – what the French call granges. There was one attached to the south-west side of the house, and another to the north-east, and between the main house and the latter there was a dilapidated lean-to, without door or windows, and with pitched roof already falling in. The only ingress was a hole about three feet square. What it had been originally used for I never knew – evidently as a place to throw debris.

The funny thing was that not all the six gables belonged to the same family. This is one of the results of the code Napoléon, and the equal distribution of a heritage among all the children. The grange at the south-west side was a separate piece of property, and the friend who had discovered the place purchased that to have a hold on the place.

Mildred had misgivings. She managed to silence them but later recalled how 'they all came back to me, and when I had to shake myself very sharply to rid myself of a tendency to accept the affair as foredained [*sic*].' With hindsight, once the war started in August 1914, Mildred would of course wonder if it was all just meant to be – her fate – her destiny.

However, that was as yet in the future. She now needed to think about how she was going to refurbish the house and make it habitable. She resigned herself to renovating perhaps just the main living room, and using that until such time as finances would allow her to complete other rooms. She was lucky in that she had furniture in her Paris apartment that would fit in her new home. In the habit of writing to an old friend in Boston, her tales of acquiring La Creste were no exception:

In the meantime – from the first idea of leaving Paris had entered my mind I had written to my American friend, to whom all my life I had had the habit of telling almost everything – not everything – never the worst – I kept that for myself. So sometime before the lease was ready, he knew all about the place [La Creste], and exactly what I thought. Then one day I got a letter from him telling me that he viewed with many misgivings my retirement from my scene of activities [in Paris], but adding:

'If you are determined to do it, I suppose you must, but not until the little shanty has been made comfortable. You see, if you outlive me, you will be a little better off than you are now. I have meant, for a long time, to tell you this. If you should die before I do, I should always regret that you had missed your tiny heritage. So all things considered - your age among others – I don't see why you should not have a part of it now, and let me have the joy – while I am living – of seeing you play with it. So go ahead with your game and make the place habitable. Of course you are quite mad – but thy will be done!'

For Mildred it was another miracle of good fortune, one which would allow her to renovate the complete house before moving in. 'So that is how it happened,' she enthused, 'that one cold Sunday in January 1914 I found myself standing on the hilltop at Huiry, with a lease in one hand and a cheque in the other, and the feeling of "I am monarch of all I survey in my soul" while the village mason and carpenter stood in front of me, waiting for me to open the door with a huge key and tell them what I wanted done.' Reality would soon bring her back to earth with a bump.

Making the journey up the hill again in that rickety, uncomfortable *diligence* carriage, she experienced the harshness of the exposed French countryside in winter. It chilled Mildred to the bone, the damp creating an ache in her joints she could never recall experiencing before – made worse by attempting to walk through the treacle-like mud surrounding the house, a walk that exhausted her. The mud and filth that swamped the house sucked and cloyed at her boots as if trying to drag her beneath its slimy surface. There were pools of water knee-high, as the site, and house, had never had adequate drainage to deal with the waste rainwater. It was perilous, miserable and the most attractive but unattractive house she had ever seen. She was determined to find its soul and restore its dignity – even if along the way she feared losing sight of her own. Something drove Mildred on, something even she didn't understand fully.

As Mildred started the renovations to the house she would also start to appreciate the view across the Marne Valley from her elevated position at Huiry. Looking at the panorama before her, little did she realise that it would not be so beautiful and peaceful for much longer. Had she been able to see far off into the distance, past Belgium and into Holland, she would have seen the newly completed Peace Palace in The Hague, paid for with money donated by the steel magnate, and fellow American, Guggenheim, and completed only weeks before in 1913. In theory, this was a place where heads of government could meet and talk and ensure peace would prevail in Europe and the wider world. Sadly, Kaiser Wilhelm had other ideas and his drum beats for war were becoming louder and louder as 1914 progressed. Sarajevo and an assassination would create a massive shifting of the political sands.

The constant talk of war and the unstable political situation in the Balkans created an atmosphere of great uncertainty and fear among all her friends, and the speculation in the press was unbearable. All this talk of war brought to mind another war for Mildred, a war that had raged and torn apart her own country several decades before. That was called the Civil War – how can any war be called civil, Mildred wondered at the time. She also remembered the Siege of Paris in 1871 and how it ended the Franco-Prussian War. Bismarck's newly unified Germany was the victor and it held France under its steely heel. It seemed inconceivable to her that there would be another war to endure in 1914. When war broke out, it would put Mildred, and her new house, La Creste, in the path of the invading German army as they marched on Paris.

2

YANKEE, ABOLITIONIST AND PATRIOT

I have always called myself a Bostonian …
although English blood ran in my veins …

Mildred Aldrich

Mildred had never married and had come from a farming family in Massachusetts. She was born on 16 November in 1853. There was confusion over her place of birth but Mildred confirms that she was born at a relative's home due to her mother's unexpected pregnancy complications:

The place of my birth was an accident. It was intended that I should be born elsewhere, and few people know less about their natal town than I do. My mother had gone to visit her sister-in-law, who resided in Providence, was taken ill there, and had to remain until after my birth. I have been told that I was two months old when I was brought to Massachusetts, and, so far as my memory goes, I never went back to Rhode Island … except for a funeral.

Mildred knew her ancestors came originally from England, and that 'English blood ran in my veins' but she was still rightly proud of her home city, declaring with passion:

I have always called myself a Bostonian, though in my childhood we seem to have been a wandering family, but it was in Boston that I was educated, and all the associations of the active years of my life are bound up in the city of east winds, colonial memories, and sincere aspirations for culture – distance has lent some enchantment, for they grow more and more interesting as they recede.

It is also worth looking at the world from Mildred's point of view, because she lived in a time when there were many technological and industrial advances that transformed life for the Victorian and Edwardian citizens around the world. In today's busy electronic communication age it is easy for us to forget the impact of these changes, and how different life was even up to a few decades ago. Mildred recalled how:

In the half century which preceded my birth the first ships propelled by steam had crossed the Atlantic; the first railroads were built; the first steam looms set up; the first sewing machine built; the first telegram sent; the first friction matches used. I, in my childhood, saw the first street cars running on rails in the city streets. They were horse-drawn, and primitive compared with the electric tram cars of today.

Mildred's enthusiasm for technology, advancement and education shines through as she has a very clear voice through her journals – one can hear an echo of what her voice must have sounded like as one reads her prose and is drawn in by her enthusiasm and excitement. She goes on to describe the changes that occurred whilst she grew up:

I was out of school when the telephone system was put at the public service, and when the typewriter and linotype were perfected. I remember well my first typewriter in the early eighties [1880s] – a heavy, clumsy caliograph, quite different from the pretty little five-pound machines, which we carry about with us today as easily as we carry a handbag. I saw the first 'horseless car' on the streets of Boston, to the protests of all the town and the terror of all the horses, and when it was considered, as the telephone had been, as a possible and interesting plaything for the rich, but never likely to be of practical value. I rode on the first horseless streetcar when the system was first run by [electric] motor not many years later than the advent of the horseless carriage. I remember the days when the streets were not cleared [of snow and other debris] in winter, and the days when there were lamplighters. Indeed the changes in the ways of living were radical in the period between my first recollections and the end of the last century.

Mildred's early years were filled with interesting historical events, events which would come back to her in later years and make her view them with a different eye. She clearly recalls sitting with her mother and female relatives knitting socks and scarves for the Yankee soldiers of the Civil War in the 1860s. She declares with absolute confidence that she was and always remained an abolitionist. She also had a good understanding of world events and recalls the great parliamentary struggle between Disraeli and Gladstone and how it would shape Queen Victoria's reign and elevate her to the greatness of Elizabeth I. Mildred's early life would also make her aware of France and the struggles that launched 'Napoleon the little on his seventeen years and nine months of Imperial Adventure,' also noting with irony, and not a little cynicism, how 'his Spanish wife, as leader of the world's laws of dress, bestowed upon it the hoop skirt, by which she will alone be remembered.'

Mildred consistently had an impatience for women's obsession with fashion and the subservience entailed in following current trends so unquestioningly. One suspects she never had time, or patience, for such pursuits, as she considered it unnecessary nonsense. No doubt it was actually a complete mystery to her, when there were so many other important things to concentrate on during life's journey. Indeed it set her apart from other women and also, no doubt, seems to have alienated her from normal society of the time because her attitude and ideas would have been little understood or tolerated. One suspects that the seeds of her character as an independent loner were sown in these formative years. It is little surprise that she would lose herself in literature. Her thirst for knowledge and quest to have an understanding of the wider world ignited a desire to travel and see the places she had read about. Mildred was, and would remain for the rest of her life, a woman before her time.

Another important historical event remained vividly etched in Mildred's mind, one which would also come back to haunt her. She would recall how she was at school during the 1871 Siege of Paris, which brought to an end the Franco-Prussian War:

I remember how we all worked at the Bazaar held at the Boston Theatre to aid the besieged city, at the time that Boston had as a guest the Grand Duke Michael, brother of the Grandfather of tragic Nicholas II – and I remember also, with a strange sinking heart, that at that time Bismarck [the German Chancellor] was the popular hero in Boston, and that big pictures of him were everywhere – that rugged, seamed face with its pitiless eyes under the spiked helmet – and little did I ever dream then that I should in my later days, see those spiked helmets under circumstances which would make me look back to that early winter of 1871, with a pain that was almost a personal shame to remember how gaily we took that French defeat, even while we danced to raise money for Paris, and that, so far as my memory goes, no effort was made to save France, our first friend, without whom our independence might never have been won, and no protest was made against the shameful treaty of Frankfort [sic]. We calmly let Germany claim and take her spoils of war.

The fall of Paris in 1871 brought to an end the Franco-Prussian War. The Germans were the victors, led by the incomparable Otto von Bismarck, a supreme military strategist, politician and founder of the newly unified German Empire. The initial treaty of Versailles was signed in the January of 1871, which brought to an end the hostilities and allowed Bismarck to cement his goal of unifying the German states of Prussia, Baden, Bavaria, Wurtenberg, Saxony, Hesse and, most importantly, adding the Alsace and Lorraine territories, up until then controlled by France, into his new Empire. Thus on 18 January 1871, in the Palace of Versailles's famous Hall of Mirrors, the new German Empire was proclaimed and Kaiser Wilhelm I was declared emperor. The Treaty of Frankfurt would follow on 10 May 1871, setting out the finer details of the return of the Alsace and Lorraine territories to Germany and also set the war indemnities demanded from France by the German victors at 5 billion francs. To appease public anger at the continued occupation, Bismarck, as chancellor, agreed that troops would be withdrawn from Paris, although he had intended a garrison of German troops would remain there. But troops would continue, he stated, to be garrisoned in other parts of France until the full indemnities were paid.

Bismarck and Kaiser Wilhelm I were hated for their humiliation of Paris and the French never forgave them, or the German nation, for their harsh treatment in 1871. Fighting for Paris had cost over 24,000 French military dead and wounded – in addition to nearly 150,000 captured and taken prisoner, with a further 50,000 civilian casualties. By contrast, the Prussian army, which captured Paris, had losses amounting to around 12,000 soldiers, either dead or wounded. These were huge losses of life on both sides, but particularly for the French. It was a wound that never healed and one that soured the relationship with a dominant German Empire right up until the outbreak of the Great War in 1914. To the surprise of Bismarck and the new emperor, the French wasted no time and formed the Third Republic, with a new government led by Adolph Thiers. They quickly repaid the indemnities set out in the treaty to get German troops off their territories. As a result of the loss of the Alsace and Lorraine regions, France lost over 1,600 villages and their populations. These people were given until 1 October 1872 to declare their intention to remain French or to become German citizens. If they chose to remain French they had to leave their homes and return to France. It was an act that left an open, weeping wound that further soured relations with Germany, and created an aspiration among the united French to repatriate the Alsace and Lorraine regions; this would ultimately be resolved in the next Treaty of Versailles in 1918 at the end of World War I. Bismarck was long dead [1898] by then, sacked by Kaiser Wilhelm II in 1890 after his succession on the death of his father, because Bismarck didn't agree with the new kaiser's military ambitions and plans of aggression. Kaiser Wilhelm II would himself be forced to abdicate as a result of the German defeat in 1918.

Mildred would understandably find these memories of her youth coming back to haunt her and also prick her conscience – even though as a young girl she could not have fully understood the implications of her misplaced admiration of Bismarck, it still troubled her greatly all those decades later when the prospect of seeing thousands of those same spiked helmets marching across her beloved France was too much to bear or believe possible again. In some way it felt to Mildred as if a circle was being completed and this had all been part of the foundations of her destiny. That young girl she had been in 1871 could never have imagined that she would one day in the far-off future actually live and work in France, and consider it her home – a home she loved with all her being. All the twists and turning roads of her life were leading her to a small, dilapidated house on a hill overlooking the Marne Valley in the French countryside.

Mildred's education was thorough and she was totally immersed in literature of all kinds apart from novels, which were considered rather scandalous and forbidden to her by her mother. Even the weekly maga-zines that printed Dickens's latest serialisation, *Edwin Drood*, were frowned upon. She was given permission to buy the weekly magazine with her allowance on the strict understanding that she would only read Dickens and nothing else of the contents. Unbelievably, Mildred was obedient and did exactly that. She was just so thrilled and relieved to be allowed to follow this latest work. The following extract from Mildred's journal sets out a taste of her reading as a child and during her schooling; it also highlights how, unlike today, there was no mass media apart from newspapers, magazines and books available. It was a world where the written word, eventually supplemented by the occa-sional photograph, put the wider world into perspective and was the foundation of education and knowledge:

> From a literary as well as an historical point of view the epoch in which my life opened was important. Two years before I was born Dickens brought out his masterpiece, *David Copperfield*, and the year in which I arrived on the scene saw the first publication of his *Bleak House* as well as Thackeray's *The Newcomes* and Charles Kingsleys's *Hypatia*, and all three of these men were dead before I was out of school, having worn their laurel on living brows. I was old enough to have read nearly all of Dickens and to be reading *Edwin Drood*, in serial form, when the pen dropped from his hand and left the tale unended, to my great grief. I did not read Thackeray until later. But Kingsley is associated with my High School days. I read *Hypatia* with my classic history, and *Hereward The Wake* with my early English history, and with it Bulwer-Lytton's *Harold the Last of the Saxons* and *The Last of the Barons* as well as his *Last Days of Pompeii* with the Roman, but Ernest Maltravers and that period of Bulwer-Lytton's novels were forbidden me until later, and when I was free to read them it was too late – I did not like them; they bored me. The Brontë sisters kept better. They were forbidden me at the same period, and I have few sensations more vividly remembered than my first devouring of *Jane Eyre*, when I was eighteen, a sensation that, with no effort, I can repeat every few years.

The strict censure on books is demonstrated by the attitude toward the Brontës – certainly not seen then as classics of literature as they are today. Mildred's literary education and influences leave one almost giddy but it is no surprise that, as she became a young woman, Mildred chose to try journalism as a career. Her passion was ignited from a very young age:

> George Eliot's *Adam Bede* came out when I was six years old, and she was one of the idols of the school girls of my time. I had nearly two years more of school before me when *Middlemarch* came out in serial form, and we were all very excited over it. I still remember how my New England soul was tormented when I first heard that the union of George Eliot and Lewes was without 'benefit of clergy' – it was a sort of mingling of terror at the sin and awe at the daring, tinged with an unconfessed sentiment of admiration for a courage stronger than the written law. Dearly beloved Edward Everett Hale in his careless attire, with his Christ-like face, whose 'Man Without a Country' came out while I was still in the grammar school, and over which I shed buckets of tears, as sincere as was the laughter he inspired later with his 'My Double and How He Undid Me', which I remember to have read on one of the first trips I ever made to New York alone in a Pullman car, when I had to put the book into my bag and leave it unfinished, because it made me laugh so that I was ashamed to be seen in public unable to control my risibles. *Little Women* came out in the same year as *Innocents Abroad*. The girls of my time were, as they should have been, quite mad about Jo and Laurie and Amy and we wept ourselves sick over the death of Beth in spite of it being the fashion then in Boston to be quite 'high-browed' even among school girls.

As much as she devoured books of every kind she took exception to some and especially to Herman Melville's *Moby Dick* and declared it would always be ranked as a 'man's book' and in spite of several attempts it left her cold and uninspired. Kipling, however, she loved. 'This was the atmosphere,' declared Mildred, 'so far as books were concerned, in which I passed my school days.' She would eventually have treasured copies of all these favorite books – all read again and again – on the shelves of her private little library in the house on the hill at Huiry.

In her later years Mildred spoke little about her parents or siblings. She had two younger sisters but seemed to have left them behind once she moved to Paris in 1898. There seems to be an almost unspoken disapproval directed at Mildred; perhaps her family felt alienated from her because she failed to fit in and embrace the normal expectations of society at the time. That she never married, or had any desire to, could have added to this and caused her to drift away and establish a new life for herself in France. It has to be said that there were suggestions, because of her close association with Gertrude Stein, and later Alice Toklas, that Mildred was a lesbian and utterly disinterested in men in any sexual way as a result. Mildred was also very guarded about revealing the names of her closest friends or disclosing too much information about them – one feels that this was as much to protect their privacy as her own. From the evidence available I would say that Mildred was predominantly someone who enjoyed living an independent life, where she could be in charge of her own destiny and answerable to no one. If she ever had any kind of relationship, male or female, it didn't have any kind of significance in her life. If anything, I would say she was one of those people who was probably just disinterested in sex altogether. Happy to focus her energies on her career, her passion for life and the wider world – and anyone in it that crossed her path. Mildred loved people.

In a rare entry she does recall her family life in Boston, and it also gives us an insight into her family structure, her mother's relationship with her father, which seemed to have ended at a time when divorce would have been unthinkable and unavailable except under stringent circumstances. Her aunt and grandmother's departure to live in California resulted in an acceptance of never seeing them again – travel for such distances was not an easy option then, as it is now. These events seemed to have a profound effect on Mildred, as she recalls:

Just after I was fifteen my mother's youngest sister, who had been the first playmate I can remember to have had, married a western man and went on to California, where, soon after, my dear grandmother followed, to my great grief, and I never saw either of them again. My mother's only brother had married in Lawrence, and had his family to think of. About the same time my father decided to change the scene of his activities to New York, and for some years I only saw him for occasional weekends. It was a terrible change for me ... Having no longer any reason [because her father had left], when school vacations came, to remain near Boston, my mother took us in the summer – I had by this time two little sisters – one of them a baby in long clothes

– babies used to wear long clothes in those days until they could creep [crawl] – back to the country where she was born, and each year we spent three months on the farm in New Sharon, Maine, where my dear grandmother's younger sister lived with her family.

Mildred seemed to have relished this part of her formative years and enjoyed learning about the land and how the farm worked. She also declared with her usual passion how 'New Sharon is in a beautiful part of Maine, in the Sandy River Valley, twelve miles from Farmington, the shire town of Franklin county,' and referring to her forebears, 'the home of the Jacob Abbotts, where my grandfather had been Registrar of Deeds for years.' She also recalled how every year, knowing how tedious the journey was from Boston, her mother 'ingeniously managed to make the trip each summer something of an adventure. We never made the journey over the same route two consecutive summers.' Knowing the limitations of transport at the time, it was indeed a challenge, be it by boat, rail, carriage or usually a combination of all three with a stopover in a road tavern for the night to add to the thrill for her children. All these influences developed Mildred's love of adventure, travel and exploring the unknown. 'The roads were not very good, and we were terribly shaken up, but when one is traveling what does one expect?' stated an ever-practical Mildred:

That was the spirit of those days for us, and there were long, quiet unexciting days enough ahead of us. Those roads through the forest on the steep hillsides! What charm and variety they had. There were dense pine forests with the sunlight filtering down on the carpet of golden needles; there were forests of silver birches like tall multitudes in white breeches waving silver banners in the upper air. There were depths of delicate green maples with their underbrush of rank brakes, or a miniature forest of maiden fern, undulating gently on their thin black stems. One must have lain on the ground and looked through under that roof of feathery green to know all about the wild maidenhair that grows under the arches of a Maine forest. It was exciting, and, to our young eyes, seemed delightfully perilous – and what was the use of riding all day on top of a swaying stage coach if there was never a thrilling moment? When the not too wide road was cut into the side of a high hill – with on one hand the forest going up, up to the blue skyline high above us, and on the other side dropping down, down, to a plain, with now a pond, like a jewel as the light flashed on to it, or a river like a silver ribbon, and here and there a group of farm buildings looking picture-like in the distance ...

In later years, as she recalled these times, Mildred would wonder if those days of the stagecoach would ever return once people had tired of the automobile and wanted once again to utilise horses for transport. 'I suppose,' reflected a wistful Mildred, 'very few people will know anything about nature sounds except what they read in poetry, and that to the future generations the purring of a motor will be their only music.' She also added how:

The American farmers' life must be different today, since the automobile has become as common as the fly, and the [1920s] cinema and the phonograph have drawn people in the country nearer together. In my time people never saw one another except at the meeting-house on Sundays, and the only festivities were the apple bee and the corn husking in October. Farmers' wives had no time to waste in social amenities. But these memories of the old days were revived in my memory when I came to live under similar conditions in another land [France, 1914], where, however, if it were equally primitive, it was also quite different.

Mildred would find all the skills and experience of living on the farm in Maine invaluable when she prepared to live again in the countryside fifty years later – but this time overlooking the Marne Valley, France.

3

LA CRESTE: RENOVATION OF A RUIN

I had climbed up to the house – standing desolate in the mud.
I waded ankle deep in it to get from the road to the door,
where the mason and the carpenter waited.

Mildred Aldrich

In late January of 1914 Mildred was preparing to start the work on
La Creste to make it habitable all year and not just for summer sojourns.
It was going to be a monumental task and one that would take every
cent of her recent inheritance and every ounce of energy, along with all
the patience and fortitude that she still possessed. Mildred was determined but found herself at a loss as she stood there in the cold and mud
trying to convey an enthusiasm she didn't feel for the sake of the bewildered looking mason and carpenter – who seemed to wear expressions
that told of a desire to be anywhere but on this hill, outside La Creste,
with an American woman they considered utterly insane. In that brief
moment, Mildred might well have agreed with them:

By this time the penetrating damp of a rainy French winter had set
in. I had come up from Esbly in a rattling so-called diligence. It was
an up-hill climb – they called it five miles – and it had taken over an
hour. From the little village at the foot of the north – Voisins – I had
climbed up to the house, standing desolate in the mud. I waded ankle
deep in it to get from the road to the door, where the mason and
carpenter waited. It was lucky that the mental vision I had of what

I was to do was what I saw and not the actual, time-stained, sad jumble of buildings before me. I cannot today even recover a memory of it as it was then. In the six months I spent getting it ready to live in, it found its soul.

Those months would indeed be challenging and Mildred would later confess that she couldn't recall how dilapidated the house was at the outset. Little did she realise it, but the six months of hard work spent renovating La Creste she would eventually come to consider as 'probably not only the happiest time I ever had, but the happiest I shall ever have.'

Mildred imagined what she wanted done to the interiors, what walls to knock down to open up two dark rooms into one and the furniture she imagined adorning every room. The décor would be classic and a brand new bespoke staircase was to be constructed to complete the picture. Then the reality set in, bringing Mildred to earth with a rather heavy thud:

As I stood alone in it for the first time, I had a great vision. As I stood on the red tiled floor of the smoke stained living room I saw it all done in white enamel, with black rafters. I saw the old staircase well thrown into the room and a new staircase sweeping in a beautiful curve up to the bedroom floor. All the furniture that was going into that room was black and the tapestry covers were on a background of the same color [sic] as the red tiles on the floors. The staircase was my prettiest dream – the French build beautiful staircases. I saw the doors into what was to be the dining room and library broadened into wide arches and curtained in black. But loveliest of all I dreamed of a work room over the grange at the north, opening onto a wide terrace supported on four rough stone piers commanding the view of the valley of the Marne and the line of hills – that wide sweeping panorama later to become historic. In fact I saw ten rooms under those six gables – and my one regret was that the rooms were none of them as big as I would have liked, and I so love space – and then I woke up, and realised that what I was really going to have was a little house with a salon, library, a dining room and breakfast room – two rooms simply because it would be too expensive to break down the wall between the two dark rooms at the back – downstairs, with a kitchen built in the rubbish hole [a grain storage area initially accessible only from outside] between the main house and the grange on the north side. Upstairs I was to have two bedrooms – one of them, a guest room, built in the loft over the dining room, and entered from the upper turn in the staircase, and above that, in a partly finished attic, a work shop. The white salon with black curtains went out of my mind with difficulty, but as I intended to do my own work [painting and decorating] I knew that it was a folly that, however mad I was, had to be abandoned. I dreamed and woke from it all in one single afternoon. But the picture still survives.

Because of her limited funds Mildred decided to embark on the restoration of La Creste without the help of an architect. This in itself was a brave decision, especially so because she was the first to admit that she had little experience in this area. However, being ever practical, and mindful of how much she wanted to achieve with the money available, she threw herself into the project with enthusiasm and levels of energy she didn't realise she still possessed. Thankfully she had commissioned the services of a local carpenter and mason who knew the house well, and who were able to source materials at reasonable costs. Many of the locals were fascinated by Mildred simply because she was American, and also an older woman who intended to live alone. It was during these early months that Mildred began to hear that the locals had assumed she was a widow and worthy of their support and assistance for her courage to live alone in the countryside of a country not her own. Mildred allowed them to assume what they wished. In some ways it was easier than trying to explain why she wasn't, nor ever had been, married. That had been a subject she had found tiresome for most of her adult life. Apart from that, it made her feel secure among her new community, knowing they were keeping an eye on her. No doubt it also appealed to her sense of humour.

Mildred wrote fondly of this new beginning and declared it 'in spite of disappointments and disillusions, a glorious time'. She goes on to say:

I doubt if, since I had helped build my doll's apartment in my childhood, I ever had so much fun, and that in spite of rarely getting just what I wanted. I was nervous at times … I was often exasperated when the work was slow. I blundered now and then … but nothing seemed to dampen my enthusiasm for long.

The two major frustrations for Mildred would be the cost of installing drainage and also the new staircase she wanted for the house. One day the heavens opened and the rain came and came. It was obvious to even the inexperienced observer that the damp in the house was caused because there was nowhere for the water to go:

> I stood one day and saw the water rushing down those six roofs, and cataracting down all the walls like miniature Niagras [sic], and I knew then that, but for the drains that were being dug and the four drain pipes and four underground cisterns, I could never have lived in the house. It pained me at first when the masons called my attention to this necessity, to see so much of my money going into that work instead of interior decorating.

After it was explained Mildred understood completely and also realised that the ground around the house would be forever a muddy midden, especially in wet, winter weather. Once the drainage work was completed the difference was immediate, and the house itself began to dry out with the help of a good fire burning away in the grate to speed the process. The terrible mud was also banished when new brick paths were laid around the house and to the road from the front door. So that the area overlooking the Marne Valley could be fully appreciated, Mildred had it laid to lawn on the north-east side once the paths were complete. This left ample land for her vegetable garden and chickens – and even enough space in borders for planting flowers. This last desire on Mildred's part sealed her fate as an eccentric in the eyes of the local workmen and community. Nobody wasted time with the growing of flowers when food was needed.

Mildred had set her heart on a new French staircase and had always admired how beautifully they were crafted in her adopted country. In her mind she saw something elegant and curved but her carpenter soon burst that bubble of fantasy. The main problem being, he declared, was a large supporting beam that ran straight through the salon and limited the headroom for anything other than a straight staircase elevating up one wall for support. Mildred was having none of it. If she couldn't have a curved staircase she wanted one that elevated a few steps, turned on a small landing to access one bedroom, then elevated again to the next bedroom level. The carpenter was adamant; the headroom was not suitable to achieve this:

After long arguments, I told him to do nothing until he heard from me. I measured the height of the beam from the floor, the space between the two floors, the width of the old well – that could not be changed – and in my primitive way, I figured it out on a big sheet of paper and with a ruler. After days of work I got a flight of stairs that could have two turns – one from the salon, and one to the upper landing, with the height and depth of each tread. It was a terrible task for an inexpert person, an architect could have done it better in five minutes.

Mildred did herself an injustice with that self-deprecating remark, but it was typical of her modesty where such matters were concerned. She knew what she wanted and, while willing to compromise in some areas, she was determined to get what she wanted – not what she was told to have. Mildred now had to take her plans to the carpenter, and hope he took no offence at proving him wrong, so he could construct them to her own drawings:

I sent the drawing, with the measurements out to the carpenter, and when I went to his shop the next Sunday, there it was drawn to scale in white chalk on the floor. I was delighted. I had on a long coat, and I remember that I picked up my skirts with both hands and on my toes I tripped up the chalk design, stepping on each tread, and at the top I jumped off.

It was at this moment that Mildred's carpenter actually appreciated her sense of humour and enjoyed the joke with her. Mildred felt it was the first time any of the local French felt they could enjoy a lighter moment with her and not have to act reverently in her presence. For that at least Mildred was relieved – and because she would get her staircase if not her white enamel walls!

I don't claim it was a beautiful flight of stairs, but it was a deal better than the one planned. It is not the easiest I ever went up and down, but I do claim that it is an easy one to fall down, and I ought to know – I have fallen down it myself, which is surely proof.

Quite how Mildred fell down her stairs and why – or how many times – she fails to specify. However, it would seem feasible that whilst doing her own painting and decorating she may have had the odd slip once that staircase was installed. As the work progressed through the winter months, Mildred began to have concerns about the viability of the house. 'Sometimes that winter I expected to perish as I stood about on frozen ground, and now and again the work stopped. Then the spring began to promise warmer days ...' Her doubts were soon swept away by the love she had for La Creste and the determination to complete the renovations so she could move in:

> As I look back at that winter I realise what a period of self control it was – so much I had wanted to do, and expected to do was impossible. Some of the mistakes I made are a daily trial to me still. Yet I think, in spite of everything, I managed to get some self-expression into the house. It sometimes mocks at me, but I wink it away. Now and then I think that if I had the opportunity earlier I might have found in it [interior designing] the suggestion of a better career than the one I followed, but I never regret anything.

As Mildred was still travelling between her Paris apartment and La Creste she relied on the services of a local man named Pierre who, along with his rickety *diligence* carriage and grumpy donkey, Ninette, collected and returned her to and from the station at Esbly. After so many journeys she knew them both well and, in spite of the discomfort, enjoyed their company and was thankful they made themselves available to her. On those journeys Pierre would sometimes mention his wife, whom it transpired was many years younger than him. Their marriage, Mildred decided, appeared to be more about convenience than any great passion. His wife's name was Amélie, and Mildred little realised what an important part of her life she would become.

The matter of furniture and decoration eventually came to the fore. As her funds were now even more limited after the added drainage costs, Mildred decided that the furniture from her Paris apartment would have to suffice and with this another thought occurred to her. To help make her feel comfortable in La Creste she decided on a plan:

> When I abandoned my scheme of a white salon I decided to repeat in the new home the color [sic] scheme of the Paris apartment – apple green walls and wood work. I had always liked it and thought it was as good for my nerves as it was for my eyes. Some of those who saw it thought it made the room too dark, as the windows were not

large, but I argued that for a house into which the sun was to pour in summer all day from all sides the effect of shade would be welcome, and that in winter, when one had to light up [with candles] at half past three or four, it made little difference.

It also offered some cosy comfort on those dark winter nights and days so in the end Mildred, as ever, did as she pleased and listened to nobody's objections or advice.

Whilst all this activity was going on to renovate La Creste there were worrying rumours and then articles in the newspapers about Kaiser Wilhelm's aggressive posturing and obvious willingness for war. Over recent years he had poured millions of marks into an attempt to create a fleet of warships that would rival if not dominate and outnumber those of the United Kingdom – much to the concern and annoyance of his cousins King George V and Tsar Nicholas II. Wilhelm had also diverted huge resources into building up the German army and its equipment. This, many speculated, could only be for one purpose. Although nobody wanted to use the word 'war', it was on everyone's mind.

Many believed that Kaiser Wilhelm, whose mother was Queen Victoria's daughter, Victoria, was freed from the family control exerted over him first by his grandmother until her death in 1901, and then by his uncle Bertie, King Edward VII, until his sudden death in 1910. This left Wilhelm to spiral out of control, free from familial shackles, and able to fulfil his ambition to create an empire greater than that of his English family. Many believed that his withered arm, damaged at birth and useless, soured his mind and made him determined to prove his warrior status by dominating and controlling his European neighbours. Fate contrived to aid his ambitions.

In London, the Kaiser's aggressive war posturing was seen as slightly ridiculous, not helped by Wilhelm's love of over-the-top, heavily plumed military dress uniforms, with rows of medals lined up on his breast. This served to create more of a comic caricature than a serious threat. As a result, his actions and rhetoric were not initially taken that seriously by the government of the day. King George V seemed alone in his fear that Wilhelm was out of control and becoming a real threat to the Royal Navy and European peace. The aggressive rumblings of discontent in the Balkans were about to erupt.

Mildred would have kept herself informed of this news, as would many of her friends including Gertrude Stein. It was about this time that Stein and others began to wonder if it was safe for Mildred to actually move into La Creste, as planned in the June of 1914, feeling she would be better to stay in Paris so she could evacuate to England, or back to America, if the worst happened and war did come. Mildred would have none of it and continued with her plans unabated. She had more important things to worry about. The time was fast approaching when she would have to vacate her Paris apartment and arrange the removal of her furniture and belongings:

> By the middle of April, when the weather began to be fine, although the house was by no means ready, all my plans to move were completed. I had regarded the moving as the bugbear. It was the easiest part of the job. The professional mover came into Paris, looked the apartment over – told me to leave it exactly as it was – touch nothing – pack my clothes and house linen when I was ready to leave – otherwise leave books on the shelves, pictures on the walls, china in the closets, kitchen untouched.

With that worry behind her she found herself once again having feelings of doubt about moving out of the city she loved so much. It was not a doubt about La Creste or her love of the new home but a slight fear about being able to adjust to a different way of life. 'Almost without my own volition,' she mused, 'I would find myself in a corner with myself, and, in spite of myself, the past and the present of me looked each other in the face, and just for a second, it took conscious pluck for me to grin.'

Her conflicting emotions were understandable considering the upheaval and relocation and all its implications. Moving home is always stressful; for Mildred it was exhausting but also difficult because she had to be resigned to close her old life and to begin a new chapter – one that she wasn't at all sure she would completely enjoy. She also wondered if she would be able to cope without seeing her friends on a daily basis – outwardly she remained adamant it is what she wanted, inwardly she wondered what would happen if she found she missed them and Paris:

> Now and then, as the evenings got longer in May [1914], and I sat on the balcony of the little Paris home, where I had lived for twelve years, I wondered what the twilights would be like when I was alone on the hilltop. I loved the twilight. In Paris, however, up above the

tree tops, where the street noises were a little softened, there was always audible – night as well as day – that never silent 'voice of the city' which had been in my ears all my life.

Whenever these misgivings came to the forefront of her mind, La Creste always managed to banish them as soon as she arrived at the house to check on progress. By this time the house was, Mildred noted, 'starting to look exactly as I had planned,' that is after she resigned herself to the reality of its design possibilities as opposed to those borne out of her initial fantasy. As the work took shape she began to relish the day she could finally move in – and her joy at the prospect of her own garden and all the space it also offered knew no bounds:

> I had built a kitchen, with red tiled floor, which was [perfect], as it was open right through from the front garden to the orchard behind, and in the corridor which led to the dining room I had built my W.C. I had opened an arch between the two dark rooms at the west of the salon and put in a window. I should have liked to throw the two rooms into one, but as the rafters rested on the division wall, that would have been a more costly undertaking than I could afford.

A special room that Mildred had been determined to locate in the new house at whatever cost was her library and study. It amused her that the location had once been shelter for the livestock of previous owners. 'I laid red tiles on the little room where the cow once lived and built book shelves all round it, painting them apple green like the salon.' This would become one of her favourite rooms, one in which she would find her voice and inspiration and begin writing again.

Since Mildred had also decided to use her existing furniture from the Paris apartment, she knew that it would blend perfectly with her favourite colour scheme, as she had already trialled it in Paris:

> The first time I saw the paint on the walls I realised that the familiar color [sic] scheme was going to carry a note over from the old life to the new, which would do much to bridge the change – and it did. I had not originally intended to carry that note so far as I was obliged to. I had hoped to plane and stain the beams and rafters, but they were so worm eaten that it was impossible to do anything but paint them the same green as the rest of the room, putting white between.

It was during these last weeks of work on the house that Mildred met for the first time a young woman who would become a life-long friend. She also lived at Huiry a little way up the hill, and was the wife of the old man who, along with his grumpy donkey, Ninette, had collected and returned Mildred to the train station in his bone-shaking *diligence* carriage on numerous occasions over several months. She had heard of her but never met her. Their meeting came as a result of Mildred's friends almost insisting that she employ some kind of daily help or companion, as they feared she would struggle to live alone without company. No doubt they were also fearful at her living isolated and alone, especially when taking into account her health problems andthe ever-present rumblings of war. Mildred was aghast to be considered so in need of support – and stubborn in her refusal to even consider such a proposal. She could manage quite well alone. Or so she thought:

> I had planned not only to live alone, but to do, if possible, without any service at all. Soon the friends, who, in greater numbers than I expected, came out to watch the progress of the house, began to see objections to that. There was no [mains] water in the house. It all had to be drawn from a well in the garden at the south – a well so deep that it had been little used – it having always been easier to bring water down [by hand] from the top of the hill. At first I did not give this much thought. Then one day – in the presence of a friend who had come out from Paris – I drew up from the well my first and only bucket of water – or rather I tried to – it took us both to get it up. Then I knew that someone else had to draw water at any rate. Then everyone began to dictate – 'I had to have a femme de ménage'. It was 'all very well for me to live alone – to sleep alone in the house – to wait on myself if I wanted to – but I could neither draw [from the well] nor carry water', and no one could see why I 'should scrub brick floors'.

Rather annoyed at this constant carping and insisting by her friends, Mildred would have cheerfully thrown them all down the said well and told them to mind their own business and, in her usual indomitable way, carried on doing exactly what she had intended all along. However, she bit her tongue, smiled and just got on with things if it pleased them or not. She was also ever mindful of the mystery person or persons who had actually provided her pension, so felt awkward at offending anyone lest it should be her benefactors. That she even had such thoughts made her feel slightly uncomfortable and shook the foundations of her cherished independence.

Mildred had been promised that she could move in during early June. It did not seem to her that that would be possible, as so much remained to be done when March turned into April 1914:

> The plot of garden at the east and north of the house had been cleared and planted with lawn grass, and the tiny green blades were just coming up through the brown earth. The old hedge on the roadside had been cleaned and clipped and the holes filled in, whilst privet had been planted round the two other edges on that side. The interior was still in the hands of the carpenters.

One day Mildred was sitting eating her lunch on the sill of an upstairs window, in the room that would become her bedroom, when she first saw and spoke to Amélie.

Mildred described seeing a 'pretty, slender woman in a clean print frock and broad hat'. As she approached the house Mildred remembered thinking she seemed somewhat different and at odds with the other people she had met thus far on the hill. She would never have imagined that this pretty young woman was the wife of the old man, Pierre. After all, he and 'the other types that I had seen were all peasant types. They had on clothes and that was all that could be said for them.' But Amélie seemed different:

> She began to pick her way through the mud and debris of the mason's work, and the piles of brick which were soon to pave the terrace ... she was so slight, so easy on her feet. She looked up, and with a pretty smile said: '*Bon jour, Madame. Voulez-vous une femme de ménage?*'
>
> I looked down at her upturned face – I liked her – so smiled back, and said: '*Peut-être – mais plus tard.*'
>
> '*Voulez-vous de moi – pensez-vous?*' she asked.'
>
> In spite of all my resolutions I thought that I did, but I answered: '*C'est bien possible – mais plus tard. Savez-vous faire la cuisine?*'
>
> She laughed as she answered: '*Pas beaucoup.*'
>
> I laughed as I said: '*N'importe*', and added, '*Attendez un peu. Quand je suis prête de m'installer, je vous causerai. On vous appelle,*' and she answered '*Amélie*', and I told her that I would see her later,

and she said: '*Merci, Madame. Au 'voir, Madame*', and began to pick her way back through the mud and rubbish without the smallest suspicion of how important that few minutes had been to me.

Mildred had taken little notice of the surrounding houses and cottages whilst the work was going on but eventually noticed that they were all in need of some kind of repair or other and had matured into their picturesque surroundings so as to look perfectly placed and create an atmosphere redolent of quiet, rural French countryside. A few weeks after that first meeting with Amélie, Mildred wondered where she could find her. She hadn't thought to ask exactly where she lived:

> At the corner above the house lived the gardener who had planted my lawn and set out the hedge, so I went to the door and asked if they knew anyone named Amélie, and was told that she lived in the court [yard] just back from the road – in a house whose back faced the south side of my little house across a field wild with black currant bushes and waving in the air later every flowering vine of weeds the country knows. There I found her sweeping out her court and feeding her chickens, and learned that this was her husband's house. When she saw me she burst into tears, declaring that she had thought that I had forgotten or was going to bring a domestic from Paris.

Mildred was a little taken aback at such an emotional reception, as she had not reckoned on Amélie assuming she had been forgotten about, it was just a mater of timing. In spite of this Mildred still warmed to her and found her dramatics somewhat charming and amusing. Mildred did not want a full-time domestic or live-in help. Apart from the cost, which was out of the question, she didn't want the intrusion or responsibility; this she quickly explained to Amélie:

> I simply wanted someone to draw water, and to help me a bit mornings, and on the spot I made all the arrangements – I was to pay her 40 francs a month – and there my responsibility ended. I had neither to house her, feed her, nor clothe her. I gave her money to buy brushes and soap ... and instructions to clean out the house, and wash the windows, and assured her that in not later than two weeks I should come out with my stuff.

Mildred had an odd premonition about her future relationship with Amélie and this new life she was embarking on – thinking that nothing would ever be the same again. She shook this off and decided that surely she was deserving of some peace and had earned the right to become one of life's spectators, a detached spectator at that, after everything she had been through. These thoughts left her with a feeling of definite uncertainty. A couple of weeks later Mildred returned to the house, as planned, to check all the remaining work had been completed and the house cleaned:

> I had come out with one of my oldest friends. A woman I had known in Boston when she was a girl – she was younger than I. We had come early, bringing a lunch basket, and were to finish putting up the books in the library. We found the house clean and sweet – the freshly curtained windows open to the sun – all the floors washed – not a speck of dust anywhere, and in the dining room a small square table had been placed with a clean napkin on it – a carafe of fresh water – a bunch of roses in the middle and the necessary service for two people. Two small chairs were drawn up to the table.

Ever mindful of maintaining her independence, Mildred was less than happy that Amélie had taken it upon herself to provide this service when she specifically made it clear she did not want this kind of help. 'My first gesture was one of anger,' fumed Mildred, 'why couldn't she mind her own business? When I wanted that sort of service I would ask for it – it was officious.' Her friend found it all very amusing and roared with laughter at Mildred's indignant sulk.

'All right, Duchess, you've fallen on your feet again. The last scruple I had about the affair [Mildred living alone] is gone. You are going to have a sympathetic service about you, in spite of yourself.'

'I don't want it,' cried Mildred in a rage.

'You have not wanted a great many things,' replied her friend, 'that you have accepted – and with fairly good grace. If you can accept the bad with a smile – and I have seen you do it – where's the harm of accepting a bit of good in the same spirit.'

Mildred reluctantly agreed with her friend that what she said made sense of sorts. However, Mildred was still full of misgivings, which seemed odd given her normal acceptance of fate. One can only assume that the stress of moving after all the months of renovations had tired her and caused her to become fractious and irritable – and also a little tired of her friends fussing over her and examining every aspect of her life as if she were a decrepit maiden aunt:

> I expect they were perfectly right, but it was not at all what I planned, and I knew, an hour later, when Amélie came and cleared away the lunch table, that once again I had changed my background, but I had changed nothing else. I have never been able to decide whether it was cowardly to accept – or the most trying sort of courage not to protest against a sort of fate which I had not courted and which I felt a bit foolish to emphasise.

This incident gives an interesting insight into Mildred's reactions and also the way she would overanalyse her own and others' behaviour towards her. She seemed afraid of not being in total command of her life and reacted badly if she felt anyone was trying to organise her or control her in any way. It was misplaced where Amélie was concerned, as they would form a friendship that would be mutually supportive during the terrors that would disrupt their respective lives on the hilltop at Huiry in the months and years to come. Mildred would look back at this day and realise how utterly wrong she had been, her behaviour childish and ridiculous. She would also in time thank God that Amélie came into her life as a friend and supported her without question.

4

FIRST DAYS ON THE HILLTOP

During those first days I reflected on my life in Paris – and everything that had brought me to La Creste.

Mildred Aldrich

'Well, the deed is done,' wrote Mildred on 3 June 1914, to her friend in Boston. 'I have not wanted to talk with you much about it until I was here. I know all your objections. You remember that you did not spare me when, a year ago, I told you that this was my plan … I did not decide to come away into a little corner of the country, in this land in which I was not born, without looking at the move from all angles. Be sure that I know what I am doing, and I have found the place where I can do it. Some time you will see the new home, I hope, and then you will understand.'

Finally, and much to her relief, the house was finished and Mildred at last moved in to her new home. However, due to the increasing tensions across Europe, especially from the ever-posturing and aggressive Germany, the threatening drums of war were becoming louder and more sinister. As a result, Mildred's friends back in the United States and the inimitable Gertrude Stein in Paris, along with other well-meaning friends, were putting pressure on Mildred to abandon moving to the house until such time as they deemed it safe to do so. Mildred, as ever, would not hear of it. She recalls the first couple of days in her new home in her journal, and it is both poignant and tragic in as much as a century later we know what is coming. Mildred was blissfully unaware that the German invasion was just a few weeks away:

The moving when it came was a great adventure. The packing and casing was all done between six o'clock in the morning of the second day of June, and four o'clock in the afternoon, when two long covered vans – the size of railway baggage cars, each drawn by three horses, started on their 25 mile journey [from Paris] by road for Huiry, and I went to spend my last night in Paris with a friend [Gertrude Stein].

At eleven o'clock the next morning, as I drove up the hill from the station I passed my household effects on their way up the hill, and at six o'clock that night everything was in place – the china in the buffets, kitchen stuff on the walls, and beds made. If the pictures had been hung the little house would have looked as if I had been living in it a long time – except that the paint was preternaturally clean. I had known just where everything was going, and everything went just where I planned as if the old house and old furniture had always expected to come together.

And after I had had my first supper, and sat out on the terrace in the soft June twilight I had such a home feeling as I never had. The few country noises – the passing of the farm wagons returning from the fields, the twittering of the sparrows preparing for bed, the singing of the finch, perched on the ridge pole above my head and turning his curious little head from side to side as he eyed me between his four note phrases, and the sweeping and sailing of the swallows – the most beautiful bird flight that I know – assuring me at once that I should never be lonely. And the next morning, after a good night of sleep, I woke to find Amélie smiling at me from the door way, waiting to ask if she should bring up my coffee, and to assure her that she should do nothing of the kind. I had never been fine lady enough to take my coffee in bed, and I was surely not going to begin it in the country.

It took forty-eight hours only to get my trunks unpacked and stored away, and to get pictures hung and I remember very well waking on my third morning and looking around my little room – at the pictures of old friends, and at the wall on the one side where hung the children of my friends – the second and third generation who were inheriting the world – and saying to myself: 'Is it here that I am to finish – here in this beauty? It is better than I dared hope – far better than I deserve – thank God.'

It was in these early few days that Mildred would naturally reflect on what she had achieved in the years she had lived in Paris. Having seen everything from the best seats for theatre productions, and arts exhibitions, as critic, reviewer or social correspondent, it would be awful to accept less than such luxury. Now, she could not hope to afford to pay for the best seats herself as her income made it impossible. Better to have nothing and not allow the treasured memories to be tarnished by such frustration, although frustration had been a constant companion throughout her journalistic career in a field dominated by men – men who little understood women like Mildred.

Following her arrival in Paris in 1898 Mildred had carved out a career for herself as a writer and journalist, writing articles as foreign correspondent for the *Boston Herald* and *The New York Times* newspapers. She had worked for the *Herald* whilst living in Boston and also its subsidiary magazine, *Mahogany Tree*. Indeed it was this latter publication she attempted to save and develop as owner and editor, but unfortunately it proved to not be viable financially and it was soon closed down. This was a great frustration and disappointment for Mildred, but she still worked as a writer for the *Herald*. Unable to progress in her chosen journalistic career because she was a woman, she decided to spread her wings and try her luck in Europe. It suited her independent spirit and sense of the unknown and, aside from being a fashionable adventure for those able to afford it; it would have also allowed Mildred freedom from the social pressures in Boston to conform to expectations and enter a marriage market she had not the slightest interest in, nor ever would.

Apart from her writing talents, Mildred also spoke and could write fluent French – which would open a new career opportunity for her eventually – and she had always felt an affinity with what would become her adopted country. No doubt this was as a result of her love of literature and her passion for reading – never was she without several of her favourite books, which she would read again and again. Many of these had created vivid pictures in her mind of Paris and France generally, as well as London, in a way that made them feel familiar but also spurred her to visit and explore the locations that she had only seen described in books. This Mildred did with her usual energy and enthusiasm.

Once she arrived in Europe in 1898 Mildred visited both London and Paris. But Paris stole her heart and she quickly established herself

among the arts, theatre and literary elite of the city – a city that in many
ways was dominant in culture and theatre at the time because it was
less morally oppressive than London, and certainly allowed freer and
more avante-garde thinking and activities for the artistically inclined.
She began writing articles, mainly society gossip and theatre opening-
night reports and critical reviews, for the *Boston Herald* and *The New
York Times*. These weekly and monthly columns had titles like 'Paris
Stage Matters', 'News of Literary Paris' and 'Notes From Paris'. A few
examples remain in *The New York Times*' archives and the following quotes give a flavour of her style of writing. It is also interesting to
see how the columns seemed to ache with the weight of such detailed,
lengthy reporting – a style we would find almost too dense to read comfortably for any length of time today. This in many ways reflects the fact
that newspapers of that period had no competition with radio or televi-
sion, so were the main source of information and as a result people's
attention spans were much longer – our own has diminished because of
the media saturation that we are bombarded with from every direction.

An early article is a good example of the kind of reporting Mildred
undertook prior to arriving in Europe. On 31 July 1892, Mildred wrote
of the adverse weather affecting her home city of Boston, Massachusetts:

> The heat this week melted the pride clean out of Bostonians, who
> have been wont to boast the claims of ... summer comfort. This city
> has fared even worse than its near neighbours throughout the present
> month. From 3 to 24 no rain fell. Not since the time of the famous
> world's peace jubilee in 1872 has Boston endured such an infliction
> of torrid weather.

It is fairly average reporting for a newspaper dominated by mainly
local issues. It is also interesting that even in 1892 people were wondering why extreme weather was affecting them, so climate change
fears are perhaps not that new. Mildred carries on by highlighting the
health consequences of the heat wave:

> Matters have been rendered much worse in the vicinity of the Back
> Bay by the plague of a malaria-breeding tract of land near Chester
> Park, just beyond the Back Bay fens. A piece of marshy land has been
> allowed to collect stagnated water, which in its turn has collected
> matter even more offensive [sewage], until the stench from that

region has become more deadly and unbearable ... public sentiment is fully aroused.

At the very end of the article there is an announcement as to the future of the subsidiary magazine: 'The weekly publication *Mahogany Tree*, that has been issued for six months under composite editorship, has been bought by Miss Mildred Aldrich, who is to issue the first number under her control Sept. 10 [1892]' As we know, it was not a success and the magazine went out of business within a year. This was maybe the spur that made Mildred decide to travel and seek her fortune and career in Europe.

Once in Paris she began reporting on the literary and artistic activities of the city. She had a much more interesting list of potential subjects to write about and her columns took the style of society and gossip weekly or monthly articles.

'Gay Mid-Season at Aix' was the title of an article Mildred wrote for *The New York Times*, as foreign correspondent, published on 20 August 1898, not long after her arrival in Paris: 'Aix-les-Bains ... this famous French watering place is just entering the second midseason of its year. The lull that for two months follows the departure of the English from Aix, which is always crowded with them in May – they stop on their way north after the winter on the Riviera is over. The town is [now] full of French people and Americans.' The crowds gave 'King George of Greece an enthusiastic reception' and she added that famous personalities of the time, whose names have faded from popular recall today, were also present and worth a mention, such as: ' Julia Marlow, Loi Fuller, Sibyl Sanderson Terry and Col. Ochiltree taking the baths.' Sibyl was the daughter of the famous actress Ellen Terry.

In November 1901 Mildred was regularly reporting on the Parisian opening nights of new plays and also offering reviews of the same for *The New York Times*. Her articles were a mix of society gossip and features on leading personalities of the time who were in attendance. Under the headline of 'Paris Stage Matters' she reported on the 'Successful Appearance of Mlle. Toutain as Yvette at the Vaudeville.' This was a famous theatre 'opening night' of an eagerly anticipated play, adapted from a story by Guy de Maupassant, Mildred continues:

Several interested persons who chanced to be passing through the Parc Monceau Saturday were witnesses of a very pretty scene, when

Mlle. Toutain [famous actress and beauty of the time], who was that evening to create the role of Yvette at the Vaudeville [Theatre], visited the monument of its author, Guy de Maupassant, and placed on the marble seat beneath his bust her tribute of flowers.

Mildred paints some lovely pictures as she reports these events although at times, it has to be said, her prose does slip into a dramatic and sentimental vein. However, more than a hundred years later, they are full of life and utterly charming inasmuch as they give voice and open a window to that lost age of pre-World War I France:

The French are very prone to these little acts of superstition, intending to propriate Fortune [*sic*]. Even in the university quarter, the haunt of free thinkers, the walls of the two churches the students most frequent – St. Severin and the Chapel of the Sorbonne – are covered with votive tablets, placed there in gratitude for success at examinations. It always strikes foreigners – who judge all students in Paris by the crowds that make demonstrations, political and otherwise, around the statue of Etienna Dolet, in the place Maubert – as singular to read on these little marble tablets the devout thanks to some saint for a student's success in obtaining some honor [*sic*] in a scientific school, or even for his Ph.D.

Mildred then added a reference to a familiar story:

Americans who go, on the Fourth of July, to the grave of Lafayette in the sad little cemetery in the convent grounds of Picpus, which Victor Hugo made famous in Les Misérables, and which have changed little since Jean Valjean and Cosette took refuge there, may have noticed a wreath [in memory of them] hanging against the wall ...

Mildred went on to declare that Mlle. Toutain's performance was brilliant and successful, and that she was supported by a cast dominated by 'Rosa Bruck, who is the cousin of Sarah Bernhardt,' no less, and that overall the story and its adaptation into a play is 'a great success behind the footlights'.

In February 1902 Mildred produced an article titled 'Notes From Paris' for *The New York Times* and the *Boston Herald*. The opening section of the article reported on the celebration mass for the repose of the soul of King Louis XVI, held at the church of St Germain 'formerly the royal chapel to the Palace of the Louvre.' It was noted with some dismay that 'the mass, ordered by the Royal Committee of Paris, was attended by 500 prominent Parisians openly committed – either by politics or sentiment – to the interests of the exiled [royal] house of France, and, considering the scant publicity given the occasion, it was a goodly number.' Goodly or not, it would seem that the general population had little time for any cause that would support a restoration of a monarchy held in little esteem then – or even in its time.

By this time many of Mildred's various articles for *The New York Times* and the *Boston Herald* seemed to have been dominated by theatre news, celebrity gossip and the exploits of various actresses and actors, today largely forgotten, and other trifles of gossip from the French capital. One section in 1902 deals with an interview Mildred conducted with a famous but aged actress, then in her eightieth year, named Adelaide Ristori. Much of the interview revolves around Ristori's view of another, younger, Italian actress, Eleonora Duse. Duse, who, Mildred remarks, 'interests the world outside of Italy more than anyone else on the Italian stage', had clearly upset Ristori:

> At the beginning ... her career attracted me by her temperament and the sincerity of her art. I thought then that she was gifted with an artistic spirit, and I longed for the time when she should appear in the heroic roles.
>
> It seemed to me that, with her undoubted genius, she would contribute something noble and lofty to her art – and then to my great grief I saw her led away by the works of that monstrosity, D'Annunzio. When Duse first went to Paris a French journalist asked me what my opinion was of her talent. Even then I prophesised that the wrong road on which she had already entered could lead to no good. I was not mistaken, for since then, in spite of her remarkable gifts, she has not contributed one worthy creation to the theatre. It is a great pity, and I grieve deeply for it.

As scathing as that assessment is by Ristori, perhaps Duse had the last laugh, as she is certainly better remembered today than her harsh critic and fellow actress.

Mildred found herself drawn more into the literary and theatrical circles of Paris and as a result she began to find demand for her articles drying up in the USA. Around this time she lost her work at both *The New York Times* and the *Boston Herald*. In the face of this frustration Mildred came up with a plan to see if this sudden lack of work had anything to do with her being a woman, which she suspected was probably the case. The truth lay somewhere in between, inasmuch as the articles she was producing were becoming too orientated towards the expectations of a literary elite and less suitable for more general consumption by those less aware, educated or interested in Europe's higher culture.

She devised a plan that helps us understand her spirit and determination, and also her paranoia where work was concerned in an industry dominated by men. In essence she decided to test the levels of discrimination against women. Mildred set about writing an article as a male boulevardier and duly created herself an appropriate male pseudonym: H. Quinn. The article reported on the society and theatre gossip of the time and, as she had done before, painted a broad picture of life in the Parisian capital for the readers back in the United States. On the whole not too dissimilar, or so she thought, to those she had been producing in the previous two years. She duly sent off the article to an eminent New York newspaper and, she recalled, within a few days had received a telegram to say the article had been accepted and asking for details of a bank for payment to be made for the piece accepted, as well as commissioning several others over the next months. Mildred recalled the fun she had writing the articles. Although the deception made her feel a little uneasy, she carried on with considerable success for some time.

Mildred then received a telegram informing her the editor of the newspaper was coming to Paris and would like to meet his new foreign correspondent. As H. Quinn didn't exist, Mildred decided to turn up at the office at the allotted date and time and come clean. This she did, to great jollity and hilarity. The meeting was amiable and the editor praised her for the skill she possessed and thanked her profusely for her efforts and hard work. However, she remarked: 'As I left the office and made my way down the stairs to the street, I knew that I would never write for that famous New York newspaper again. And I never did.' Disillusioned, Mildred decided to just move on and concentrate on other employment possibilities.

To occupy her time, and also to try to resolve her problem of earning a living now the newspaper work had been cut off, she focussed on her contacts in the theatre circles of Paris. As she was fluent in written and spoken French it wasn't long before she was asked to translate

French plays into English for consideration as properties suitable for London or New York productions. She soon realised that French plays and comedies rarely allow for successful translation into English and that the subject matters were not those that always appealed to more conservative playgoers in London's West End and on Broadway.

There were exceptions and one collaboration that did bear some fruit, and certainly longevity in that it is still remembered, was the association she enjoyed with the Belgian playwright Maeterlinck and his play *L'Oiseau Bleu*. She translated the play into English and, as *The Blue Bird*, became famous in London and New York. Audiences were charmed by its fairy-tale morality. Mildred was also involved in the London production as a producer and agent for the play's performance rights but she made little money from it when the deal went bad. As a consequence the play's run was shorter than expected.

This new career would bring Mildred into the circles of the famous London producer Frank Curzon and also the Broadway producer Charles Frohman. Curzon and Frohman strove to outdo each other, each attempting to secure properties the other was interested in producing. Mildred found it to be an association fraught with difficulties, financial collapse and continual manipulation in a way that infuriated her. Mildred found the professional theatre world even more volatile than the cut-throat newspaper industry that had so unceremoniously discarded her. Indeed, where theatre matters were concerned, Mildred was shrewd enough by this time to say: 'I would not go on my oath concerning anything regarding the theatre.' Mildred was certainly fearless to the outside observer and stood her ground, with no qualms about expressing her sometimes very fixed opinions.

Mildred found herself acting as an agent for a playwright named Wolff, whose latest work was a farce that had proved very successful in Paris. She recalled how 'Of course I had one of my attacks of optimism. I, as far as I can remember, thought the play would be rushed on, and I was distressed when silence settled over it, and a torrent of water went under the bridge before the footlights went up on *The Secret of Polichinelle*.'

Frank Curzon was interested enough to demand a meeting about the script. There had been initial anger that Mildred had secured the agent rights to the play for England. The deal was a result of some trickery by Mildred's boss, Hackett, a producer, on those holding the play's rights for the USA and Canada. As a result, Mildred would act on behalf of playwright Wolff through her boss Hackett in England. But the play caused her nothing but frustration, as she remembers vividly in her journal:

One cold night about nine o'clock a man in livery came to my door – I was then living temporarily in the Porte Dauphine quarter – with a pencilled note which said that my presence was required immediately [at an address in the centre of Paris to discuss the play] ... It was mad but I had to laugh ... my first impulse to send the man away – but after all I was in the business [play agent], and if this was the way the game was played ... so I put on a clean pair of white gloves – I expected to find him [Wolff] at a café on the Champs-Élysées, smoking his cigarette with perhaps Georges Faydeau or Gaston Le Roux [*sic*] and enjoying his little coup of treating the independent American woman [as a comrade].

At my door I found what looked like a private Victoria [carriage] with a coachman in the same livery as the lackey, who opened the door for me, and then mounted the box. Away the two horses sped up the Avenue du Bois and down the Champs- Élysées, but to my surprise they went the whole length and crossed the Place de la Concorde to the Grand Boulevard and only stopped at the most famous of cafés [Maxims] in that quarter. There the footman opened the door of the carriage ... and led the way across the sidewalk and up the red carpeted stairs and flung open with a flourish the door to one of the private banqueting rooms, ushered me in, announced me, and closed the door behind me.

From the long table across the far end of the big room a dozen men sprang to their feet, and from the head of the table Wolff came forward with both hands outstretched ... If I was ever quite as mad as I was at that moment I have no recollection of it. However, it was no time or place to show any sort of feeling. I declined the place at the table – everyone sat down – I could at least with dignity deprive Wolff of playing his little scene to an audience, so at the end of the room he was forced to explain that his London 'friend' had made an appointment with Frank Curzon for [two days time] and I was to go to London ... to do the business part.

Mildred insisted she could not go to London – and furthermore didn't want to. But the playwright, Wolff, insisted she help as promised.

'I don't see,' he said, 'how I am going to succeed without your aid. I shall look very foolish walking round London with a French play under my arm which no one can read.'

Mildred considered this as she attempted to suppress what she called her 'New England prudishness' at even being in such an establishment. To aid her escape as quickly as possible she finally agreed to go to London and read the play to Curzon once Wolff sent her a telegram to say he was there and all had gone to plan – and the meeting arranged with Curzon:

I found the footman waiting to conduct me down to the carriage. As I went slowly down the long flight of red velvet stairs (the landing was full of waiters attached to the service of the other dining rooms) Wolff seemed intent on giving me as telling an exit as possible. He leaned over the balustrade and called down to me ['My dear I am sorry to have subjected you to this dire fait']. I shook my head and made no effort to laugh in his face ... I knew it would not do for me to laugh. I might lose my balance and fall down those red velvet stairs. I was never very sure on my feet. The only time I ever fainted quite away I chose the foyer of the Comédie-Française for the act ... but felt to tumble down these stairs, at this time, would be an anti-climax [at Maxims]!

Mildred's opinion of Wolff was not great to say the very least. It would be fair to say she disliked him intensely but her professional façade kept her personal feelings and opinions in check. In her journal she refers to him as 'that ugly little monkey of an up-to-date boulevardier', adding rather tersely 'that all of whose life had to be treated as if it were a scene from one of his [immoral] plays'. In spite of this antipathy and resentment at Wolff bringing her to such a decadent place, she duly received a cable from London and rather grudgingly set off on her way to the capital:

I expected to read the play to Frank Curzon – in English from a French manuscript. I don't know why I felt I had to do it. Perhaps because I imagined that a London production might benefit Hackett. I arrived in London in the afternoon – found Wolff and his tall English friend at the station waiting for me. They had been trotting about London together for forty-eight hours ... I had no idea what they had been doing in that time, and I did not ask them, which, as it developed later, was a mistake.

That night Mildred read the play again in preparation for the following day's meeting with Curzon. She wanted to get it done and return
to Paris as quickly as she could. She was beginning to loathe Wolff's
company. The next morning Wolff was waiting for Mildred at her
hotel, where he informed Mildred he would be going with her and
sitting with her as she read the play. She refused this request without
a moment's thought and was irritated that Wolff should suggest he
was offended and wanted 'to hear [her] read in [her] pretty voice, the
words he had written with so much emotion'. Mildred was adamant
and saw Curzon alone for the reading:

> That did not touch me a bit. I knew him too well by now, so I gave
> him his choice – he could let me do the trick alone – or I would take
> the noon train for Paris, and leave him to finish the business alone
> … that settled the question. They both escorted me to the theatre,
> but I went into Curzon's office alone. He received me very kindly –
> and I remember him as good an audience as I ever had to listen to a
> reading – and I have had many.
>
> He sat at his desk, and I sat at a little table in the middle of the
> room. I read rapidly – giving him the action of the play as well as the
> dialogue, and I got most of the laughs. Long before I had finished
> I knew that I had landed it. He asked but one question – at the end
> of the first act – while he was waiting for a glass of water to be
> brought to me, he came over to me and asked if he might look at
> the manuscript, and he leaned over my shoulder to do so, and then
> remarked:
>
> 'You have no English notes to help you?'
>
> I had not – it was a clean French script. I might have explained that
> I had already translated it once … but I was in a hurry.
>
> When I said 'Quick Curtain' at the end, he said without a moment's
> hesitation 'That's all right', and ringing his bell ordered Mr Wolff to
> be sent up – and up he came – his tall English friend came also – and
> was told his play was accepted … that the contract would be ready
> for his signature at eleven the next morning, and his check [sic] for
> the sum agreed on advance royalties.

With that Mildred left them and returned to her hotel to pack for her
journey back to Paris. A few hours later Wolff turned up with his English friend to inform Mildred he had sold the rights to the play to the

management, Maude and Harrison, of the Haymarket Theatre as they had offered more money by way of advance. Mildred was furious. She quickly informed him that this double-cross would cost him dearly, as neither Curzon nor any other management in London would now produce the play because of his unprofessional behaviour. Once his scheme came to light he was finished and so was his play. Wolff was adamant that he was entitled to sell his play to whoever was willing to pay him the most money. Mildred agreed, but told him 'your play will never be played in London' under any contract. Mildred returned to Paris and put the matter behind her:

> For several weeks I heard no more of the matter. Then one day Wolffs's brother-in-law came to me – Wolff did not dare to come himself – and begged me to go to London and try and arrange the matter, to get the manuscript from Maude & Harrison and transfer it back to Frank Curzon, as I had said from the first would have to be done, if the play ever saw the light in London, and he passed me over the money for my expenses. I called attention to the fact that there was a sum to be refunded to the Haymarket people over and above the amount of Curzon's check [sic], and was begged to 'fix that somehow,' as of course Wolff had long ago spent the money, and hadn't any just then – he never did have any.

Mildred, to her credit, went to London and sorted the whole mess out with the Haymarket and Curzon. '[I] delivered the script back to Curzon,' recalled Mildred, 'and except that I was paid to do the literal translation with the business and mise-en-scène from which the London version, under the title of *Everybody's Secret* was made.' Once it was all over, Mildred realised she had not added a clause in the contract to ensure she received a 1 per cent commission on Wolff's royalties – which eventually cost her several hundred dollars. Wolff never offered to put this right:

> When sitting on the train returning to Paris, I said to myself: 'Well, there are people – or I am given to understand that there are – who make their living doing this sort of thing. I wonder how they do it? I wonder why they do it? Probably because they like it. Well I don't.' And I never did.

Mildred continued to work translating plays for producers who wished to stage them in the UK or USA with varying degrees of success. All that can be said is that Mildred managed to make a small living from these various contracts. In time she felt very disillusioned with the newspaper world and even began to question her own abilities as a writer and wondered if her talent, or lack of it, was to blame for the shortage of commissions. Eventually she decided to stop writing altogether and, much to the despair of her friends in Paris and Boston, refused to reconsider in spite of their urgings. She found an outlet for writing in her private journals and her letters to friends.

Little did she realise it but everything that had gone before the first days of June 1914 were but a preparation for the most important mission of her life. Fate had placed her in this time and place in preparation for her to witness and preserve for history the events she was destined to witness that would change the world. Archduke Franz Ferdinand, the heir to the Austro-Hungarian throne, and his devoted wife, Sophie, were currently holidaying in Vienna prior to embarking on a state visit to Sarajevo on 28 June 1914, just three weeks away. In the meantime, Mildred was enjoying her first days' living in La Creste, perched on the hill at Huiry, overlooking the beautiful Marne Valley. As she sat in her garden and gazed across the valley the heat and brightness of the sun made the landscape shimmer – the heat haze creating a distorted view, reminding her of the Impressionist paintings she had seen in the galleries and salons of Paris. Far off in the fields she could see the red headscarf of a farmer's wife as she helped him with the harvest – the horse drawing their cart ambled listlessly in the intense heat. For a moment the farmer's wife shielded her eyes against the sun and seemed to look up towards Mildred, holding her gaze for a moment; she then looked away and carried on with her chores. The gentle heat-hum of summer added to the sensation of seemingly endless hot days:

Remember one thing. I am not inaccessible, I may now and then get an opportunity to talk again, and in a new background. Who knows? I am counting on nothing but the facts about me. So come on, Future [sic]. I've my back against the past. Anyway, as you see, it is too late to argue. I've crossed the Rubicon, and can return only when I have built a new bridge.

5

ASSASSINATION AND GERMAN INVASION

Sophie is my entire happiness ... I sit with them and admire
them the whole day because I love them so.
Archduke Franz Ferdinand, heir to the Austro-Hungarian throne, on
his wife and children.

'This will only be a short letter. It looks, after all, as if the Servian [sic]
affair is to become a European affair,' Mildred wrote in late July 1914
to Gertrude Stein, who was visiting friends in England. She punctuated
the letter ominously by ending with 'what looked as if might happen
during the Balkan War [in 1913] is really coming to pass – a general
European uprising. I am sitting here this morning, as I suppose all
France is doing, simply holding my breath to see what England is going
to do. Just imagine what it will mean!'

The omens were all there, but nobody seemed to see them. A royal
visit was arranged for 28 June 1914 in the city of Sarajevo. Franz Ferdinand and his wife Sophie Chotek von Chotkowa and Wognin were
a rare royal couple in the early twentieth century in that, despite being
pawns in the game of politically arranged imperial marriages, they
actually loved each other. The date for the royal visit was their wedding
anniversary. It was also St Vitus' day, which marked the anniversary
of the 1839 battle between the Serbs and the Ottoman forces, where
the Serb forces were defeated on the Field of Blackbirds – Kosovo –
thus bringing to an end the Serbian empire. This was also an important
St Vitus' day for Serb nationalists because it was the first since Kosovo's

liberation in the second Balkan War in 1913. It was the perfect opportunity for a few amateur but hard-line terrorists to take advantage of a significant date and make their mark in history. What better way to do so than by attacking the hated autocratic ruling royal family. Franz Ferdinand's public reputation was not a good one. He was disliked for his abruptness and overt rudeness towards officials and those who came into close contact with him. He distrusted everyone until they proved themselves. However, behind the scenes in his private life, he was a warm and affectionate husband and father.

As that fateful day approached, the security surrounding the royal couple was minimal. Franz and Sophia were in good spirits because they had enjoyed a few private days in the area and, whenever they met the general population, they were feted and treated with respect and adoration. It never occurred to them or their royal protection guards that they were in any danger. In Germany the Kaiser was feeling more and more threatened by, and sandwiched between, the power of his cousins, Tsar Nicholas of Russia to the east, and King George V to the west in England. Between them sat a very nervous Holland, Belgium and France. The latter's allegiance lay with Russia, but its security and borders were weak and threatened by Germany's increasing aggression and paranoia.

Mildred was still establishing herself and her routine in the new home – although she kept a close eye on all the news in the daily newspapers delivered from Paris. She had also very quickly formed a very close bond with Amélie and was busily telling her friends in Boston, via letter, all about her new companion. 'Never in my life,' wrote Mildred, 'anywhere under any circumstances have I been so well taken care of.' This was a complete turnaround for Mildred, as initially she had seen Amélie's unrequested ministrations and organisation of her domestic affairs as an impertinence at the very least – and an intrusion into her independence at worst. This initial reaction was quickly forgotten and a bond based on affection and respect soon developed. She also wanted to reassure her friends, who had been pleading with her to return to Boston because of the worsening 'European situation', or at the very least move back to Paris where evacuation would be easier and safer should that be necessary:

I have a *femme de ménage* – a sort of cross between a housekeeper and a maid-of-all- work. She is a married woman, the wife of a farmer whose house is three minutes away from mine. My dressing-room window and my dining-room door look across a field of current bushes to her house. I have only to blow on the dog's whistle and she can hear. Her name is Amélie, and she is a character, a nice one, but not half as much of a character as her husband – her second.

She is Parisian ... Her first husband ... died years ago when she was young ... She has had a checkered career, and lived in several smart families before, to assure her old age, she married this gentle, queer little farmer.

Abelard was many years older than Amélie and the marriage was, as Mildred had surmised after talking to him during those bone-rattling journeys, more one of convenience than passion, providing Amélie with a sense of security for the future:

She is a great find for me ... but the thing [their arrangement] balances up beautifully, as I am a blessing to her, a new interest in her monotonous life, and she never lets me forget how much happier she is since I came here to live. She is very bright and gay, intelligent enough to be a companion when I need one, and well-bred enough to fall right into her proper place when I don't.

As to the matter of her security and her friends' natural concern, Mildred was quick to try and allay their fears and reassure them that in spite of the general uncertainties she was safe in her new house:

Don't harp on that word 'alone'. I know I am living alone, in a house that has four outside doors into the bargain. But you know I am not one of the 'afraid' kind. I am not boasting. That is a characteristic and not a quality. You would laugh if you could see me 'shutting up' for the night. All the windows on the ground floor are heavily barred. Such of the doors as have glass in them have shutters also. The window shutters are primitive affairs of solid wood, with diamond-shaped holes in the upper part. First, I put up the shutters on the door in the dining-room which leads into the garden on the south side; then I lock the door. Then I do a similar service for the kitchen door onto the front terrace, and that into the orchard, and lock both doors. Then I go out the salon door and lock the stable and the grange and take out the keys. Then I come into the salon

and lock the door after me, and push two of the biggest bolts you
ever saw.

Mildred ends her letter on a lighter note, her sense of the dramatic and
her humour to the fore:

After which I hang up the keys, which are as big as the historic keys
of the Bastille ... I always grin, and feel as if it were a scene in a
play; it impresses me so much like a tremendous piece of business –
dramatic suspense – which leads to nothing except my going quietly
upstairs to bed.

The dawn of 28 June had arrived and Franz and his wife Sophia
were to travel to Sarajevo by train, arriving mid morning. They were
greeted enthusiastically at the train station and as they travelled on
the main road by the river to the City Hall to meet dignitaries for
lunch. It seems incredible that none of the plans for their visit were
scrutinised and tightened by their security contingent. Did no one
consider that travelling in an open carriage so close to the crowds
was unwise considering the unrest and political instability of recent
years? The radical nationalistic organisations had certainly become
more vocal and explicit in their anti-monarchy rhetoric and in their
propaganda publications in the months leading up to the royal visit.
All of this seemed to have gone unheeded.

As their carriage made its way through the cheering crowds one of a
handful of nationalists took his chance and primed his bomb. After he
hurled it at the royal carriage he ran to the bridge, swallowed cyanide
powder, then tried to shoot himself. The shot grazed his head and the
cyanide powder didn't work. He threw himself off the bridge into the
river but, as the river level was low in summer, he fell onto the dry
sandy bank still alive. A crowd pounced on him and began to beat him
until the police arrived and arrested him. The royal carriage had passed
by the time the bomb exploded. Several of those following in the security car were killed or injured along with several in the crowd. Unbeknown to everyone there had been at least five assassins each awaiting
their chance, but their nerve failed them or the opportunity was lost
because of the crowd getting in the way. The royal couple's carriage,
after Franz had offered help to the injured, sped up at the insistence
of his security team and arrived at City Hall, where they were greeted

by a dignitary who, oddly, delivered a speech of welcome that ignored the attempt just made on the royal couple's lives. The Crown Prince was furious and made his feelings known. They promptly moved into City Hall for pre-planned meetings and a luncheon party. At this time it was decided to return the royal couple to the train station by a direct route instead of the planned one. Unbelievably, it was also decided they would travel back to the station in the open carriage:

> The morning paper – always late here – brings the startling news of the assassination of the Crown Prince of Austria. What an unlucky family that has been! Franz Josef must be a tough old gentleman to have stood up against so many shocks. I used to feel so sorry for him when fate dealt him another blow that would have been a 'knock out' for most people. But he has stood so many, and outlived happier people, that I begin to believe that if the wind is tempered to the shorn lamb, the hides, or the hearts, of some people are toughened to stand the gales of fate.

On that return journey the royal couple's fate was truly sealed. As their carriage made its way back to the train station by the direct route as agreed, they were surprised when the driver made a right turn into, ironically, Franz Josef Street, to follow the original and longer route. Nobody had told the driver the route had changed. Travelling along this circuitous route the royal couple came within sight of another assassin, Gavrilo Princip, leader of the gang, who had positioned himself at the front of the crowd at a point where the road turned, requiring the carriage to slow down. As it did so, Princip stepped forward and fired several shots at point-blank range into the royal couple. Both were fatally wounded. Their carriage sped off, and by the time it arrived at the Konak Palace Sophie was already dead. Franz died a few minutes later. His last words to his already dead wife in the carriage were: 'Sophie, Sophie, don't die, stay alive for our children.' On being asked if he was injured he uttered these final words: 'It's nothing ...' Then he lost consciousness. His pillion guard held his collar to keep him sitting upright as the carriage sped past the confused crowds:

> Well, I imagine that Austria will not grieve much, though she may be mad over the loss of a none too popular crown prince, whose morganatic wife could never be crowned, whose children cannot

inherit, and who could only have kept the throne warm for a while for who now steps into line a little sooner than he would have had this not happened. If a man will be a crown prince in these times he must take the consequences.

Mildred's opinion of this tragic event seems quite harsh, but in her times the unstable Balkan regions had caused much turmoil across Europe, turmoil that had created a feeling of uncertainty and created a tangible threat of war. Mildred would conclude her reporting of this event by stating: 'We do get hard-hearted, and no mistake, when it is not in our family that the lightning strikes. The "Paths of Glory lead but to the grave," so what matters is, really, out of by what door one goes?'

However, after she had had time to reflect on what had happened in Sarajevo, Mildred revised her opinion when the enormity of what was happening as a result began to dawn on her:

Alas! I find that I cannot break myself of reading the newspapers, and reading them eagerly. It is all the fault of that nasty affair in Servia [sic]. I have a dim recollection that I was very flippant about it in my last letter to you. After all, woman proposes and politics upset her proposition. There seems to be no quick remedy for habit, more's the pity. It is a nasty outlook. We are simply holding our breaths here.

Germany had devised a plan for invading France as early as 1905, called, after its author, the Schlieffen Plan. This plan was a carefully constructed military strategy to ensure a swift invasion of France, by sweeping through neutral Belgium, and then cutting straight to Paris via the Marne Valley. This would ensure a quick, clean surrender once the Kaiser's invading army captured the capital. Once Paris fell, then the French would surrender – at least that was the belief. The plan had its critics within the German military.

'The Schlieffen plan was based on a number of fragile assumptions,' according to contemporary historian, Holger H. Herwig, in his book *1914*. '[That] the Russians would take at least forty days to mobilise; that the Dutch and Belgian railroad systems would assure his speed of advance; that the element of surprise would throw the French (and British) off their guard; and that the German railroad system would be able to expeditiously transfer the bulk of the armies from west to east in time to stall the Russian steamroller.' He ended by stating that 'Schlieffen's blueprint was riddled with hedge words such as "if", "when", "perhaps" and "hopefully".' It was a classic best-case scenario, and 'audacious, yes, [an] overly audacious gamble, whose success depended on many strokes of luck'.

After the assassination in Sarajevo, Kaiser Wilhelm II and his ministers began to feel there was a chance to make their move, cloaked in an excuse of national protectionism. The Austro-Hungarian emperor was distraught at the assassination of his son and heir, and felt there was no other option than to declare war on Serbia. As a result there were noises from Russia that they would not tolerate this course of action. The Kaiser dithered, not wanting to offer the unconditional support for military action he had previously assured would be forthcoming. In reality the Kaiser had sought an assurance from the British government that it would remain neutral should Germany support and assist a war between Austro-Hungary and Serbia. This was refused by London immediately; the government would not even discuss the request. The Kaiser and his ministers were concerned that their power in Europe would be seriously diminished if any conflict involving Russia and England erupted as a result of Austro-Hungary declaring war with Serbia – the Russians would immediately mobilise against them and this would be followed by the French who were their allies and bound by a treaty. One of Kaiser Wilhelm's ministers urged calm. He was then seriously chastised.

'Who authorised him to do so?' demanded an enraged and embarrassed Kaiser. 'This is utterly stupid! It is none of his business, since it is entirely Austria's affair what she intends to do. Later on, if things went wrong, it would be said: Germany was not willing!' He ended with a rather chilling statement. 'It was high time a clean sweep of the Serbs was made.' This news would have been received in Belgrade with mounting concern.

The Kaiser then made sure that Emperor Franz Josef received an assurance that he could count on 'the full support of Germany'. The Kaiser also made it clear that 'this action should not be delayed', adding that 'Russia's attitude would be hostile in any event, but he [the Kaiser] had been prepared for this for years, and if it should come to a war between Austria-Hungary and Russia, [they] should be confident that Germany would stand by [their] side with the customary loyalty of allies'. The missive ended on a more thoughtful note. 'The Kaiser,' it stated, 'would regret it if [they] failed to exploit the present moment, which is so advantageous to us.' The Kaiser had finally made up his mind and had stopped dithering. It would seem that his concerns were entirely for his own position and that of Germany. He wanted to make sure the situation was favorable for his own military and political ambitions.

By 28 July 1914, Emperor Franz Josef had finally made up his mind and officially declared war on Serbia. Sitting in his study in the imperial villa he signed the declaration with a quill pen; an act of old-fashioned tradition and dignity that hindsight would see as one of the final actions of this doomed monarchy, a monarchy so rooted in the past that it propelled itself towards inevitable self-destruction and oblivion. The Emperor's declaration read thus:

> To my peoples! It was my fervent wish to consecrate the years which, by the grace of God, still remain to me, to works of peace and to protect my peoples from the heavy sacrifices and burdens of war. Providence, in its wisdom, has otherwise decreed. The intrigues of a malevolent opponent compel me, in the defence of the honour of my Monarchy, for the protection of its dignity and its position as a power, for the security of its possessions, to grasp the sword after long years of peace.

Austro-Hungarian troops mobilised on 30 July, supported by their allies Germany on 1 August, quickly followed by the Russians and their ally France. It meant that Germany was now at war with Russia and France.

On 30 July 1914 Mildred was writing in her journal with some frustration:

> It is an odd thing. It seems it is an easy thing to change one's environment, but not so easy to change one's character. I am just as excited over the ugly business as I should have been had I remained near the boulevards, where I could have got a newspaper half a dozen times a day. I only get one a day, and this morning I got that one with difficulty. My *Figaro*, which comes out by mail, has not come at all.

Desperate for news of the latest developments, she managed to get a copy of the paper by traveling to the station at Couilly and purchasing a second-hand copy. She was not disappointed and read the latest news with mounting horror. 'Well, it seems that the so-called "alarmists" were right,' she wrote with some sarcasm. 'Germany has NOT [sic] been turning her nation into an army just to divert her population, nor spending her last mark on ships just to amuse herself...'

In London the government, via Lord Kitchener at the War Office, immediately instructed Sir John French that, should England be drawn into the war, he would command the British Expeditionary Force. However, there was the hope that maybe this would not come to pass. Some of Prime Minister Asquith's cabinet argued that those countries concerned should resolve their differences alone, and in spite of the entente that existed between Britain, Russia and France, there was no obligation on Britain even if Germany invaded France. To others this was a betrayal not worthy of such a great nation. They argued that if France was invaded by Germany, then Britain would have no choice but to declare war on Germany. Britain would also, under such circumstances, have no option but to honour its treaty obligations with Russia and France. As it transpired the Germans did invade, but they did so by implementing Schlieffen's plan and storming through neutral Belgium into France, an action that changed everything for Great Britain.

At Huiry, Mildred was desperate to keep up with the latest news and, in spite of frustrations and wild rumours, she still managed to get hold of the newspapers. 'I am sitting here this morning,' she wrote, 'as I suppose all France is doing, simply holding my breath to see what England is going to do.' At this stage there was no certainty that Great Britain would automatically enter the war. Mildred also admitted that she often referred to Great Britain as 'England' without realising this identified only the English and excluded the Scottish, Welsh and Irish subjects of the country. An error she apologised for. The prospect of war still seemed surreal and almost unbelievable even at this stage:

I imagine there is small doubt about it. I don't see how she [Great Britain] can do anything but fight. It is hard to realise that a big war is inevitable, but it looks like it. It was staved off, in spite of Germany's perfidy, during the Balkan troubles. If it has to come now, just imagine what it is going to mean! It will be the bloodiest affair the world has ever seen – a war in the air, a war under the sea as well as on it, and carried out with the most effective man-slaughtering machines ever used in battle.

Mildred's focus was also on those who lived around her and the effect a war would have on her, and her new neighbour's lives. 'The tension here is terrible,' she wrote in her diary. 'The faces of the men are stern, and every one is so calm – the silence is deadly. There is an absolute suspension of work in the fields. It is as if all France was holding its breath.' This intense atmosphere brought to mind that time in her youth when she had, as a young girl, raised money after the defeat of France in the Franco-Prussian War. The consequences of that defeat still haunted France and retribution was perhaps now possible if this war happened:

I have felt as if I could bear another one [war], if only it gave Alsace and Lorraine back to us – us meaning me and France. France really deserves her revenge for the humiliation of 1870 and that beastly Treaty of Frankfort [*sic*]. I don't deny that 1870 was the making of modern France, or that, since the Treaty of Frankfort [*sic*], as a nation she has learned a lesson of patience that she sorely needed. But now that Germany is preparing – is really prepared to attack her again – well, the very hair on my head rises up at the idea.

Meanwhile in London, Lord Kitchener, the Secretary of State for War, had also dispatched a directive on 29 July 1914 to the General Officer Commanding at Aldershot Barracks, Lieutenant General Douglas Haig, to put in place 'precautionary measures' for possible mobilisation of troops. Haig recorded in his diary that 'All our arrangements were ready, even to the extent of having the telegrams written out. These merely had to be dated and despatched.' Haig seems to have been exceptionally well organised:

On 2 March last 'Mobilisation Orders for the Aldershot Command', having been brought up to date, were sent out ... consequently when the telegram containing the one word 'Mobilise' ... was received at 5.30 p.m. on 4 August, these orders were put in force and methodically acted upon without friction or flurry. Everything had been so well thought out and foreseen that I, as 'C in C' Aldershot, was never called upon for a decision. I had thus all my time free to make arrangements for my own departure for the front, to visit Field Marshall French's GHQ [General Head Quarters] now established at Hotel Metropole in London, and to ponder over the terribly critical military situation as it gradually developed day by day.

Great Britain declared war on Germany on 4 August 1914 as a result of the invasion of neutral Belgium. The Kaiser's generals were following the Schlieffen plan to invade France and capture Paris for a quick surrender. In London, Sir John French had also received instructions from Lord Kitchener concerning the dispatch of the British Expeditionary Force:

> The special motive of the Force under your control is to support and cooperate with the French army against our common enemies. During the assembly of your troops you will have every opportunity for discussing with the Commander-in-Chief of the French Army [General Joffre], the military position in general and the special part which your Force is able and adapted to play. It must be recognised from the outset that the numerical strength of the British Force and its contingent reinforcement is strictly limited, and with this consideration kept steadily in view it will be obvious that the greatest care must be exercised towards the minimum losses and wastage.
>
> Therefore, while every effort must be made to coincide most sympathetically with the plans and wishes of our Ally, the gravest consideration will devolve upon you as to participation in forward movements where large bodies of French troops are not engaged and where your Force may be unduly exposed to attack.
>
> Should a contingency of this sort be contemplated, I look to you to inform me fully and give me time to communicate to you any decision which His Majesty's Government may come to in this matter. In this connection I wish you distinctly to understand that your command is an entirely independent one, and that you will in no case come under the orders of any Allied General.
>
> In minor operations you should be careful that your subordinates understand that the risk of serious losses should only be undertaken where such risk is authoritatively considered to be commensurate with the object in view.

Kitchener's directive seemed to leave Sir John French with little room for manoeuvre and also limited his ability to lead from the front with his French allies. It would also put an enormous strain on the relationship between himself and General Joffre. Joffre believed from the outset until a few months later that Sir John was just ignoring his orders (Joffre believed that French and the BEF were under his command) and

London was too weak to make Sir John follow orders. Naturally Joffre was furious when he realised some months later that French had been told from the start by Kitchener that he was not to take orders from any 'Allied General'. It would seem that from the outset the War Office was taking a precautionary stance, perhaps in the hope that it would all be over quickly and they could recall the BEF home.

Meanwhile, Haig had written to a military friend:

I agree that we ought not to despatch our Expeditionary Force in a hurry to France. Possibly had there been a chance of supporting her at the very beginning, our help might have been decisive. That moment seems to have been allowed to pass. Now we must make an Army large enough to intervene decisively – say 300,000. With the necessary reserves at home for wastage [possible dead and wounded] say 200,000. On what principle would you set about incorporating the less regular forces with our existing 6 divisions? I know nothing about the policy at the WO [War Office] at present … How rapidly events move! I hardly liked looking at last week while our Government 'waited'! How much longer will the German Empire last?

On 5 August Haig drove to London and had a medical examination at the War Office and was declared fit to serve at home and abroad. He then made his way to a more important meeting. One he recorded in his diary:

At 4 p.m. I attended a War Council at 10 Downing Street. Mr Asquith (the Prime Minister) was in the Chair. He began with a brief statement of the circumstances in which he had summoned this Council. The Germans had crossed their frontier into Belgium early yesterday (4 August). War had actually been declared between England and Germany, between Russia and Germany and between France and Germany, but as yet Austria was not technically at war with any country except Serbia. One unexpected factor in the situation was the neutrality of Italy. It must now be assumed that Italy would not stand in with Germany and Austria … Sir John French gave in outline a pre-arranged plan which had been worked out between the British and French General Staffs. Briefly stated, it was hoped that the Expeditionary Force would mobilise simultaneously with the French, and would be concentrated behind the French left at Maubeuge by the fifteenth day of mobilisation. The intention then was to move eastwards towards the Meuse, and act on the left of the French against the German right flank ...

The events, which led to the various declarations of war, had been rapid. Mildred was aghast at the speed it had all come to pass and she found herself almost bemused by the avalanche of imaginings that crashed through her mind. She wanted to run and lock herself in her house and leave the world behind when she heard the lone drum beating in the distance, the sign that war had been declared, calling to arms able-bodied men. Nobody needed to hold their breath any longer – Great Britain had decided, and for that Mildred was grateful, for her beloved France might yet be safe. Had Great Britain sat on the sidelines, Mildred feared that France would have been doomed to German domination and occupation once again. In her diary she recalled the moment when she read the proclamation of war in the village:

> I had a cold chill down my spine as I realised that it was not so easy as I had thought to separate myself from life. We stood there together – a little group of women – and silently read it through – this command for the rising up of a Nation. No need for the men to read it. Each with his military papers in his pocket knew the moment he heard the drum what it meant, and knew equally well his place. I was a foreigner among them, but I forgot that, and if any of them remembered they made no sign. We did not say a word to one another. I silently returned to my garden and sat down. War again! This time war close by – not war about which one can read, as one reads it in the newspapers ... but war right here if the Germans can cross the frontier.

Unbeknown to Mildred the Germans had already crossed into Belgium. They intended to trample that nation under foot to enable them to cross the border into France en route to Paris via the Marne Valley. The Kaiser's brother, Prince Henry, had reported a conversation he had with his cousin King George V just prior to the mobilisation and declarations of war. 'I don't know what we shall do, we have no quarrel with anyone, and I hope we shall remain neutral,' declared King George V. 'But if Germany declares war on Russia, and France joins

Russia, then I am afraid we shall be dragged into it. But you can be sure that I and my government will do all we can to prevent a European war.' It was all too little and far too late. It is also doubtful that King George V even said this to Prince Henry as no official documentation can confirm it.

'I passed a rather restless night,' Mildred wrote in her diary, 'I fancy everyone in France did. All night I heard a murmur of voices, such an unusual thing here. It simply meant that the town was awake and, the night being warm, every one was out of doors.'

Mildred noted another unusual activity in her diary:

All day today aeroplanes have been flying between Paris and the frontier. Everything that flies seems to go right over my roof. Early this morning I saw two machines meet, right over my garden, circle about each other as if signalling, and fly off together. I could not help feeling as if one chapter of Wells' *War in the Air* had come to pass. It did make me realise how rapidly the aeroplane had developed into a real weapon of war ... it is awe compelling ... how these cars in the air [will] change all military tactics.

As Mildred marvelled at yet another technological advance in her lifetime, she was unaware that those aeroplanes zooming over her head between Paris and the frontier were collecting intelligence to identify the direction the mighty German army would take: their objective to capture Paris. The Kaiser's Chief of General Staff, Helmuth von Moltke, and General Alexander von Kluck would spearhead the attack.

The mood at Huiry was sombre but expectant, as Mildred noted in her diary: 'We have had a sort of intermittent communication with the outside world ... after a week of deprivation, we began to get letters and an occasional newspaper, brought over from Meaux by a boy on a bicycle.' She goes on to recall a memory of long ago that her present situation brought to the forefront of her mind once again:

I am old enough to remember well the days of our Civil War, when regiments of volunteers, with flying flags and bands of music, marched through our streets in Boston, on the way to the front. Crowds of stay-at-homes, throngs of women and children lined the sidewalks, shouting deliriously, and waving handkerchiefs, inspired by the marching soldiers, with guns on their shoulders, and the strains of martial music, varied with the then popular 'The Girl I Left Behind Me,' or 'When This Cruel War is Over'. But this is quite different. There are no marching soldiers, no flying flags, no bands of music. It is the rising up of a Nation as one man – all classes shoulder to shoulder, with but one idea – 'Lift up your hearts, and long live France'.

Ever since 4 August, all our crossroads have been guarded, all our railway gates closed, and also guarded – guarded by men whose only sign of being soldiers is a cap and a gun, men in blouses with a mobilisation badge on their left arms, often in patched trousers and sabots, with stern faces and determined eyes, and one thought – 'The country is in danger'.

The Kaiser's army had planned an invasion route to Paris that would lead them along the Marne Valley right past Mildred's garden at Huiry. The first major battle of the war would be fought below Mildred's house. It was only matter of time before the soldiers arrived:

So, after less than a month of peaceful digging in the soil I stood one morning on the lawn, which I had just mowed for the first time myself – and gazed off to the north-east and shivered, as I said to myself – I did not dare say it out loud – 'war'. What was it going to mean to us here, between the frontier and Paris?

6

MOBILISATION AND PREPARATIONS

In my own heart, I know that [Sir John] French is quite unfit for this great Command at a time of crisis in our Nation's History.
But I thought it sufficient to tell the King that I had 'doubts' about his selection

> Lieutenant General Sir Douglas Haig to King George V –
> 11 August 1914

Haig had met the King and Queen at Aldershot on that August afternoon, as mobilisation plans were well underway to get the British Expeditionary Force on the move and across the channel. The King was in a positive and jolly mood and seemed delighted with everyone he met. Haig was concerned, as in his opinion the King seemed to not 'give the impression that he fully realised the grave issues both for our Country as well as for his own house'. As the royal family had predominantly German roots and familial ties, Haig feared that the King and Queen had not considered the implications this would have on them and their family. All things German were fast becoming very unpopular and that included any Germans who found themselves in foreign lands. Haig recorded in his dairy the events of that afternoon:

The King & Queen arrive at Aldershot at 12 noon. His Majesty joins me in an open car and we motor around the lines. The troops turn out and line the roads and give their Majesties a cheer as they pass along … The King seemed delighted that Sir John French had been appointed to the Chief Command of the Expeditionary Force. He asked my opinion. I told him at once, as I felt it my duty to do so ...

Haig was much younger than Sir John and perhaps he saw French as a bit of a dinosaur in his military and tactical abilities. Whatever the reason, Haig was pretty direct in expressing his less than shining opinion of Sir John to the King. 'I had grave doubts, however, whether his temper was sufficiently even,' continued Haig, 'or his military knowledge sufficiently thorough to enable him to discharge properly the very difficult duties which will devolve upon him during the coming operations with Allies on the continent.'

The King and Queen went on to have a private lunch with Haig and his wife, Doris, before returning to London with much food for thought. Haig's comments on Sir John made little difference, because nothing changed and the King continued to give him his full support. Haig consoled himself with his position:

> But in all my dreams I have never been so bold as to imagine that when war did break out, that I should hold one of the most important commands in the British Army. I feel very pleased at receiving command of the First Army and I also feel the greatest confidence that we will give a good account of ourselves, *if only* our High Command give us a reasonable chance.

The British Expeditionary Force began to arrive in France on 12 August, giving Sir John a chance to meet with his Allied generals and officers – including Joffre. The meeting seems to have done nothing to improve communication or indeed cooperation between the two forces. Meanwhile, the German army, led by Helmuth von Moltke (Chief of the General Staff), General Alexander von Kluck (Chief of Staff 1st Army), General von Kuhl, Eric Ludendorf (Deputy Chief of Staff 2nd Army) and General Karl von Bullow (2nd Army), was on the move across Belgium, following the long-mooted Schlieffen plan. Kluck was determined to to proceed into France as quickly as possible – then a swift march to Paris and capitulation. Or at least that was the often discussed and hoped for outcome. The French and BEF forces had other plans.

On 15 August Haig crossed to France on the SS *Comrie Castle* determined to do his country proud in spite of his misgivings about his Commander-in-Chief. Meanwhile Sir John had been divulging his thoughts about Joffre and his men. In his rather old-fashioned way he felt that French officers were not exactly gentlemen, and he was not afraid to make his thoughts clear to anyone who would listen. '*Au fond*, they are a low lot, and one always has to remember the class these French generals mostly come from.' English snobbery perhaps, but it was the system that Sir John had lived through. There was also animosity between Joffre and Sir John simply because of the crossed wires over who was in control of the combined Allied forces and who should take orders from whom and when. Blame for many of these difficulties lay at the door of Kitchener for not making sure his directive to Sir John was known officially to Joffre and the French Command. It was a far from positive start for either man. However, Sir John did respect the soldiers of France:

> These Frenchmen are gloriously brave, and I love them, but their leaders try me very hard sometimes. They always look at things from their own point of view, and consequently expect me to do the impossible ...

In France there was also much anti-German feeling, and those nationals in the country fled as quickly as possible to their own country to avoid retribution from the French populace. On 10 August Mildred recorded in her diary the problems being caused by German saboteurs as they fled back to their homeland:

> What makes things especially serious here, so near the frontier, and where the military movements must be made, is the presence of so many Germans, and the bitter feeling there is against them ... [Just] when the troops were beginning to move east, an attempt was made to blow up the railroad bridge at lie de Vilenoy, between here and Meaux. The three Germans were caught with the dynamite on them – so the story goes – and are in the barracks at Meaux.

By this time France was also under martial law and everyone had to carry passports and residents' permits, and show them on request or face the prospect of being marched to the nearest police station or barracks. The press was also heavily censored, which was a frustration for everyone, especially Mildred, but necessary:

> Meaux is full of Germans, the biggest department shop there is a German enterprise. Even Couilly has a German or two, and we

had one in our little hamlet. But they've got to get out. Our case is
rather pathetic. He was a nice chap, employed in a big fur house in
Paris. He came to France when he was fifteen, has never been back,
consequently has never done his military service there. He has no
relatives in Germany. Even though he is an intimate friend of our
mayor, the commune preferred to be rid of him. He begged not to be
sent back to Germany, so he went sadly enough to a concentration
camp, pretty well convinced that his career here was over.

The worst of it for Mildred was the interminable waiting, waiting and
more waiting to see what was going to happen and when. Rumours were
spreading, and stories of sabotage and German infiltrators, even reports
of German cavalry hiding in the woods, ran amok. It was impossible to
separate fact from dramatic French fiction in those August days. Making
the situation worse was the terrible heat. It was the hottest August anyone
could remember. This of course made the work in the fields even harder
for the farmers who, in spite of the advancing Germans, had to continue
with their harvest. Many were laying vegetables in their cellars, barrelling
apples and preserving as much of the summer fruit harvest as possible.
Mildred and Amélie worked hard to gather the blackberries growing in
the land between their houses and preserve them. Planting vegetables
was also imperative, as the railroads had been given entirely over to the
military and no produce of any kind was being sent from Paris. The local
shops were bare and would remain so. 'We can do without many things
in this life,' declared an ever practical Mildred, 'but we all need food.'
If it wasn't available to purchase, then they would have to grow their own.
At least they had their livestock, pigs, chickens, goats and rabbits, to provide them with some meat and goats' milk if all else failed.

In those early days Mildred did consider getting a slow train to Paris
to stock up on flour, sugar and tea. On this trip she would also be able to
make sure she had a reserve of money from the bank that she could hide
in the house and quickly bring to hand if she had to evacuate at short
notice. She had been thinking of this since war was declared and how
she could achieve it. Whatever, it would have to include Amélie and her
aged husband, Abelard. It amazed Mildred how they had become such
a fixture in her life in such a short time. The problem was that all trains
had been commandeered by the military.

On 19 August, Haig recorded in his diary the deterioration of the
situation and the seemingly unstoppable German push through Belgium.

'I gather that the Belgium Army is falling back on Antwerp while the Germans are crossing in considerable strength ... This looks as if an effort is to be made to turn the French left ... The neighbourhood of Waterloo and Charleroi should then be the scene of another great battle.' Kluck's army was advancing through Belgium and was about to clash with the British Expeditionary Force at the French city of Mons. But Mildred's concerns were more local:

> The latest news from Couilly concerned the barber who occupied a shop in one principal street in the village, which is, by the way, a comparatively rich place. He had a front shop, which was a café, with a well fitted up bar. The back, with a well-dressed window on the street, full of toilette articles, was the barber and hair-dressing room, very neatly arranged, with modern set bowls and mirrors, cabinets full of towels, well-filled shelves of all the things that make such a place profitable. You should see it now. Its broken windows and doors stand open to the weather. The entire interior has been 'efficiently' wrecked. It is a systematic work of destruction as I have ever seen. Not a thing was stolen, but not an article was spared. All the bottles full of things to drink and all the glasses to drink out of are smashed, so are the counters, tables, chairs, and shelving. In the barber shop there is a litter of broken porcelain, broken combs, and smashed-up chairs and boxes among a wreck of hair dyes, perfumes, brilliantine, and torn towels, and an odor of aperitifs and cologne over it all.

Mildred goes on the say that nobody seemed to know who was responsible or even how this happened during the night. 'It was found like that,' everyone says. The barber and owner had fled, never to be seen again. 'Everyone goes to look at it,' Mildred noted, 'no one enters, no one touches anything. They simply say with a smile of scorn, "Good – and so well done".' It was chilling but inevitable considering the stories beginning to seep through from invaded Belgium.

In Paris, at the general headquarters of the BEF, Sir John was to get a shock directive from Kitchener, still based at the War Office in London. Kitchener was not always popular because of the way he issued demands and directives that cared little for the morale of his staff or his generals. Sir John was told that his nemesis, Sir Horace Smith-Dorrien, had been given the command of II Corps of the British Expeditionary Force in spite of Sir John requesting another be given the post. Sir John, known for his volatile temper and rages, exploded with indignation at this deliberate slight. It was a development he could do little about, and he had no choice but to work with Smith-Dorrien. On 18 August, Sir John met with his commanders – though Smith-Dorrien was not present – and he presented them with his 'probable but tentative plans' in light of intelligence to confirm that masses of German troops were approaching the Meuse: should they attack as expected 'we shall advance on the line Mons-Diant to meet it'.

On 19 August two aircraft from the Royal Flying Corps made their first ever flights to gather intelligence and to help track German movements. These planes would have flown back and forth over Mildred's house as they carried out their missions between Paris and the frontier. All this activity, along with the waiting, and the interminable heat, created a strange other-worldly feeling to life at Huiry and from her hilltop position Mildred would watch the planes buzz over her house and off into the distance as they became smaller and smaller. The thought most often in her mind was the wish that she knew what they were doing. It was perhaps just as well she didn't. Mildred did however manage to get some news that lifted her spirits after having had no real news for weeks.

About this time Mildred recorded in her diary her feelings about Belgium, its plight and the arrival of the BEF:

I have Belgium on my soul. Brave little country that has given new proof of its courage and nobility, and surprised the world with a ruler who is a man, as well as a King. It occurs to me more than ever to-day in what a wonderful epoch we have lived. I simply can't talk about it. The suspense is so great. I heard this morning from an officer that English [Great British] troops are still landing, though he tells me that in London [the public] don't yet know the Expedition has started. If it is true, it is wonderful.

Lack of hard news had frustrated everyone, but this news of the BEF caused much excitement and relief. 'Everything is quiet here. Our little commune sent two hundred men only [to enlist in the French Army], but to take two hundred men away makes a big hole, and upsets life in many ways.'

Mildred had also managed to come by some information as to what had happened to Belgium. It seemed unbelievable to her that

Germany's kaiser had demanded access through that little country to enable his armies to invade France. He also wanted the Belgian king to assure him that the German troops would have a free and safe passage through Belgium, unhindered and unopposed by his own forces.

> The noblest and most deathless gesture was that of little Belgium when, without a moment of hesitation, she threw herself in front of that marching horde of Germans, contemptuously despising the bargain offered her by the nation which had already broken faith, and knowing she had only the strength to delay the passage she could not check, chose death rather than dishonor ... I consider it to be of an indelible stain on the honor of every government – mine or any other – which did not immediately proclaim that act as the eternal shame of Germany.

The stories of German atrocities towards Belgian women and children had also begun to trickle through to French civilians, creating real fear and horror. Mildred was shocked and found it hard to believe that German soldiers were so ill-disciplined as to rape and plunder as they marched over their Belgian captives. There were also stories of German soldiers cutting off the hands of small boys to ensure they could not be soldiers when they grew up. It was horrific and frightening. Refugees began to pass through the valley, fleeing from Belgium, and what a sorry sight they were. Cars and carts packed with weary and stunned women, children, the elderly and the frail, dozens of them in a continual stream of the dispossessed rattling along hot and dusty roads. They also began to get sight of the first wounded French and British troops being sent back from the front to Paris. It was heartbreaking to witness, but it seemed to create a steely resolve in Mildred and Amélie.

'Amélie walked to Esbly, and came back with the news they were [also] rushing trains full of wounded soldiers and Belgian refugees through towards Paris, and that the ambulance there was quite insufficient for the work it had to do.' Mildred and Amélie hatched a plan to help in whatever way they could:

> So Monday and Tuesday we drove down in the donkey cart to carry bread and fruit, water and cigarettes and to 'lend a hand.' It was a pretty terrible sight. There were long trains of wounded soldiers.

There was train after train crowded with Belgians – well dressed women and children (evidently all in their Sunday best) – packed onto open trucks, sitting on straw, in the burning sun, without shelter, covered with dust, hungry and thirsty.

As they did their best to help, Mildred began to realise this was just the start of something much more serious. Standing on the train platform she heard a drum beating on the road outside and sent Amélie to see what it was. She came back to say they were asking all inhabitants to take all their guns and revolvers to the nearest collection point before sundown. This news sent a shiver through Mildred: 'it flashed through my mind that the Germans must be nearer than the official announcements had told us.'

It would get worse. As Mildred noticed another set of wagons approaching the station, she asked Amélie to find out what it was. 'While I was reflecting a moment, Amélie ran down the track to the crossing to see what it meant, and came back at once to tell me that they were evacuating the towns to the north of us.' Mildred was shocked by the news. 'I handed the basket of fruit I was holding into a coach of the train just pulling into the station , and threw my last package of cigarettes after it; and, without a word, Amélie and I went out into the street, untied the donkey, climbed into the wagon, and started for home.'

On that journey home Mildred and Amélie would witness refugees, now from the French towns and villages, being evacuated to save them from the German advance. Mildred reflected that the invading force seemed unstoppable based on what she was witnessing. For the first time she allowed herself to admit she was afraid:

By the time we got to the road which leads to Montry, whence there is a road over the hill to the south, it was full of the flying crowd. It was a sad sight. The procession led in both directions as far as we could see. There were huge wagons of grain; there were herds of cattle, flocks of sheep; there were wagons full of household effects, with often as many as twenty people sitting aloft; there were carriages; there were automobiles with the occupants crowded in among bundles done up in sheets; there were women pushing overloaded handcarts; there were women pushing baby-carriages; there were dogs and cats, and goats; there was every sort of vehicle you ever saw, drawn by every sort of beast that can draw, from dogs to oxen, from boys to donkeys. Here and there was a man on horseback, riding along the line, trying to keep it moving in order and to encourage the weary. Everyone was calm and silent. There was no talking, no complaining.

The whole road was, however, blocked, and, even had our donkey wished to pass, which she did not, we could not. We simply fell into the procession, as soon as we found a place. Amélie and I did not say a word to each other until we reached the road that turns off to the Chateau de Conde; but I did speak to a man on horseback, who proved to be the intendant of one of the chateaux at Daumartin, and with another who was mayor. I simply asked from where these people had come, and was told that they were evacuating Daumartin and all the towns on the plain between there and Meaux, which meant that Monthyon, Neufmortier, Penchard, Chauconin, Barcy, Chambry – in fact all the villages visible from my garden were being evacuated by order of the military powers … I turned to look at Amélie for the first time. I had had time to get a good hold of myself.

'Well, Amélie?' I said.

'Oh, *madame*,' she replied, 'I shall stay.'

'And so shall I.' I answered; but I added, 'I think I must make an effort to get to Paris to-morrow, and I think you had better come with me. I shall not go, of course, unless I am sure of being able to get back …'

'Very well, *madame*,' she replied as cheerfully as if the rumble of the procession behind us was not still in our ears.

Mildred and Amélie organised themselves very quickly. Amélie arranged for her elderly husband, Abelard, to go and stay with relatives in Paris. This they were able to arrange on one of the last trains into Paris. It was on the return journey that they discovered that Meaux was also being evacuated. Mildred also remembered:

Just after we left Esbly I saw first an English officer, standing in his stirrups and signalling across a field, where I discovered a detachment of English artillery going towards the hill. A little farther along the road we met a couple of English officers – pipes in their mouths and sticks in their hands – strolling along as quietly as if there was no such thing as war. [...] The sight of them and their cannon made me feel a bit serious. I thought to myself: 'If the Germans are not expected here

– well it looks like it.' We finished the journey in silence, and I was so tired when I got back to the house that I fell into bed, and only drank a glass of milk that Amélie insisted on pouring down my throat.

Once they had returned, it was decided that Amélie would close her house and move in with Mildred at La Creste – this would also mean that the wood and coal they had could last longer if only one house was heated and one kitchen active. Mildred wished she had asked the English soldiers more questions, but thought they would probably not have told her anything anyway. Mildred had also been able to withdraw a reserve of money from the bank in Paris that would be vital should they have to leave in a hurry. They had also managed to bring back a good supply of dry goods that Amélie immediately stored away for future use.

The next day Amélie began to bury all her china, linens and valuables in a hole in the floor of her barn. This was to stop them being looted. She wanted to bury Mildred's books and valuables too but Mildred refused to even consider it. She was adamant that her books would be buried only when she was.

> Naturally I gave a decided refusal to any move of that sort ... my books and portraits are the only things I should be eternally hurt to survive ... I refused to listen. I had no idea [of considering] putting my books underground to be mildewed ... I felt a good deal like the Belgian refugees I had seen, – all so well dressed; if my house was going up, it was going up in its best clothes. I had just been uprooted once – a horrid operation – and I did not propose to do it again so soon.

The argument ceased when they heard the sound of artillery explosions in the distance. The sound of aeroplanes zooming and buzzing over the roof was also adding to the tension. If they could hear artillery, however far off, it meant only one thing. The Germans were advancing on Paris, and fast.

The BEF did temporarily stop Kluck's advance at Mons on 23 August, but the small British force was soon overwhelmed by the sheer size of the German army and Kluck's forces thundered into France, heading towards Paris. On 24 August, Joffre gave orders for the French army to retreat in the face of the German advance. The next day, 25 August, Joffre began to form a new army with troops transferred from Alsace and Lorraine. Sir John believed the French army was a beaten force. By 26 August, at the Battle of Le Cateau, the BEF gave Kluck's army a bloody nose during hard fighting. However, Kluck's army continued to advance and declared the BEF defeated. By the end of August it seemed that the Germans were unstoppable and the French and BEF spent forces. The German Supreme Headquarters reported the 'allied armies in full retreat' and that they were 'incapable of offering serious resistance'.

The casualties, evacuees and refugees Mildred had seen pouring through the Marne, fleeing to Paris, were displaced by the military action attempting to halt the German advance. Towns and villages were evacuated because the French military believed that the Germans would destroy them and everyone still living in them. The precaution turned out to be wise and undoubtedly saved thousands of civilian lives.

Haig recorded in his diary: 'General Joffre arrives, looking very worried, so are his Staff. All the Fifth French Army has been defeated and is falling back. Sr J. French decides that our army must fall back … retreat to begin at once …'

'It is too sad losing so many good fellows,' Haig wrote to his wife on 3 September, 'without materially affecting the result of the campaign. I should like to see the whole of our Expeditionary Force moved entirely forward to Ostend, where we could operate on our own against the German lines of communication which pass through Belgium. The French are most unreliable. One cannot believe a word they say as a rule!' He ended his letter with a more personal detail. 'I must tell you what a comfort the little spirit lamp and tin in the leather case has been. I use it for Maggi soup usually twice a day, and of course the luncheon box is always in use.' Joffre would have been horrified if he had known how little respect his British allies held him and his army in.

Mildred's friend Gertrude Stein found herself, much to her frustration, trapped in England at the outbreak of the war. Mildred believed that, as much as Gertrude complained by letter of her plight and her refusal to evacuate, she was in fact a little jealous and more than a little annoyed to find herself detached from history in the making in her beloved France. Mildred rather rubbed salt into that wound by writing:

Oh the things I have seen and felt since I last wrote to you over two weeks ago. Here I am again cut off from the world, and have been since the first of the month. For a week now I have known nothing of

what was going on in the world outside the limits of my own vision.
For that matter since the Germans crossed the frontier our news of
the war [at the Front] has been meagre. We [get] the calm, constant
reiteration – 'Left wing – held by the English – forced to retreat a little'.

All the same, the general impression was, that in spite of everything,
'all was well'. Mildred had also noticed there was a picket (armed British soldier) at her gate and patrolling the lane.

The next day Mildred and Amélie were surprised to hear a knock
at the door. It was a young girl from the village down the hill. She had
come on the instructions of her mother to inform them of what was
happening in the villages. 'Of course you know,' she said to Mildred,
'that every one has left Couilly; all the shops are closed, and nearly
every one has gone from Voisins and Quincy.' She asked if they were
staying, and then informed them that her mother had sent her to offer
them a seat in their wagon, 'a chance to go with us' if they wanted
to. Mildred thanked her, but told her they were staying. 'I was really
touched,' remembered Mildred, 'and I told her so.'

Mildred returned to the dining room to find Amélie, in spite of her
mistress's decision, packing away the silver and odd bits of china that
she thought valuable and worth hiding:

> I was too tired to argue. [While] I stood watching her there was a
> tremendous explosion. I rushed into the garden. The picket, his gun
> on his shoulder, was at the gate.
>
> 'What was that?' I called out to him.
>
> 'Bridge,' he replied. 'The English divisions are destroying the
> bridges on the Marne behind them as they cross. That means that
> another division is over.'
>
> I asked him what bridge it was, but of course he did not know.
> While I was standing there, trying to locate it by smoke, an English
> officer, who looked of middle age, tall, clean-cut, rode down the
> road on the chestnut horse, as slight, as clean-cut, and well groomed
> as himself.

On 4 September 1914, Haig recorded in his diary a meeting with
Sir John: 'I stated that our troops were tired out, that we could hold
a position but that they could not attack or move at the "double".
Smith-Dorrien had arrived and concurred in all I said.' On that same

day Joffre ordered a French counter-attack that would result in the Battle of the Marne. It was agreed that the BEF would advance and slip into a gap between the German armies.

The next day, 5 September, Haig's diary entry reported that 'the day was cooler: the troops marched with more life [after a good rest].' A note had arrived from GHQ in Paris from Sir John, asking Haig to pay particular attention to it. 'The latter [part] was to the effect that the French were really going to stand and attack [at Marne Valley]! This time there was to be no doubt about it: they would fight to the death!' Haig concluded from this that 'if the French advance, and if the Germans don't attack before the French organise their forces for an attack, then the situation seems favourable for us'.

As the British forces arrived at the Marne they were joined by more of the French army. Their joint objective was to stop the Germans advancing on and capturing Paris. Joffre and the French High Command were determined to fight to prevent a repeat of the capitulation that ended the Franco-Prussian War in 1870. They would rather die than face that humiliation again. Sir John, still trying to go against Kitchener's orders for the BEF to remain at the front, wanted to minimise what he thought would be a disaster. He believed that the French army was outclassed and faced certain defeat at the hands of the Germans, especially bearing in mind Kluck's ruthlessness. He thought it would be wiser for the BEF to retreat to the channel ports.

The British troops were ready to fight, and fight hard. They were in good spirits in spite of marching miles across country and fighting with limited rations. The smell of thousands of unwashed male bodies, intensified by the sweltering heat, seemed to drift and cling to the countryside. British soldiers could be heard singing lustily a familiar song, 'The Girl I Left Behind Me', with alternative lyrics of their own invention:

Oh, oh, oh, we don't give a F**k,
For old von Kluck!
And all his German army!

7

THE FRENCH MIRACLE

The first description that any one we knew received
in England of the battle of the Marne came in a letter from
Mildred. We were delighted to receive it, to know that
Mildred was safe, and to know all about it.

Alice B. Toklas & Gertrude Stein

Mildred formed her first relationship with an officer of the British
Expeditionary Force as it arrived, along with French troops, in preparation for a battle to stop the German advance at the Marne Valley.
Mildred's garden gave a panoramic view across the valley and was
therefore ideally placed to witness this momentous moment – if and
when it occurred. If the Germans succeeded in advancing past the
Marne, Paris would lie open before them. It was unthinkable and why
Joffre was determined to fight to prevent that happening, and to push
the Germans back as far as possible so that he could make Paris safe.

The enormity of what was happening around Mildred was beginning to make her realise that she had to be prepared for any situation.
She had decided to pack some emergency items – clean underwear,
chocolate, cigarettes and money – into a hat box that she placed by
the stairs for easy access in a hurry. She also insisted that Amélie pack
a small case of similar items for an emergency departure. Once that
was taken care of, they watched and waited as the BEF soldiers arrived
in greater numbers. Around 3 September 1914, she first saw Captain
John Edmund Simpson astride his horse as he trotted down the lane

outside her house. Mildred's account of their meeting that afternoon, and the following morning, as she first reported it in her letter to Gertrude Stein, and other friends in the United States, is worth recounting in full:

He rose in his stirrups to look off at the plain before he saw me. Then he looked at me, then up at the flags flying over the gate – saw the Stars and Stripes – smiled, and dismounted.'

'American, I see.' He said.

I told him I was.

'Live here?' said he.

I told him that I did.

'Staying on?' he asked.

I answered that it looked like it.

He looked me over a moment before he said, 'Please invite me into your garden and show me that view.'

I was delighted. I opened the gate, and he strolled in and sauntered with a long, slow stride – a long-legged stride – out onto the lawn and right down to the hedge, and looked off.

'Beautiful,' he said, as he took out his field-glass, and turned up the map case which hung at his side. 'What town is that?' he asked, pointing to the foreground.

'I told him it was Mareuil-on-the-Marne.

'How far off is it?' he questioned.

I told him that it was about two miles, and Meaux was about the same distance beyond it.

'What town is that?' he asked, pointing to the hill.

I explained that the town on the horizon was Penchard – not really a town, only a village; and lower down, between Penchard and Meaux, were Neufmortier and Chauconin.

All this time he was studying his map.

'Thank you. I have it,' he said. 'It is a lovely country, and this is a wonderful view of it, the best I have had.'

'For a few minutes he stood studying it in silence – alternatively looking at his map and then through his glass. Then he dropped his map, put his glasses into the case, and turned to me – and smiled. He had a winning smile, sad and yet consoling, which lighted up a bronzed face, stern and weary. It was the sort of smile to which everything was permitted.'

'Married?' he said.

You can imagine what he was like when I answered right up [Mildred disliked people asking if she was married and tended to be sharp in her response to such enquiries], and only thought it was funny hours after – or at least I shook my head cheerfully.

'You don't live here alone?' he asked.

'But I do,' I replied.

He looked at me bravely for a moment, then off at the plain.

'Lived here long?' he questioned.

I told him that I had lived in the house only three months, but that I had lived.in France for sixteen years.

Without a word he turned back toward the house, and for half a minute, for the first time in my life, I had a sensation that it looked strange for me to be an exile in a country that was not mine, and with no ties. For a penny I would have told him the history of my life. Luckily he did not give me time. He just strode down to the gate, and by the time he had his foot in the stirrup I had recovered.

'Is there anything I can do for you, Captain?' I asked.

He mounted his horse, looked down at me. Then he gave me another of his rare smiles.

'No,' he said, 'at this moment there is nothing that you can do for me, thank you; but if you could give my boys a cup of tea, I imagine that you would just about save their lives.' And nodding to me, he said to the picket [soldier on guard at her gate], 'This lady is kind enough to offer you a cup of tea,' and he rode off, taking the road down the hill to Voisins.

I ran into the house, put on the kettle, ran up the road to call Amélie, and back to the arbour to set the table as well as I could. The whole atmosphere was changed. I was going to be useful.

I had no idea how many men I was going to feed. To this day I don't know how many I did feed. They came and came and came. It reminded me of hens running toward a place where another hen had found something good. It did not take me many minutes to discover that these men needed something more substantial than tea. Luckily I had brought back from Paris an emergency stock of things like biscuit, dry cakes, jam, etc, for even before our shops were closed there was mighty little in them. For an hour and a half I brewed pot after pot of tea, opened jar after jar of jam and jelly, and tin after tin of biscuit and cakes, and although it was hardly hearty fodder for men, they put it down with a relish. I have seen hungry men, but never anything as hungry as these boys.

Most of the BEF soldiers had marched into France from Belgium and had been fighting the Germans most of the way. They were hungry, tired, foot-sore and ill prepared to face Kluck's formidable army. The refreshments that Mildred gave them so willingly, with Amélie's help, were more than appreciated. Not least because she could also speak English, and was happy to exercise her maternal instincts on all these young boys:

> I knew little about military discipline – less about the rules of active service; so I had no idea that I was letting these hungry men – evidently hunger laughs at laws – break all the regulations of the army. Their guns were lying about in any old place; their kits were on the ground; their belts were unbuckled. Suddenly the captain rode up the road and looked over the hedge at the scene. The men were sitting on the benches, on the ground, anywhere, and were all smoking my best Egyptian cigarettes, and I was running round as happy as a queen, seeing them so contented and comfortable. It was a rude awakening when the captain rode up the street.
>
> There was a sudden jumping up, a hurried buckling up of belts, a grab for kits and guns, and an unceremonious cut for the gate. I heard a volley from the officer. I marked a serious effort on the part of men to keep the smiles off their faces as they hurriedly got their kits on their backs and their guns on their shoulders, and, rigidly saluting, dispersed up the hill, leaving two very straight men marching before the gate as if they never in their lives had thought of anything but picket duty.
>
> The captain never looked at me, but rode up the hill after his men. A few minutes later he returned, dismounted at the gate, tied his horse, and came in. I was a bit confused. But he smiled one of those smiles of his, and I got right over it.
>
> 'Dear little lady,' he said, 'I wonder if there is any tea left for me?'
>
> Was there! I should think so; and I thought to myself, as I led the way into the dining-room, that he was probably just as hungry as his men.
>
> While I was making a fresh brew he said to me: 'You must forgive my giving my men Hades right before you, but they deserved it, and

know it, and under the circumstances I imagine they did not mind taking it. I did not mean you to give them a party, you know. Why, if the major had ridden up that hill – and he might have – and seen that party inside your garden, I should have lost my commission and those boys got the guardhouse. These men are on active service.'

Then, while he drank his tea, he told me why he felt a certain indulgence for them – these boys who were hurried away from England without having a chance to take leave of their families, or even to warn them that they were going.

'This is the first time that they have had a chance to talk to a woman who speaks their tongue since they left England; I can't begrudge it to them and they know it. But discipline is discipline, and if I had let such a breach of it pass they would have no respect for me. They understand. They had no business to put their guns out of their hands. What would they have done if the detachment of Uhlans [German Cavalry] we are watching for dashed up the hill – as they might have?'

Before I could answer or remark on this startling speech there was a tremendous explosion, which brought me to my feet, with the inevitable, 'What's that?'

He took a long pull at his tea before he replied quietly, 'Another division across the Marne.'

Then he went on as if there had been no interruption: 'This Yorkshire regiment has had hard luck. Only one other regiment of the Expedition has had worse. They have marched from the Belgian frontier, and they have been in four big actions in the retreat – Mons, Cambrai, Saint-Quentin, and La Fere. Saint-Quentin was pretty rough luck. We went into the trenches a full regiment. We came out to retreat again with four hundred men – and I left my younger brother there.'

I gasped; I could not find a word to say. He did not seem to feel it necessary that I should. He simply winked his eyelids, stiffened his stern mouth, and went right on; and I forgot all about the Uhlans – 'At La Fere we lost our commissary on the field. It was burned, and these lads have not had a decent feed since – that was three days ago. We have passed through few towns since, and those were evacuated, – drummed out and fruit from the orchards on the roadsides is about all they have had – hardly good feed for a marching army in such hot weather. Besides, we were moving pretty fast – but in order – to get across the Marne, toward which we have been drawing the Germans, and in every one of these battles we have been fighting with one man to their ten.'

I asked him where the Germans were.

'Can't say,' he replied.

'And the French?'

'No idea. We've not seen them – yet. We understood that we were to be reinforced at Saint-Quentin by a French detachment at four o'clock. They got there at eleven – the battle was over – and lost. But these boys gave a wonderful account of themselves, and in spite of the disaster retreated in perfect order.'

Then he told me that at the last moment he ordered his company to lie close in the trench and let the Germans come right up to them, and not to budge until he ordered them to give them what they hate – the bayonet. The Germans were within a few yards when a German automobile carrying a machine gun bore down on them and discovered their position, but the English sharpshooters [snipers] picked off the five men the car carried before they could fire a shot, and after that it was every man for himself – what the French call '*sauve qui peut*'.

The Uhlans came back to my mind, and it seemed to me a good time to ask him what he was doing here. Oddly enough, in spite of several shocks I had had, and perhaps because of his manner, I was able to do it as if it was the sort of tea-table conversation to which I had always been accustomed.

'What are you doing here?' I said.

'Waiting for orders,' he answered.

'And for Uhlans?

'Oh,' replied he, 'if incidentally while we are sitting down here to rest, we could rout out a detachment of German cavalry, which our aeroplane tells us crossed the Marne [river] ahead of us, we would like to. Whether this is one of those flying squads they are so fond of sending ahead, just to do a little terrorising, or whether they escaped from the Battle of La Fere, we don't know. I fancy the latter, as they do not seem to have done any harm or to have been to anxious to be seen.'

I do not need to tell you that my mind was acting like lightening [*sic*]. I remembered, in the pause, as I poured him another cup of tea, and pushed the jam pot toward him, that Amélie had heard at Voisins last night that there were horses in the woods near the canal; that they had been heard neighing in the night; and that we had jumped to the conclusion that there were English cavalry there. I mentioned this to the captain, but for some reason it did not seem to make much impression on him; so I did not insist, as there was something that seemed more important which I had been getting up the courage to ask him. It had been on my lips all day. I put it.

'Captain,' I asked, 'do you think there is any danger in my staying here?'

He took a long drink before he answered.

'Little lady, there is danger everywhere between Paris and the Channel. Personally – since you have stayed until getting away will be difficult – I do not really believe there is any reason why you should not stick it out. You may have a disagreeable time … at all events, I am going to do what I can to assure your personal safety – no one really knows anything except orders given out – it is not intended that the Germans shall cross the Marne here. But who knows? Anyway, if I move on, each division of the Expeditionary Force that retreats to this hill will know you are here. If it is necessary, later, for you to leave, you will be notified and precautions taken for your safety. You are not afraid?'

I could only tell him, 'Not yet,' but I could not help adding, 'Of course I am not so stupid as to suppose for a moment that you English have retreated here to amuse yourselves, or that you have dragged your artillery up the hill behind me just to exercise your horses or to give your gunners a pretty promenade.'

He threw back his head and laughed aloud for the first time, and I felt better.

'Precautions do not always mean a battle, you know'; and as he rose to his feet he called my attention to a hole in his coat, saying, 'It was a miracle that I came through Saint Quentin with a whole skin. The bullets simply rained about me. It was pouring – I had on a mackintosh – which made me conspicuous as an officer, if my height had not exposed me. Every German regiment carries a number of sharpshooters [snipers] whose business is to pick off the officers. However, it was evidently not my hour.

As we walked out the gate I asked him if there was anything else I could do for him.

'Do you think,' he replied, 'that you could get me a couple of fresh eggs at half-past seven and let me have a cold wash-up?'

'Well rather,' I answered, and he rode away.

As soon as he was gone one of the pickets called from the road to know if they could have 'water and wash'.

I told them of course they could – to come right in.

He said they could not do that, but that if they could have water at the gate – and I did not mind – they could wash up in relays in the road. We drew buckets and buckets of water, and you never saw such a stripping and such a slopping, as they washed and shaved – and with such dispatch. They had just got through, luckily, when, at about half-past six, the captain rode hurriedly down the hill again. He carried a slip of white paper in his hand, which he seemed intent on deciphering.

As I met him at the gate he said: 'Sorry I shall miss those eggs – I've orders to move east,' and he began to round up his men.

I foolishly asked him why. I felt as if I were losing a friend.

'Orders,' he answered. Then he put the slip of paper into his pocket, and leaning down he said: 'Before I go I am going to ask you to let my corporal pull down your flags. You may think it cowardly. I think it prudent. They can be seen a long way. It is silly to wave a red flag at a bull. Any needless display of bravado on your part would be equally foolish.'

All this time he had been searching in a letter-case, and finally selected an envelope from which he removed the letter, passing me the empty cover.

'I want you,' he said, 'to write me a letter – that address will always reach me. I shall be anxious to know how you came through, and every one of these boys will be interested. You have given them the only happy day they have had since they left home. As for me – if I live – I shall some time come back to see you. Good-bye and good luck.' And he wheeled his horse and rode up the hill, his boys marching behind him; and at the turn of the road they all looked back and I waved my hand, and I don't mind telling you that I nodded to the French at the gate and got into the house as quickly as I could – and wiped my eyes. Then I cleared up the tea mess. It was not until the house was in order again that I put on my glasses and read the envelope that the captain had given me:

Capt. J.E. Simpson
King's Own Yorkshire I., VIth Infantry Brigade
15th Division, British Expeditionary Force

And I put it carefully away in my address book until the time should come for me to write and tell 'how I came through'; the phrase did disturb me a little.

I did not eat any supper. Food seemed to be the last thing I wanted. I sat down in the study to read. It was about eight when I heard the gate open. Looking out I saw a man in khaki, his gun on his shoulder, marching up the path. I went to the door.

'Good evening, ma'am,' he said. 'All right?'

I assured him that I was.

'I am the corporal of the guard,' he added. 'The commander's compliments, and I was to report to you that your road was picketed for the night and that all is well.'

I thanked him, and he marched away, and took up his post at the gate, and I knew that this was the commander's way of letting me know that Captain Simpson had kept his word. I had just time while the corporal stood at the door to see 'Bedford' on his cap, so I knew that the new regiment was from Bedfordshire.

For Mildred the meeting with Captain Simpson and his boys was just the start. She had been strangely charmed by this wistful, almost ethereal, captain of the BEF – and he never left her mind. In the days prior to the war if any man had addressed her as 'My dear little lady,' they would have received a curt reply from Mildred, as she would have found it insulting and patronising. However, he was a rare exception and she didn't really know why. As new regiments arrived, with their officers, she fed and watered the boys as best she could and with what little she had. It was a constant toil of boiling kettles and washing towels as the men stripped, washed and shaved on the trestle table set up by her gate. The overpowering smell of so many unwashed male bodies seemed to ease temporarily – however, the stench clung and lingered like a fog, creeping into every nook and cranny.

As the hours passed Mildred began to realise that Captain Simpson had been trying to ease her fears about having stayed. He knew, with a fair degree of certainty, what was to come. He also knew that there was no way Mildred could escape at such a late stage and that she was trapped on the hill, with British artillery behind her house, a target for German artillery shells. The explosions that seemed far off were now getting closer and closer – there were more huge explosions in the valley below as the BEF destroyed the bridges crossing the Marne in an attempt to halt the German advance and prepare for the offensive.

Moltke had instructed his 2nd Army to move in behind his 1st Army to give it cover on its exposed flank when it moved on the Marne river. Kluck chose to ignore this order and attempted to continue with his own rapid attack to try and cross the Marne. This exposed the right flank and made it vulnerable to an attack from Joffre and the French army divisions. Joffre planned an offensive to begin on 7 September but Sir John French was reluctant to allow the BEF to get involved. By 5 September Sir John had capitulated and the BEF joined the offensive with the French north of Meaux. The Battle of the two Morins ensued and Kluck skilfully moved his troops. The BEF cut off Kluck's path. The hope was that the Germans would eventually begin to retreat.

Haig recorded in his diary: 'Officers arrived from the Sixth French army saying that they were hard pressed on the Ourcq [river] and asking us to push on to their support. This report gave colour to the belief that this army of the French had been beaten and that the Germans had brought up fresh troops which had been besieging Maubeuge.' He added, 'I sent out aeroplane reconnaissance and so I was able to send word to divisions to continue the march and that the enemy was [actually] in full retreat ... the enemy was running back. It was the duty of each one of us to strain every effort to keep him on the run.'

Mildred was for the first time conscious of the fact that she was cut off from her friends and the outside world as the battle for the Marne began to rage below in the valley. The BEF had destroyed most of the bridges by this stage and had also stopped the trains by destroying the tracks at the main crossing; in addition they had cut all the telegraph wires to prevent them being used by the Germans. The sound of artillery explosions and rifle fire began to predominate along with the smell of cordite, stale smoke, burning wood and fear:

Almost everyone ... I knew on this side of the water was either at Havre waiting to sail, or in London, or shut up in Holland or Denmark; that except for the friends I had at the front I was alone with my beloved France and her Allies. Through it all ran a thought that made me laugh at last – how all through August I had felt so outside of things, only suddenly to find it right at my door. In the back of my mind – stood the question – what was to become of all this.

Sir John French, Commander of the BEF, reported events in despatches to Lord Kitchener and the King:

Retreat from the Aisne to the Marne: On 1 September, when retiring from the thickly wooded country to the south of Compiègne, the First Cavalry Brigade was overtaken by some German Cavalry [probably those hiding in woods near to Mildred's house and Voisins]. They momentarily lost a Horse Artillery battery, and several officers and men were killed or wounded. With help, however, some detachments from the Third Corps operating on their left, they not only recovered their own guns but succeeded in capturing twelve of the enemy's ...

On 3 September the British Forces were in position south of the Marne between Lagny and Signy-Signets. Up to this time I had been requested by General Joffre to defend the passage of the [Marne] river as long as possible, and blow up bridges in my front. After I made the necessary dispositions, and the destruction of the bridges had been affected, I was asked by the French Commander-in-Chief to continue my retirement to a point some 12 miles rear of the position I then occupied, with a view to take up a second position behind the Seine [river] ... In the meantime the enemy had thrown bridges and crossed the Marne in considerable force, and was threatening the allies all along the line of the British Forces and the Fifth and Ninth French Armies ...

Mildred, unaware of the military disasters unfolding, was kept busy looking after the countless soldiers of the BEF and the French soldiers that passed through on their way to the front. The constant barrage of explosions in the near and far distance punctuated the days and never ceased to make Amélie jump – much to everyone's amusement and her embarrassment. Mildred now found herself acquainted with Captain Edwards and Major Ellison of the Bedfordshire Light Infantry. Their men waited until the officers were out of sight and then they set up an area to wash in Amélie's courtyard as it was a little more private than the trestle table in the road:

As Amélie had put all the towels underground, I ran back and forward between my house and hers for all sorts of things, and, as they slopped until the road ran tiny rivulets, I had to change shoes and stockings twice. I was not conscious till afterwards how funny it all was. I must have been a good deal like an excited duck, and Amélie like a hen with a duckling. When she was not twitching my sash straight, she was running about after me with dry shoes and stockings, and a chair, for fear '*madame* was getting too tired...'

The boys she spoke to were sad because they had watched their mail wagon burn on the battlefield below – with all their mail from home in it. Mildred's heart ached for them and the forlorn looks on their faces – it had been so long since they had heard from their loved ones at home. She wished she could do more but contented herself with easing their plight, albeit temporarily:

> We were like old friends. I did not know one of them by name, but I did know who was married, and who had children; and how one man's first child had been born since he left England, and no news from home because of the burning mail wagon. One of them was only twenty, and had been six years in the army, – lied when he enlisted; how none of them had seen war before; how they had always wanted to, and 'Now,' said the twenty-year-older, 'I've seen it – good Lord – and all I want is to get home,' and he drew out of his breast pocket a photograph of a young girl in all her best clothes, sitting up very straight.

Mildred began to get on with tidying up the mess and collecting all the wet towels to wash and dry for the next batch of unwashed bodies. As she did a young soldier came up to her, smiled rather shyly and said after gathering the courage:

'I take it you're a lady?'

'I am glad you noticed it,' she replied giving him a reassuring smile.

'No, no,' he said, 'I'm not joking. I may not say it very well, but I am quite serious. We all want to say to you that if it is war that makes you and the women you live amongst so different from English women, then all we can say is that the sooner England is invaded and knows what it is to have a fighting army on her soil, and see her fields devastated and her homes destroyed, the better it will be for the race. You take my word for it, they have no notion of what war is like; and there ain't no English woman of your class could have, or would have, done for us what you have done this morning. Why, in England the common soldier is the dirt under the feet of women like you.'

Such bitterness and honesty made Mildred feel at times uncomfortable and lacking in anything constructive to say in response or reassurance.

Mildred was too tired and too happy to feel anything in the heat and moment of the busy days. But these comments made her think deeply once she was alone at night and these boys faces seemed to parade across her mind and haunt her night-time hours. She wondered constantly about Captain Simpson and where he could be, and if he was safe; and also if his boys were still doing themselves proud. It made her heart ache, but daily there were departures and new arrivals – her meeting with them all so fleeting but permanently etched into her life. And these intense, fleeting meetings were accompanied, always, by the sound of explosions and gunfire.

Amélie told her that the Uhlans, the German cavalry unit, had been seen at the bottom of the hill in Voisins and there was now a concerted effort to find them. They would be laying low as they would be unable to cross the river easily now most of the bridges had gone and because it seemed pretty certain that Kluck's army had been halted on the other side of the river. Captain Edwards came to see Mildred and she could not stop herself from asking some direct questions. All the English officers seemed so laid back, calm and almost indifferent. They were, she decided, masters at hiding their true feelings behind their rigid yet charming façades. Maybe it was the English 'class' system that made them so:

While I was making the tea, he walked about the house, looked at the pictures, examined the books. Just as the table was ready there was a tremendous explosion. He went to the door, looked off, and remarked, as if it were the most natural thing in the world, 'Another division across. That should be the last.'

'Are all the bridges down,' I asked.

'All, I think, except the big railroad bridge behind you – Chalifert. That will not go until the last minute.'

I wanted to ask, 'When will it be the "last minute" – and what does the "last minute" mean?' But where was the good? So we went into the dining room.

As he threw his hat onto a chair and sat down with a sigh, he said, 'You see before you a very humiliated man. About half an hour ago eight of the Uhlans we are looking for rode right into the street below you, in Voisins. We saw them, but they got away. It is absolutely our own stupidity.'

'I fancy I can tell you where they are hiding … the horses had been heard in the woods at the foot of the hill since Tuesday; that there was a cart road, rough and winding, running in towards Conde for over two miles; that it was absolutely screened by trees, had plenty of water, and not a house in it – a shelter for a regiment of cavalry.' And I had the impertinence to suggest that if the picket had been extended to the road below it would have been impossible for the Germans to have got into Voisins.

'Not enough of us,' he replied. 'We are guarding a wide territory, and cannot put our pickets out of sight of one another.' He went on to say they believed about twenty four were in the vicinity but had run out of ammunition. He then changed the subject.

On about 3 September Mildred recorded in her journal, and wrote to Gertrude Stein, who was still trapped across the channel in London, a letter she was not sure could even be posted, let alone delivered. That said, Mildred was determined to try to keep communication open between them– if only as a way of preserving the day-to-day events for history should her house and belongings fall victim to the German artillery shells that exploded ever closer. This account recalled a briefing she was given by Captain Edwards when he looked her in the eye and said: 'You want to know the truth?' 'Yes,' replied Mildred:

'Well, this is the situation,' Captain Edwardes said to me, 'as near as I can work it out. We infer from the work we were given to do – destroying bridges, railroads, telegraphic communications – that an effort is to be made here to stop the [German] march on Paris; in fact, the Germans are not to be allowed to cross the Marne at Meaux, and march on the city by the main road from Rheims to the capital. The communications are all cut. That does not mean that it will be impossible for them to pass; they've got clever engineers. It means we have impeded them and may stop them. I don't know. Just now your risk is nothing. It will be nothing unless we are ordered to hold this hill, which is the line of march from Meaux to Paris. We have had no such order yet. But if the Germans succeed in taking Meaux and attempt to put their bridges across the Marne, our artillery behind you there on the top of the hill, must open fire on them over your head. In that case the Germans will surely reply by bombarding this hill.

In the silence that followed, Mildred recalled that she watched him slowly lift his china tea cup and sip his tea without even looking to see how she had reacted to this honest appraisal. She had asked and he had answered honestly. Perhaps, Mildred thought, it would have been better not to know; but that thought she quickly dismissed. In her initial shock she remembered how 'I involuntarily leaned against the wall behind me, but suddenly thought, "Be careful. You'll break the glass in the picture of Whistler's mother, and you'll be sorry." It brought me upstanding, and he didn't notice. Isn't the mind a queer thing?'

He finished his tea, and rose to go. As he picked up his cap he showed me a hole right through his sleeve – in one side, out the other – and a similar one in his puttee, where the ball [bullet] had been turned aside by the leather lacing of his boot. He laughed as he said, 'Odd how near a chap comes to going out, and yet lives to drink tea with you. Well, good-bye and good luck if I don't see you again.' And off he marched, and I went into the library and sat down and sat very still.

As Mildred sat there wondering what was going to happen, she recalled a couple of stories about recent events at the front that Captain Edwards had told her. One was about a pretty chateau they had dined in near Saint-Quentin. The French owners could not do more for the British soldiers and had prepared a wonderful meal during which the daughters had waited on them amid sumptuous surroundings and fine antique furniture. Towards the end of the meal the alert sounded and the soldiers rushed off to engage in battle with the advancing Germans. They did not have the chance to thank their hosts. A few hours later they returned but 'there was not one stone standing on another', Edwards told Mildred, 'and what became of the family' he had no idea.

The other story was equally chilling and involved how the Germans managed to cross the river at Saint-Quentin in spite of the best efforts of the British to prevent them. The engineer had packed explosives under the bridge supports and, helped by Captain Edwards, had rolled the charge wire well back and sat ready to touch off the mine. He pressed the button. Nothing happened, the charge had failed. The engineer was distraught and Edwards said to him, 'Brace up, my lad – give her another chance.' The engineer tried again and nothing happened. Then the engineer got up and ran towards the bridge and fired six shots into the explosives, knowing that if he succeeded he would be blown up with it. But nothing happened and he was dragged back 'weeping with rage' as the Germans crossed the bridge. She also remembered his words when she pressed him for any kind of information: 'Only three men in this war know anything of its plans – Kitchener, Joffre, and French. The rest of us obey orders …'

Mildred was shaken rudely from her thoughts by a pounding on the front door which, under current circumstances, was alarming in itself. When she answered the door, determined to scold the caller for startling her, she was greeted with a kind-faced and boyish corporal who had come to ask if he could survey the surrounding woods from her window in the roof. Mildred took him upstairs and he informed her that the Germans they were hunting (the Uhlans) had been spotted by the aeroplanes 'not a thousand feet from this house' and he went on to tell her quite matter of factly, as if it were perfectly sane and normal:

> You know that we are the sacrificed corps, and we have known it from the first – went into the campaign knowing it. We have been fighting a force ten times superior in numbers, and retreating, doing rear-guard action, whether we were really outfought or not – to draw the Germans where Joffre wants them. I reckon we've got them there. It is great strategy – Kitchener's, you know.

Mildred made no reply, but wondered how true his statement was. History would eventually make it clear, she decided.

Before long Mildred noticed a flurry of activity on the road and went out to find soldiers were placing tree trunks across the road at intervals to prevent anyone storming the hill – especially the German cavalry still hiding somewhere in the area. She was told to lock all but her main front door and even to keep the shutters barred at her windows. The artillery fire and explosions were now constantly in the background and everyone seemed to just accept it as normal. It also seemed to grow in both intensity and volume, which had unnerved Mildred more than anything else. She took it as a good sign that the British artillery battery positioned behind her house were not, as yet, joining in. Perhaps it was only a matter of time. A corporal marched up and asked her very earnestly is she was afraid at all. She answered not and then he said, 'My orders are not to expose you uselessly …'. Mildred was unsure, amidst a fit of giggles, if he meant her or her house. Uselessly or not, she was here to stay, whatever happened. Down in the valley, unbeknownst to

Mildred, the Germans had started throwing temporary bridges across the river.

Sir John French, in his despatches to Kitchener and the King, gave an outline of the disposition of the armies on 5 September:

I met the French Commander-in-Chief [Joffre] at his request, and he informed me of his intention to take the offensive forthwith, as he considered conditions were very favourable to success. General Joffre announced to me his intention of wheeling up the left flank of the 6th [French] Army, pivoting on the Marne and directing it to move on the [river] Ourcq; cross and attack the flank of the 1st German Army, which was then moving in a south-easterly direction east of that river. He [Joffre] requested me to effect a change of front to my right – my left resting on the Marne and my right on the 5th Army – to fill the gap between the army and the 6th. I was then to advance against the enemy in my front and join in the general offensive movement … I should conceive it to have been about noon on 6 September, after British Forces had changed their front to the right and occupied the line Jouy-Le-Chatel-Faremoutiers-Villeneuve Le Compte, and the advance of the 6th French Army north of the Marne towards the [river] Ourcq became apparent, that the enemy realised the powerful threat that was being made against the flank of his columns moving south-east, and began the great retreat which opened the battle above referred to. On the evening of 6 September, therefore, the fronts and positions of the opposing armies were roughly as follows:

ALLIES
6th French Army – Right on the Marne at Meaux, left towards Betz.
British Forces – On the line Dagny-Coulommiers-Maison.
5th French Army – At Courtacon, right on Esternay.
Cavalry Troops – Between the right of the British and the left of the French 5th Army.

GERMANS
4th Reserve and 2nd Corps – East of the Ourcq and facing that river.
9th Cavalry Division – West of Crey.
2nd Cavalry Division – North of Coulommiers.
4th Corps – Rebais.
3rd and 7th Corps – South-west of Montmirail.

All these troops constituted the 1st German Army, which was directed against the French 6th Army on the Ourcq, and the British Forces, and the left of the 5th French Army south of the Marne. The 2nd German Army 99th, 10th, 10th R. and Guard was moving against the centre and right of the 5th French Army ... The French 5th Army threw the enemy back to the line of the Petit Morin river [adjacent the Marne] after inflicting severe losses upon them, especially about Montceaux, which was carried at the point of bayonet ... [their 2nd, 9th and Guard] Cavalry Divisions suffered severely.

Mildred had retired to bed exhausted on Friday 4 September. She woke to open her shutters before 4 a.m. on 5 September. She recalled that it was a lovely day and noted, probably with irony, how perfect the weather had been again all week. She went downstairs and looked from her window and couldn't see the picket at her gate, which was strange. She went outside 'but there was no picket there' and furthermore 'there was the barricade, but the road was empty.' Amélie appeared in a terrible state and told Mildred that the British soldiers marched off an hour or two earlier after an officer arrived with fresh orders. It was disquieting indeed because 'so far as anyone could discover,' reported Mildred, 'there was not an English soldier, or any kind of soldier, left anywhere'.

This was Saturday morning, September 5, and one of the loveliest days I ever saw. The air was clear. The sun was shining. The birds were singing. But otherwise it was very still. I walked out on the lawn. Little lines of white smoke were rising from a few chimneys at Joncheroy and Voisins. The towns on the plain, from Monthyon and Penchard on the horizon to Mareuil in the valley, stood out clear and distinct. But after three days of activity, three days with soldiers about, it seemed, for the first time since I came here, lonely; and for the first time I realised that I was actually cut off from the outside world. All the bridges in front of me were gone, and the big bridge behind me. No communication possibly with the north, and none with the south except by road over the hill to Lagny. Esbly evacuated, Couilly evacuated, Quincy evacuated. All the shops closed. No government, no post-office, and absolutely no knowledge of what had happened since Wednesday. I had a terrible sense of isolation.

Soon after this Mildred would find herself confronted by her worst nightmare:

> Amélie woke me this morning to tell me that all the British boys had gone. The Germans had advanced upon us! It was an awful feeling. A German regiment marched up the hill, an Officer requested to see me. I put the most calm expression on my face that I could think of. Underneath I was more than a little scared. Amélie had locked herself in the larder by this time, and no amount of coaxing from me would bring her out! I walked down to the gate; they were very polite, perfect English. They wanted to know their position on the map. Cheek, I thought! Well, I didn't allow them in my garden, and they certainly got no cups of tea from me!

That day was the most trying for Mildred. She couldn't believe she was watching Germans wearing those awful helmets with spikes on marching up her hill and past her house. Her fear was that she and Amélie would be trapped in a German-controlled area and that their fate would be insufferable should it remain occupied territory for any length of time. The battle raged in the valley as the Germans crossed the Marne on their temporary bridges and engaged with the French and British. Mildred knew that the allied armies were outnumbered and had only a fraction of the resources the mighty German army had – and that the Germans were determined to humiliate France as they had done in 1870 by capturing Paris. Mildred described that first day:

> As near as I can remember, it was a little after one o'clock when the cannonading [artillery] suddenly became much heavier, and I stepped out into the orchard, from which there was a wide view of the plain. I gave one look; then heard my self say, 'Amélie,' – as if she could help, – and I retreated. Amélie rushed by me. I heard her say, '*Mon Dieu.*' I waited but she did not come back … the battle had advanced right over the crest of the hill … Monthyon and Penchard were enveloped in smoke. From the eastern and western extremities of the plain we could see the artillery fire, but owing to the smoke hanging over the crest of the hill on the horizon, it was impossible to get an idea of the positions of the armies … By the middle of the afternoon Monthyon came slowly out of the smoke. That seemed to mean that

the heaviest firing was over the hill and not on it – or did it mean that the battle was receding? If it did, then the Allies were retreating. There was no way to discover the truth. And all this time the cannon thundered in the southeast, in the direction of Coulommiers, on the route into Paris by Ivry.

Mildred, surveying the scene through her field glasses, marvelled at the sight of a farmer and his wife in the far distance still gathering their harvest in spite of everything, determined that 'the grain had to be got in.' The French were resilient if sometimes foolish:

It was about six o'clock when the first bomb that we could really see came over the hill. The sun was setting. For two hours we saw them rise, descend, explode. Then a little smoke would rise from one hamlet, then from another; then a tiny flame – hardly more than a spark – would be visible; and by dark the plain was on fire, lighting up Mareuil in the foreground, silent and untouched.

At nightfall Mildred and Amélie, who now stayed with Mildred in the house, locked themselves in. Mildred retired to her bedroom upstairs and watched from her window. Once alone, and staring uncomprehendingly out into the valley below, the shadow of the faces of all those boys came back to haunt her as she witnessed the battle:

The shelling went on for hours. [The] worst thing was not knowing how my boys were doing. All I could see were the plumes of smoke curling up after each explosion, the whole plain was ablaze lighting up the village in the background. All the haystacks caught fire by 10 o'clock, they stood out like a procession of huge torches across my beloved panorama. It went quiet in the early hours, an eerie quiet. The night was quite beautiful. As I looked from my window, all I could think of were those fine young men – the slaughter. Looking into the night, all I could picture in my mind were my boys – 'my boys' – laying dead beneath the stars … All those boys, so many so young. I cried that night for all their mothers.

In London, Gertrude Stein had received some of Mildred's letters and was anxiously waiting for fresh news. She was fully aware of the danger Mildred was in, and admired her for staying in spite of everything.

Travel was banned, so Stein and her friend Alice Toklas could do little but wait for news. Toklas remembered how:

The Germans were getting nearer and nearer Paris and ... Gertrude Stein could not leave her room, she sat and mourned. She loved Paris, she thought neither of manuscripts nor of pictures, she thought only of Paris and she was desolate ... The first description that any one we knew received in England of the Battle of the Marne came in a letter to Gertrude Stein from Mildred Aldrich.

8

PARIS IS SAVED!

The troops have done splendidly, and when one considers the
continuous marching and retreat, I believe it will be hard to find an
instance in our annals in which troops have shown a finer spirit,
or fought with greater determination …
                              Sir Douglas Haig to Sir John French

Mildred recorded in her journal that on 7 September she did not
awake of her own accord but due to the noise of a heavy artillery
bombardment at just after 5 a.m. Having rushed into her garden to
look off in the direction of the valley and the cathedral city of Meaux,
she decided that, in spite of the noise, the battle was receding. This
could only mean one thing – the Germans were in retreat, and, she
guessed, involved in heavy fighting near Lizy-sur-Ourcq, north-east of
the city. 'The cannonading was a violent, as incessant, as it had been
the day before,' she noted, 'but it was surely further off.'

Amélie, peering off into the distance intently, agreed with her and
then, as she had not been able to collect any milk the previous day,
decided it was safe to walk to Voisins and collect some from the farm –
confident that she wouldn't encounter the enemy. Amélie had been gone
but a few minutes when she ran back up the hill shouting Mildred's
name. Mildred feared the worst and thought they must have read the
situation wrong, and Amélie had the Germans snapping at her heels.
But no. '*Madame, un anglais, un anglais!*' she shouted. Following right
behind her was a British soldier – as soon as he saw Mildred he 'waved
his cap' and his face lit up with a sunny smile.

'We went together to meet him,' recalled Mildred. 'As soon as he was near enough, he called out, "Good-morning. Everything is all right. Germans been as near you as they will ever get. Close shave."' On asking if he knew where they were, he replied, 'Retreating to the northeast – on the Ourcq.' Amélie couldn't restrain herself any longer and, wrapping her arms round his neck, kissed him on both cheeks with delight. He thanked her as he blushed a scarlet red.

Mildred then became aware of a great number of British soldiers coming down the hill. Asking the soldier what was happening, he told her they were 'scouts' under the orders of 'Colonel Snow's division', clearing the way for the advance. He continued, 'You've a whole corps of fresh French troops coming out from Paris on one side of you, and the English [British] troops on their way to Meaux.' Mildred asked about the bridges being destroyed on the Marne river and he answered, 'The pontoons are across. Everything is ready for the advance. I think we've got 'em.' As he went on his way Mildred noted that 'he laughed as if it were all a game of cricket.'

Sir John French, in his despatches to Kitchener and the King, said:

On 8 September, the enemy continued his retreat northward, and our army was successfully engaged during the day with strong rearguards of all arms on the Petit Morin River, thereby materially assisting the progress of the French Armies … on both sides the enemy was thrown back with heavy loss … Several machine guns and many prisoners were captured, and upwards of two hundred German dead were left on the ground.

In London, Gertrude Stein was still morose and inconsolable at the thought of Paris falling to the Germans. Stein and Toklas had not had any more word from Mildred and they worried about her fate – wondering if she was dead or alive, even if her little house had survived. A letter arrived by some miracle and Alice Toklas rushed to tell Stein the latest news from the Marne.

'I came up to her room,' recalled Toklas. 'I called out, it is alright Paris is saved, the germans [*sic*] are in retreat. She turned away and said, don't tell me these things. But it's true, I said, it's true. And then we wept together.'

Meanwhile back at Huiry, Mildred was suffering from a kind of post-traumatic stress after realising that she was safe. She recorded in her journal her feelings:

I came into the house and lay down. I suddenly felt horribly weak. My house had taken on a queer look to me. I suppose I had been, in a sort of subconscious way, sure that it was doomed. As I lay on the couch in the salon and looked round the room, it suddenly appeared to me like a thing I had loved and lost and recovered – resurrected in fact; a living thing to which a miracle had happened. I even found myself asking, in my innermost soul, what I had done to deserve this fortune. How had it happened, and why, that I had come to perch on this hillside, just to see a battle, and have it come almost to my door, to turn back and leave me and my belongings standing here untouched, as safe as if there were no war – and so few miles away destruction extending to the frontier.

With all this racing through her mind she could still hear the artillery explosions and smell the smoke, the stench of death and of unwashed bodies:

Yet out there, on the plain, almost within my sight, lay the men who had paid with their lives – each dear to some one – to hold back the battle from Paris … I instinctively thought of Captain Simpson, who had left his brother in the trenches at Saint-Quentin, and still had in him kindly sympathy that had helped me so much.

Another miracle that had done so much to support the Battle of the Marne was accomplished by hundreds of taxi and bus drivers who had bravely brought troops and supplies to the front. It would go down in French history as one of their most remarkable achievements.

General Gallieni, commander of a French Infantry division, was ordered to march his exhausted men another 37 miles (60 km) to join their comrades on the front and to support the Battle of the Marne. Gallieni was furious that his men were expected, under Joffre's orders, to march so far and then fight. He hatched a plan and, using his powers as Military Governor of Paris, requisitioned all the taxis in Paris to transport his men to the Marne, thus ensuring they had energy to fight once there. As a result, 1,200 Paris taxis transported the men through the night and then returned to collect more. The taxi drivers were all aged over 50 and they worked without stopping for over 40 hours to complete their task and get the troops to the front in a state fit to fight. The taxis were used up until 15 September to transport officers back and forth and to bring the wounded back to Paris's hospitals. This didn't come free – Gallieni insisted that the taxi drivers calculate their normal rates and finally ended up paying a combined bill of over 70,000 francs for their services.

Mildred had a mutual friend with Stein and recalls that their friend, Nellie Jacott, who also lived in France, and was there throughout, told her in a letter, with no sense of irony, how the taxi requisition affected her:

> You know, she said, I always come to town once a week to shop and I always bring my maid. We come in the street-car because it is difficult to get a taxi in Boulogne and we go back in a taxi. Well we came in as usual and didn't notice anything and when we had finished our shopping and had our tea we stood on a corner to get a taxi. We stopped several and when they heard where we wanted to go they drove on.

The taxis were heading in the opposite direction to Nellie and the drivers were sworn to secrecy – which is why they failed to explain their refusal to oblige her. 'Of course we understood later, when we heard about Gallieni and the taxis,' said Nellie and added, 'and that was the Battle of the Marne.'

Mildred was aghast that Nellie had so little understanding and even less sympathy for the disaster that had unfolded, where men had died in their hundreds it not thousand so that she could have shops to go to. It bewildered Mildred how ridiculous women like Nellie were – interested only in the latest fashion and not having their comfortable lives disrupted in any way.

Another Parisian friend of Mildred's noticed, whilst he sat at a café in a near deserted city, several huge wagons pulled by weary-looking horses trundling along, with Banque de France written across the side. Soldiers were guarding them. 'That was the gold going away,' his letter recalled, 'just like that, before the Battle of the Marne.'

Once the Germans had been pushed back and were on the retreat, the city of Meaux was finally free of the invaders. The fighting at the River Ourcq had been ferocious and bloody and, although in retreat, the Germans fought to the last man to hold their ground. They were desperate to turn retreat back into an advance but it proved impossible. The sheer will and determination of the Allies succeeded, in spite of the greater strength and numbers of the enemy.

Sir John recorded in his despatches on 10 September:

The fighting of this army in the neighbourhood of Montmirail was very severe. The advance was resumed at daybreak on the 10th up to the line of the Ourcq, opposed by strong rearguards of all arms ... [they] drove the enemy northwards. Thirteen guns, seven machine guns, about 2,000 prisoners, and quantities of transport fell into our hands. The enemy left many [thousands] dead on the field. The French 5th and 6th Armies had little opposition. As the 1st and 2nd German Armies were now in full retreat, this evening marks the end of the battle which practically commenced on the morning of the 6th instant; and it is at this point in the operations that I am concluding the present despatch.

Sir John was certainly relieved that the disaster he had anticipated had not occurred and by some 'miracle' the Germans had been halted at the Marne and turned back. Paris was saved, but at great cost. Sir John said in despatches:

Although I deeply regret to have had to report heavy losses in killed and wounded throughout these operations, I do not think they have been excessive in view of the magnitude of the great fight, of which I have only been able to briefly describe, and the demoralisation and loss in killed and wounded which are known to have been caused to the enemy by the vigour and severity of the pursuit.

Sir John also made it clear the strain his men were under by adding:

In concluding this despatch I must call your Lordship's attention to the fact that from Sunday, 23 August, up to the present date (17 September), from Mons back almost to the Seine, and from the Seine to the Aisne, the army under my command has been ceaselessly engaged without one single day's halt or rest of any kind.

Kitchener had been ruthless in his demands on Sir John and had put him under pressure to do exactly what he commanded from the comfort of the War Office in London. Kitchener had also put Sir John in an intolerable position with his French counterpart, Joffre, by insisting that he should not take any orders from the Frenchman. Sir John did

not like Joffre and the feeling was mutual. That they managed to agree
and coordinate troops in combined operations was a miracle in itself.
The BEF had nearly captured Chemin de Dames ridge, but failure to
secure this made Sir John order his troops to entrench.

By 20 September, Haig noted in his diary, 'our troops have now been
a week in the trenches. It is well nigh impossible for them to have a hot
meal, and the weather has been very wet and cold. I am therefore most
anxious to withdraw the men in turn from the trenches for rest and
food.' The troops would remain firmly entrenched until they began
moving to Flanders fields and Ypres in the weeks and months to come.

Mildred was still very aware of what was going on. Although the
battle had moved away from her immediate vicinity, she still had a
panoramic view from her garden and was able to see the explosions in
the distance and hear the now almost continual boom of artillery, the
buzz of aeroplanes swooping and zooming over her roof, and the distant sound of gunfire. She was also kept busy with French and British
troops going to and from the front. It was exhausting and hectic and
made her and Amélie feel thoroughly useful.

Zeppelin airships from Germany had also made an appearance and
filled everyone with dread, as there were rumours the Germans were
shooting civilians and also dropping explosives from these floating
ships. Sir John included mention of these aircraft in his despatches:

> In view of the many statements being made in the Press [sic] as to the
> use of Zeppelins against us, it is interesting to note that the Royal
> Flying Corps, who have been on reconnaissances on every day since
> their arrival in France, have never seen a Zeppelin, though airships of
> a non-rigid type have been seen on two occasions. Near the Marne,
> late one evening, two such were observed over German forces.
> Aeroplanes were dispatched against them, but in the darkness our
> pilots were uncertain of the airships' nationality and did not attack.
> It was afterwards made clear that they could not have been French …
> The order of the Royal Flying Corps are to attack Zeppelin at once,
> and there is some disappointment at the absence of those targets.

In the same dispatch to Kitchener and the King, Sir John included a
letter printed in a newspaper from a German soldier, 74th Infantry, to
his wife, who had been fighting since the Marne:

My Dear Wife,

I have just been living through days that defy imagination. I should
never have thought that men could stand it. Not a second has passed
but my life has been in danger, and yet not a hair on my head has
been hurt. It was horrible, it was ghastly. But I have been saved for
you and for our happiness and I take heart again, although I am still
terribly unnerved. God grant that I may see you again soon and that
this horror may soon be over. None of us can do anymore, human
strength is at an end.

It is pretty desolate in its tone and gives a good indication of how low
morale was among the German infantry. He continues his letter and
refers to Paris. 'We hear that three armies are going to get into line,
entrench, rest, and then start afresh our victorious march on Paris.
It was not a defeat, but only a strategic retreat. I have confidence in
our Chiefs that everything will be successful. Our first battalion, which
has fought with unparalleled bravery, is reduced from 1,200 to 194
men.' But there would be no march on Paris for the German army, just
entrenchment and stalemate.

'It was just after lunch that Amélie told me,' recalled Mildred, 'that
French reinforcements were marching out from the south of Paris;
that they were already coming over the crest of the hill to the south
and could be seen from the road above; that the advance scouts were
already here.' In no time at all a French officer came through Mildred's
gate and approached the house:

I had to encounter the expressions of astonishment to which I am
now quite accustomed – a foreigner in a little hole on the road to
the frontier, in a partially evacuated country. I answered all the usual
questions politely; but when he began to ask how many men I could
lodge, and how much room there was for horses in the outbuildings,
Amélie sharply interfered, assuring him that she knew the resources
of the hamlet better than I did, that she was used to 'this sort of
thing' and 'madame was not'; and simply whisked him off.

Mildred watched the efficiency with which the empty buildings and
houses above her and below in Voisins were requisitioned with fas-
cination. French officers broke open doors and soon had everything
organised, from which men would be billeted where to which horses

would be stabled where. The requisitions officer numbered doors and barns with chalk and then, when the troops arrived, he gave out the numbers to direct them to their stable and billet for the night. He also decided which of the adjacent fields would be used for how many tents and which men would occupy them. Finally, and after he had been given an obvious talking to by Amélie, the officer returned to Mildred's house. 'If you please, madame,' he said, 'I will now see what you can do for us.' Mildred invited him in – into a house recently renovated where everything was neat, clean and brand new!

> I don't suppose I need tell you that you would get very little idea of the inside of my house from the outside. I am quite used now to the little change of front in most people when they cross the threshold. The officer nearly went on tiptoes when he got inside. He mounted the polished stairs gingerly, gave one look at the bedroom part-way up, touched his cap, and said: 'That will do for the chef-major. We will not trouble you with any one else. He has his own orderly, and will eat outside, and will be no bother. Thank you very much, madame'; and he sort of slid down the stairs, tiptoed out, and wrote in chalk on the gatepost, 'Weitzel'.

When the reservist troops arrived Mildred went out to greet them and managed to talk to them. They had marched 36 miles and had missed the Battle of the Marne, only realising it was happening once they crossed the hill at Montry, when they saw the smoke in the far distance. 'I tell you,' declared a delighted Mildred, 'their faces were wreathed with smiles when they discovered that we knew the Germans were retreating.'

As she discussed the experiences of war with this new batch of French troops, it occurred to her that there was a marked difference between the English and French troops – and the way they discussed their personal experiences:

> The English never talked battles. Not one of the Tommies mentioned the fighting. [They] talked of 'home', of the girls they had left behind them, of the French children whom the English loved, of the country, its customs, its people, their courage and kindness, but not one of them had told me a battle story of any kind, and I had not thought once of opening the subject.

Among the new French troops billeted at Huiry was a young man of the Ambulance Corps, who fascinated Mildred with his charm and good looks, but mostly because he had eloquence and humour: 'with a smile in his eyes and a laugh on his lips [he] told me stories that made me see how war affects men.' One particular story concerned the recent Battle of the Marne and what he had witnessed of the German soldiers' fate:

I suppose that in the history of the war it will stand as a success – at any rate, they came across [the Marne river], which was what they wanted. We could only have stopped them, if at all, by an awful sacrifice of life. Joffre is not doing that. If the Germans want to fling away their men by the tens of thousands – let them. In the end we gain by it. We can rebuild a country; we cannot so easily re-create a race. We mowed them down like a field of wheat, by the tens of thousands, and tens of thousands sprang into the gaps. They advanced shoulder to shoulder. Our guns could not miss them, but they were too many for us. If you had seen that crossing I imagine it would have looked to you like a disaster for Germany. It was so awful that it became comic. I remember one point where a bridge was mined. We let the first divisions of artillery and cavalry come right across on to our guns – they were literally destroyed. As the next division came on to the bridge – up it went – men, horses, guns dammed the flood, and the cavalry literally crossed on their own dead. We are bold enough, but we are not so foolhardy as to throw away men like that. They will be more useful to Joffre later.

Mildred was stunned at the horror of it all and, in spite of her proximity to this carnage, she never imagined it could be described in such a matter of fact way. It seemed to add to the sense of distress for the listener. 'It was the word "comic" that did for me,' declared Mildred. 'There was no sign in the fresh young face before me that the horror had left its mark.' The young man went on to tell Mildred that he had seen the Germans attacked in a closed street area and as a result had seen 'havoc in their ranks' and how 'the air was full of flying heads and arms and legs, of boots, and helmets, swords, and guns that it did not seem as if it could be real – it looked like some burlesque.'

As September turned into October and Christmas approached, the front was now some miles off, in the vicinity of Flanders, the Ypres salient and the Somme. Mildred continued to help the troops from both the French and British divisions as they prepared to move up to the front or on their way back. Those returning always looked pale and exhausted and voiced their frustration at the entrenched lines that had now taken root and created stagnation. Those going to the front were full of determination and vigour after a deserved rest or because they were fresh-faced and had no idea of what lay ahead of them. The trench systems were becoming more and more sophisticated as time passed, with neither side advancing or retreating more than a few metres at a time. One thing was certain: the war would not be over by Christmas, as the British boys had hoped, and wildly announced, in the first weeks after war was declared.

Haig wrote to a friend:

We have had terribly hard fighting during the last week, but we have held our ground and the Germans seem to be almost more tired than we are. Our casualties I regret to say have been very heavy, but we have had to hold our ground until French reinforcements could be brought forward. Our men are very tired: they fight hard by day and then during the night dig all they can to strengthen their position so they get very little sleep. We ought to have more men. Even Territorials would do splendidly against the present German infantry.

Haig ended the letter by alluding to the situation with British officer class as being dire, 'of course officers are also badly needed as our casualties in officers have been very heavy'.

By this time the city of Meaux and the surrounding areas of the Marne valley were comparatively safe. As a result, those who had evacuated from the surrounding towns and villages began to return, albeit slowly. Some were still unable to accept that the Germans would not return and terrorise them again. The sound of heavy artillery and explosions was still a constant background noise, and would be for a long time to come. Initially this created an odd sense of detachment from the rest of the world. It also began to arouse a desire to perhaps explore the road that led to the city of Meaux and see how that city had fared since the battle with the Germans raged in its surrounding villages, farms and hamlets.

Mildred was surprised to find herself wondering what had gone wrong in the German ranks. She had always suppressed her fear that the Germans would succeed in reaching Paris due to their superior equipment and numbers, not to mention the intricate planning, preparations and scheming that had gone on for years:

> I could not help wondering if, in the game of 'snap the whip', von Kluck's right wing [advancing on the Marne] had got swung off the line by the very rapidity with which it must have covered that long arc in the great two week's offensive.

In reality it was Kluck's refusal to follow orders and his insistence on steaming forward to Paris that did for him and his troops.

Amélie was still feeling terribly downcast that the Germans had managed to advance as far as they had towards Paris. She had an absolute belief in the British and couldn't understand why they had not managed to keep the Germans back and instead allowed them to advance so far with such terrible consequences for everyone in their path. 'She had such faith in the British,' Mildred remembered, 'she has believed in a short war ...' Mildred had no idea how long the war would last, but it was clear that since the Germans and Allies had entrenched to the north at Ypres and the Somme that the war would be longer, much longer, than anyone had at first thought.

Amélie had also been affected badly by the stories she had been hearing about how prepared the Germans were and how they had lived among them for years. Mildred noticed a real change in Amélie as they climbed the hill from Voisins back to La Creste. 'She walked sadly beside me back to the garden, an altogether different person from the one who had come racing across the field in the sunshine.' Once there, she braced up enough to say:

> And only think, madame, a woman told me that the Germans who were [weeks ago before war] all chauffeurs at the Galeries Lafayette and other big shops in Paris, and that they not only knew all the country better than we do, they knew us all by name. One of them, who stopped at her door to demand a drink, told her so himself, and called her by name. He told her he had lived in Paris for years.

Mildred agreed it was a chilling thought and probably true:

> The delivery automobiles from all the big shops in Paris came out here twice a week [before the war], and some of them three times

a week. It was no secret that Paris [had been] full of Germans, and [had] been since that beastly treaty of Frankfort [*sic*], which would have expired next year. Although, that was all academic now.

Mildred had made friends with a young woman, Mademoiselle Henrietta, whose mother lived in Voisins and had refused to evacuate. Mlle Henrietta was soon to be a nurse. She had striking looks and a caring, compassionate nature. She had asked Mildred to evacuate with her prior to the German advance and had been quite distraught at her refusal. However, Mildred later discovered that Henrietta ended up staying with her mother, who had also refused to leave and wanted, much to her daughter's consternation, to 'face the enemy'.

> My little French friend from the foot of the hill came to my door. I call her 'my little friend', though she is taller than I am, because she is only half my age. She came with the proposition that I should harness Ninette [the donkey] and go with her out to the battlefield, where, she said, they were still sadly in need of help.

Mildred asked her how she knew this and was shocked to hear that reports had been brought to the hospital by the elderly men who ventured back to their villages through the woods and across the battlefields that 'there were still many wounded men in the woods who had not yet been picked up'. In would seem that these men included British, French and German troops. Henrietta also expressed concern that the small hospital at Neufmortier needed nursing volunteers to help as soon as possible. It transpired, however, that there was an ulterior motive to her request. Henrietta's mother had insisted that she could go and help only if Mildred went with her. Mildred sensed a ploy – Henrietta's mother had guessed that Mildred would not be able, or want to go:

> I knew they didn't want an old lady like me, however willing, an old lady very unsteady on her feet, absolutely ignorant of the simplest rules of 'first aid to the wounded,' that they needed skilled and tried people, that we could not only lend efficient aid, but should be a nuisance, even if, which I doubted, we were allowed to cross the Marne.

Sincerely yours
Mildred Aldrich.

Mildred Aldrich,
c. 1914. (Author's collection)

British Hussars arrive in France, 1914. A machine war, certainly – but by 1917 Britain had more than a million horses and mules in service in all theatres. About half that number died.

View of Mildred's house La Creste as it was around 1914, after her renovations were completed just before war broke out. She described the view across the Marne Valley as her 'beloved panorama'.

Mildred's house La Creste as it is today. There are plans for La Creste to be available for short lets and linked to the new First World War museum at Meaux. (Michael Lawson, 2011)

Forever Nineteen, a play about Mildred, wins an award for Best Play and Best New Theatre Company alongside *Les Misérables* in 1993. Taken on the set of *Les Misérables* at the Palace Theatre, with David Slattery-Christy (playwright), Jeff Leyton (Jean Valjean) and an unknown actor. (Author's collection, with kind permission of Cameron Mackintosh)

Above: Nicki Casey (Amélie) and Lee Wolstenholme (Ted Pratley) in *Forever Nineteen*, Buxton Festival 1993, where the play won the Best Drama Award. (Author's collection)

Left: Mildred's grave, now rather dilapidated. She was buried near La Creste at the Cimetière d'Eglise, Saint-Denis, Quincy, Voisins. (Michael Lawson, 2011)

The inscription on Mildred's grave is still visible. There are plans to have the grave restored and for La Creste to be available for short lets and linked to the new First World War museum at Meaux. (Michael Lawson, 2011)

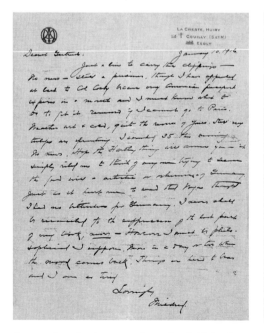

A sample of a letter written by Mildred to a friend from La Creste in 1916.

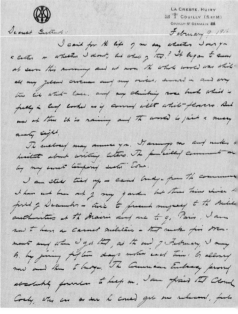

A sample of a letter written by Mildred to Gertrude Stein from La Creste in 1916.

Mildred was in a quandary. Every fibre of her being wanted to help but the thought of nursing wounded men terrified her; her stomach churned at the thought of blood. It was simply alien to her and she didn't honestly know how she would react to such horrors. Seeing dead soldiers at close quarters made her heart fill with lead and her eyes brim with salty tears. The writer and journalist however, began to come to the fore:

> All the time I was explaining myself, with that diabolical dual consciousness which makes us spectator and listener to ourselves, in the back of my brain – or my soul – was running this query: 'I wonder what a raw battle field looks like? I have a chance to see if I want to – perhaps.' I suppose that was an attack of involuntary, unpremeditated curiosity. I did not want to go.

Henrietta argued her case and was near to begging Mildred to reconsider. Her disappointment and distress was hard to bear. 'She argued that we could "hunt for the dead", and "carry consolation to the dying". I shook my head. I even had to cut the argument short by going into the house. I felt an imperative need to get the door closed between us.' In truth Henrietta had tapped into Mildred's own insecurities:

> The truth was that I had a sudden, cinematographical vision of my chubby self – me, who cannot walk half a mile, nor bend over without getting palpitation – stumbling in my high-heeled shoes over the fields ploughed by cavalry and shell – breathlessly bent on carrying consolation to the dying. I knew that I should surely have to be picked up with the dead and dying, or, worse still, usurp a place in an ambulance, unless eternal justice – in spite of my age, my sex, and my white hairs – left me lying where I fell – and serve me good and right!

In spite of her disgust at her own lack of courage, Mildred consoled herself with the thought that had there been wounded and dying men in her garden she would have done her best to minister to them without hesitation. She would help and not allow anything to deter or put her off:

> But for me to drive deliberately nine miles – we should have had to make a wide detour to cross the Marne on the pontoons – behind a donkey who travels two miles an hour, to seek such an experience,

and with several hours to think it over en route, and the conviction that I would be an unwelcome intruder – that was another matter.

I am afraid Henrietta will never forgive me. She will soon be walking around in a hospital, looking so pretty in her nurse's dress and veil. But she will always think that she lost a great opportunity that day – and a picturesque one.

In spite of this setback Mildred carried on doing what she could for the troops heading to and from the front. The stories they heard about the conditions in the trenches, and what the soldiers had to endure in such awful surroundings, seemed almost unbelievable to them. Equally the behaviour of the Germans and what they did to people's evacuated homes was beyond the pale. To act in such a vile way would never be forgotten – using homes as toilets and smearing human faeces on the walls and furniture was the worst of it, although deliberately destroying possessions and defiling them with graffiti was equally repellent. It would be a long time before such mindless acts were forgiven and forgotten – if they ever were.

'All the words from the front tell us that the boys are standing the winter in the trenches very well,' wrote Mildred to Gertrude Stein. 'They've simply got to – that's all there is to that. Amélie is more astonished than I am. When she first realised that they had got to stay out there in the rain and the mud and the cold, she just gasped out that they never would stand it. I asked her what they would do then – lie down and let the Germans ride over them? Her only reply was that they would all die.'

Mildred was cheered by the arrival of a letter written some weeks before on 30 October 1914, passed by the censor, from a young officer of her acquaintance, whom she declines to name. For security reasons he was identified by initials only at the time. Mildred described him as an 'English boy … [who] had been in China and North Nigeria with [her friend] Sir Frederick Ludgard as an aide-de-camp', when they visited her in June 1914 on their way back to London to take up civil service appointments. Sadly, Mildred never rectified this and added his name, with him or others, as time passed and it would not have mattered for security reasons. However, it does nothing to detract from their insight and experience. As a result of some investigation, it would seem that the identity of this particular officer is one Noel Spicer. He certainly fits the profile, and his background and movements tally with the dates:

My dearest Mildred,

Last night I heard your account of your experiences between September 1 and 9, and it made me boil anew with disappointment that my attempts to reach Huiry on September 4 were frustrated. I was disappointed enough at the time, but then my regret was tempered by the thought that you were probably safe in Paris, and I should only find an empty house at La Creste. Now that I know that I should have found you – you!!! – it makes me wild, even after this interval of time, to have missed a sight of you. Now let me tell you how it came about that you nearly received a visit from me.

I left England August 17, with the 48th Heavy Battery (3rd Division). We landed at Rouen, and went by train, via Amiens, to Houtmont, a few kilometres west of Mauberge. There we detrained one morning at two o'clock, marched through Malplaquet into Belgium, and came into contact with the enemy at once.

The story of the English retreat must be familiar to you by now. It was a wonderful experience. I am glad to have gone through it, though I am not anxious to undergo such a time again. We crossed the Marne at Meaux, on September 3, marching due east to Siney-Signets. Funnily enough it was not until I had actually crossed the Marne that I suddenly realised that I was in your vicinity. Our route, unfortunately, led right away from you, and I could not ask to get away while we were actually on the march, and possibly going many miles in another direction. The following day, however – 4th – we retraced our steps somewhat and halted to bivouac a short distance west of a village named La Haute Maison – roughly six miles from you. I immediately asked permission to ride over to Huiry. The Major, with much regret, declined to let me leave, and, since we received orders to march again an hour later, he was right. We marched all the night. I have marked out our road with arrows on the little map enclosed. We reached a place called Fontenay about 8.30 the next morning, by which time I was twenty miles from you, and not in a condition to want anything but sleep and food. That was our farthest point south. But, sad to say, in our advance we went by a road farther east, and quite out of reach of you, and crossed the Marne at a place called Nanteuil – I got your first letter about one day's march south of Mons.

Best love, dearest Mildred. Write again.

N[oel] S[picer]

There is an obvious affection in the way this young man signs off his letter to Mildred and an equal affection in her excitement at receiving them from these boys and soldiers of her acquaintance. She was touched by the simplicity and honesty of his account and commented, 'Isn't that a calm way to state such a trying experience as that retreat?' This letter also brought to the front of Mildred's mind her meeting with Captain Edwards of the Bedfords, and it made her wonder, as she often did, how he was faring out at the front. It also occurred to her that the writer of this letter would have arrived at the same time as an event etched on her mind:

> If he had come that afternoon imagine what I should have felt to see him ride down by the picket at the gate. He would have found me pouring tea for Captain Edwards of the Bedfords. It would have surely added a touch of reality to the battle of the next days. Of course I knew he was somewhere out there, but to have seen him actually riding away to it would have been different. Yet it might not, for I am sure his conversation would have been as calm as his letters, and they read as much as if he were taking an exciting pleasure trip, with interesting risks thrown in, as anything else. That is so English. On some future day I suppose we shall sit together on the lawn – he will probably lie on it – and swap wonderful stories, for I am going to be one of the veterans of this war

By late November 1914 Mildred was writing of her frustration with the mail system and communications in general. The telegraph system was the worst as it was always being sabotaged and cut either by the Allies or by the enemy. When living in Paris, Mildred's friends marvelled at her love of sending telegrams for any reason, be it an announcement or an event; even her impending arrival would be preceded by a telegram! Those days, sadly for her, were gone. She was also frustrated at the length of time it took a letter to reach Paris, 20 miles away – ten days was normal. How long it took a letter to reach London or the USA was anyone's guess. 'We get our mail with great irregularity,' wrote Mildred to a friend, 'even our local mail goes to Meaux, and is held there for five days, as the simplest way of exercising the censorship.' She presumed the reason for this was that old news was no news.

Although the front line was now nearly 40 miles away towards Ypres and the Somme, Mildred still lived in a military zone, through which supplies along with retreating and fresh troops continually came and went. She described her drive to a nearby town, Couilly, which Amélie walked in ten minutes 'across the fields in a short and pretty walk', but that route being barred from Mildred, because she cannot climb 'that terrible hill to get back' without great breathlessness and difficulty, 'besides the mud is inches deep'. As a result she took other means of transport:

> I have a queer little four-wheeled cart, covered if I want to unroll the curtains. I call it my perambulator, and really, with Ninette hitched in, I am like an overgrown baby in its baby carriage, and any nurse I ever knew would push a perambulator faster than that donkey drags mine. Yet it just suits my mood. I sit comfortably in it, and travel slowly – time being non-existent – so slowly that I can watch the wheat sprout, and gaze at the birds and the view and the clouds. I do hold on to the reins – just for looks – though I have no need to, and I doubt if Ninette suspects me of doing anything so foolish.

On these excursions, mainly for post, foodstuffs and fuel for the fire, which took some considerable time, Mildred would often encounter military vehicles, horses and soldiers on the way to or back from the front line. Mildred must have been an odd and eccentric sight amidst this continuous hustle and bustle, and as a result she attracted some curious glances:

> On the road I always meet officers riding along, military cars flying along, army couriers spluttering along on motor-cycles, heavy motor transports groaning up hill, or thundering down, and now and then a long train of motor ambulances … simply flew by me, raising such a cloud of dust that after I had counted thirty, I found I could not see them, and the continual tooting of the horns began to make Ninette nervous – she had never seen anything like that before.

Mildred recalled that this was the 'only scenes of war' she now witnessed every day – her house now, thankfully, being some miles from the trenches of the front line. But they could still hear the constant firing of artillery and cannons in the distance. The other inconvenience for Mildred was the lack of coal for the house fire and range. The military had requisitioned coal for military purposes. The coal that was available for domestic use was all 'dust and did not burn well'. She added how one would imagine it would be easy to get wood in the countryside. 'It is not.' She declared, ' The army takes a lot of it, and those who, in ordinary winters, have wood to sell, keep it for themselves.' As a result the locals took it upon themselves to cut down some older trees in their gardens, including Mildred's, and chop them up for burning. It was green wood, not dried out, so was poor fuel 'and the smoke' was appalling, especially if the chimney or stove did not have a good draw. At times Mildred was so cold she huddled over her meagre stove in the small kitchen. Then she would be hot in the face but her back was freezing. At times she even felt like sticking her wrapped-up feet in the embers, instead of on the cast-iron stove, they were so cold. At least the hot bricks that Amélie placed in her bed provided some meagre warmth to her bed sheets before she slipped between them for the night.

All these inconveniences were as nothing compared to the alternative. Had the Germans not been pushed back at the eleventh hour, their deprivations, under the enemy's heel, would have been much worse. Counting blessings was wise and grumbling because of a little cold and discomfort unappreciated. Paris was saved from another humiliation – as was France – so everyone was thankful. The main concern now was how long it would take to end this war. Nobody knew for sure, but Mildred guessed it would 'not be a short lived one' now the trenches had created a stagnant and unmoving stand off. The scars of the recent battles at Marne, Meaux, Mons and beyond were still visible in the distance and Mildred thought of Henrietta's offer to go there to help the injured and bury the dead. Perhaps she should now consider going on that journey, seeing the recent battlefields and the damage done to the towns and villages the Germans had rampaged through. Things had moved on, time had passed and it was safer than when first suggested. Perhaps. In the distance the cannon and artillery explosions at the front still punctuated the days and nights, a constant reminder, lest they forget, that the horror continued.

9

WITNESS TO DESTRUCTION ON THE EDGE OF THE WAR ZONE

One whole street of houses was literally gutted.
The walls stand, but the roofs are off and the doors and
windows gone, while the shells seemed burned out.

Mildred Aldrich
Refers to the village of Chauconin, west of Meaux

Once it was apparent that there was no chance of the Germans returning, those who had evacuated from the surrounding towns, villages and
hamlets began to return to see what, if anything, remained of their property and possessions. Some were relieved, while others found themselves
devastated at what had not survived. In spite of this, Mildred found it
reassuring how quickly life began to return to some sense of normality
– apart from the lack of active young men who were all still in the army
fighting at the front. Women, young and old – very old in some cases –
donned their headscarves, rolled up their sleeves and just got on with the
heavy manual farm work that still needed to be done. Mildred admired
them because they had such a cheery way of getting on with things in
times of adversity. Their resoluteness of spirit and body shook her out of
her own self-indulgent moments of doubt and inspired her to tend her
vegetable patch, milk her goat or do the hundred other things she needed
to do to survive. In spite of the cold it was invigorating, and she was able
to sleep well due to sheer exhaustion.

Still the troops came and went from the front and the innumerable
military vehicles and personnel, both French and British, continued to

pass through. Mildred never got used to the sudden realisation that in the night orders had been received for the latest contingent to march to the front. On getting up they were all gone, the fields empty of their tents and horses and the lane quiet again. Until, of course, the next contingent arrived and it started all over. She would often smile as she attempted to count the number of pans of water boiled, cups of tea made and drunk, biscuits eaten, and perspiring male bodies that had been washed and shaved at her gate in the lane or in the little courtyard to the side of Amélie's house. They always smelled sweeter afterwards, that she couldn't deny. Returning from the front were the endless caravans of motor ambulances thundering to the military hospitals nearer to Paris. Mildred could not bring herself to think about the contents of those ambulances, but she was reassured that nurses like her friend Henrietta were ministering to their wounds and needs somewhere out there in the ever spinning turmoil created by war.

Mildred and Amélie made the decision to 'make a pilgrimage' to Meaux and beyond in early December 1914, to decorate the graves of those killed in the recent battles. 'You can realise how near it is,' wrote Mildred, ' and what an easy trip it [would] be in normal times, when I tell you that we left Esbly for Meaux at half past one – only ten minutes by train – and were back in the station at Meaux at quarter to four, and had visited Monthyon, Villeroy, Neufmontier, Penchard, Chauconin, Barcy, Chambry, and Varreddes.'

All the places Mildred refers to were scenes of battles and fierce fighting with the Germans as they advanced and then retreated to what were now entrenched positions on the front line. This expedition was not without its risks, as the French authorities, along with the British, had deemed this area a restricted military zone and as such did little to encourage people to move about. However, those living within the zone had perhaps a little more freedom than others from outside the area:

> The authorities are not very anxious to have people go out there. Yet nothing to prevent it is really done. It only takes a little diplomacy. If I had gone to ask for a [local] passport, nine chances out of ten it would have been refused me.

Mildred's plan was to organise a hire car for the afternoon from a woman in Meaux who she had known from before the war and knew was now operating her husband's garage whilst he was away with his regiment.

Mildred had also agreed to furnish her with all the necessary papers in case an over-zealous guard should stop them:

> They are not taxi cabs, but handsome touring-cars. Her chauffeur carries the proper papers. It seemed to me a very loose arrangement, from a military point of view, even although I was assured that she did not send out anyone she did not know. However, I decided to take advantage of [her offer].

Whilst waiting for the car and driver, Mildred talked to some locals in Meaux and learned that Archbishop Marbeau had stayed with other locals to try to minimise the damage inflicted on the city and also to try to protect people's homes and property – especially the aged and poor who did not have the means to leave even if they had wanted to. 'But never mind all these things,' Mildred recorded rather tartly, 'which the guides will recite for you, I imagine, when you come over to make the grand tour of Fighting France, for on these plains about Meaux you will have to start your pilgrimage.' She had clearly already begun to feel frustrated at the thought of future tours recounting history that was for her and all those she knew the reality of their lives.

Once in the car, Mildred began to feel a sense of anticipation at what they would actually witness. It might perhaps have been wiser to remain on her hill, viewing from a distance as she had hitherto done. Amélie also seemed unusually quiet as the car left Meaux on the main road. Within a few minutes they could clearly see a soldier standing in the road holding his hand up to stop the car. His rifle and attached bayonet glinted in the weak winter sun. The car slowly came to a halt and Mildred's heart beat a little faster:

> Were we after all going to be turned back? I had the guilty knowledge that there was no reason why we should not be. I tried to look magnificently unconcerned as I leaned forward to smile at the soldier. I might have spared myself the effort. He never even glanced inside the car. The examination of the papers was the most cursory thing imaginable – a mere formality. The chauffeur simply held his stamped paper towards the guard. The guard glanced at it, lifted his gun, motioned us to proceed – and we proceeded. It may amuse you to know that we never showed the paper again. We did meet two gendarmes on bicycles, but they nodded and passed us without stopping.

In letters to Gertrude Stein and other friends in the United States Mildred recounted the journey that afternoon and what she and Amélie did and saw. Later she would use these letters as inspiration for her book *On The Edge of the War Zone*. It is worth allowing Mildred to recount the story of that afternoon as she did in her original letters to friends, which was her way of recording the history of the moment she lived through for posterity:

> A little way out of Meaux, we took a road west for Chauconnin, the nearest place to us which was bombarded, and from a point in the road I looked back across the valley of the Marne, and I saw a very pretty white town, with red roofs, lying on the hillside. I asked the chauffeur: 'What village is that over there?'
>
> He glanced around and replied: 'Quincy.'
>
> It was my town. I ought not to have been surprised. Of course I knew that if I could see Chauconin so clearly from my garden, why, Chauconin could see me. Only, I had not thought of it.
>
> Amélie and I looked back with great interest. It did look so pretty, and it is not pretty at all – the least pretty village on this side of the hill. 'Distance' does, indeed, 'lend enchantment'. When you come to see me I shall show you Quincy from the other side of the Marne, and never take you into its streets. Then you'll always remember it as a fairy town.
>
> It was not until we were entering into Chauconin that we saw the first signs of war. The approach through the fields, already ploughed, and planted with winter grain, looked the very last thing to be associated with war. Once inside the little village – we always speak of it as '*le petit Chauconin*' – we found destruction enough. One whole street of houses was literally gutted. The walls stand, but the roofs are off and doors and windows gone, while the shells seem burned out. The destruction of the big farms seems to have been pretty complete. There they stood, long walls of rubble and plaster, breeched; ends of farm buildings gone; and many only a heap of rubbish. The surprising thing to me was to see here a house destroyed, and, almost beside it, one not even touched. That seemed to prove that the struggle here was not a long one, and that a comparatively small number of shells had reached it.

As they continued their solemn journey, Mildred recalled, their silence cut the air and it felt as if neither of them could find words to express their feelings at what they were seeing. Mildred could not have realised it at the time, but in recording this journey in her writing and letters, she was recording an eyewitness account of history:

Neufmortier was in about the same condition. It was a sad sight, but not at all ugly. Ruins seem to 'go' with the French atmosphere and background. It all looked quite natural, and I had to make an effort to shake myself into a becoming frame of mind. If you had been with me I should have asked you to pinch me, and remind me that 'all this is not yet ancient history', and that a little sentimentality would have become me. But Amélie would never have understood me.

It was not until we were driving east again to approach Penchard that a full realisation of it came to me. Penchard crowns the hill just in the centre of the line which I see from my garden. It was one of the towns bombarded on the evening of September 5, and, so far as I can guess, the destruction was done by the French guns which drove the Germans out that night.

They say the Germans slept there the night of September 4, and were driven out the next day by the French [Cavalry] which trotted through Chauconin into Penchard by the road we had just come over … Penchard is the town in which the Germans exercised their taste of wilful nastiness [using homes as toilets and spreading faeces on walls] of which I wrote you weeks ago. It is a pretty little village, beautifully situated, commanding the slopes to the Marne on one side, and the wider plains of Barcy and Chambry on the other. It is prosperous looking, the home of sturdy farmers and the small rentiers. It has an air of humble thrift, with now and then a pretty garden, and here and there suggestions of a certain degree of greater prosperity, an air which, in France, often conceals unexpected wealth. You need not look the places up unless you have a big map. No guide-book ever honoured them.

From Penchard we ran a little out to the west at the foot of the hill, on top of which stand the white walls of Monthyon, from which on September 5, we had seen the first smoke of battle … some week's ago how puzzled I was when I read Joffre's famous [order] at the beginning of the Marne offensive, to find that it was dated September 6, whereas we had seen the battle begin on the 5th. Here I found what I presume to be the explanation, which proves that the offensive along the rest of the line on the 6th had been a continuation simply of what we saw that Saturday afternoon.

At the foot of the hill crowned by the walls on Monthyon lies Villeroy – today the objective point for patriotic pilgrimages. There, on the 5th September, the 276th [French] Regiment was preparing its soup for lunch, when, suddenly, from the trees on the heights, German shells fell amongst them, and food was forgotten, while the French at St Soupplet on the other side of the hill, as well as those at Villeroy, suddenly found themselves in the thick of a fight – the battle we saw [from the garden of La Creste].

They told me at Villeroy that many of the men in the regiments engaged were from this region, and here the civilians dropped their work in the fields and snatched up guns which the dead or wounded soldiers let fall and entered the fight beside their uniformed neighbours. I give you that picturesque and likely detail for what it is worth.

At the foot of the hill between Monthyon and Villeroy lies the tomb in which two hundred of the men who fell here are buried together. Among them is Charles Peguy, the poet, who wore a lieutenant's stripes, and was referred to by his companions on that day as '*un glorieux fou dans sa bravoure*'. This long tomb, with its crosses and flags and flowers, was the scene on All Soul's Day of the commemorative ceremony in honour of the victory [just weeks before], and marks not only the beginning of the battle, but the beginning of its triumph. From this point we drove back to the east, almost along the line of the battle, the hillside hamlet of Barcy, the saddest scene of desolation on this end of the great fight.

It was a humble little village, grouped around a dear old church, with a graceful square tower supporting a spire. The little church faced a small square, from which the principal street runs down the hill to the open country across which the French 'push' advanced. No house on the street escaped. Some of them are absolutely destroyed. The church is a mere shell. Its tower pierced with huge holes. Its bell lies, a wreck, on the floor beneath its tower. The roof has fallen in, a heaped-up mass of debris in the nave beneath. Its windows are gone, and there are gaping wounds in its side walls. Oddly enough the Chemin de la Croix is intact, and some of the peasants look on that as a miracle, in spite of the fact that the High Altar is buried under a mass of tiles and plaster …

The best idea I got of the destruction was, however, from a house almost opposite the church. It was only a shell, its walls alone standing.

As its windows and doors had been blown out, we could look in from the street to the interior of what had evidently been a comfortable country house. It was now like an uncovered box, in the centre of which there was a conical shaped heap of ashes as high as the top of the fireplace. We could see where the stairs had been, but its entire contents had been burned down to a heap of ashes – burned as thoroughly as wood in a fireplace. I could not have believed in such absolute destruction if I had not seen it.

While we were gazing at the wreck I noticed an old woman leaning against the wall and watching us. Out of her weather-beaten, time-furrowed old face looked a pair of dark eyes, red-rimmed and blurred with much weeping. She was rubbing her distorted old hands together nervously as she watched us. It was inevitable I should get in conversation with her, and discover that this wreck had been, for years, her home, that she had lived there all alone, and that everything she had in the world – her furniture, her clothing, and her savings – had been burned in the house.

From Barcy we drove out into the plain, and took the direction of Chambry, following the line of the great and decisive battle of September 6 and 7. We rolled slowly across the beautiful undulating country of grain and beet fields. We had not gone far when, right at the edge of the road, we came upon an isolated mound, with a rude cross at its head, and a tiny tricolore at its foot – the first French grave on the plain. We motioned the chauffeur to stop, and went on, on foot.

First the graves were scattered, for the boys lie buried just where they fell – cradled in the bosom of the mother country that nourished them, and for whose safety they laid down their lives. As we advanced they became more numerous, until we reached a point where, as far as we could see, in every direction, floated the little tricolore flags, like fine flowers in the landscape. They made tiny spots against the far-off horizon line, and groups like beds of flowers in the foreground, and we know that, behind the skyline, there were more. Here and there was haystack with one grave beside it, and again there would be one, usually partly burned, almost encircled with the tiny flags which said: 'Here sleep the heroes.'

From here we turned east again towards Varreddes, along a fine road lined with enormous old trees, one of the handsomest roads of the [district]. Many of these huge trees have been snapped off by [artillery] shells as neatly as if they were mere twigs. Along the road, here and there, were isolated graves. Varreddes had a tragic experience. The population was shockingly abused by the Germans. Its aged priest and many other old men were carried away, and many were shot, and the town badly damaged.

We intended to go further but the weather had changed, and a cold drizzle began to fall, and I saw no use in going on in a closed car, so we turned back to Meaux. As we came back to Esbly I strained my eyes to look across the hill on which my house stands – I could just see it as we crawled across the bridge at the Iles-les-Villenoy – and felt again the miracle of the battle that swept so near to us.

I had done my best to get a tragic impression. I had not got it. I had brought back instead an impression heroic, uplifting, altogether inspiring … it was a disturbing and thrilling sight [seeing all the graves]. I give you my word, as I stood there, I envied them. It seemed to me a fine thing to lie out there in the open, in the soil of the fields their simple death has made holy, the duty well done, the dread over, each one just where he fell defending his mother-land, enshrined forever in the loving memory of the land he saved, in graves to be watered for years, not only by the tears of those near and dear to them, but by those of the heirs to their glory – children of the coming generation of free France.

Mildred was inspired by the determination and defiance of the French civilians and soldiers when faced with the aggression and horrors inflicted on them by an invading army. One could say that Mildred had slipped into the sentimental by the end of her description of the battlefields around the Marne. But what she describes is an accurate portrayal of the damage inflicted on those towns and villages but also the spirit of the French. They happily sacrificed themselves for the greater good. There were also, lest we forget, thousands of British soldiers killed in these battles and their bodies were also hastily buried alongside their French comrades.

After this journey Mildred decided that she needed to take a trip to Paris. She had been delighted to receive a letter from her friends – Gertrude Stein and Alice Toklas – informing her that they had returned to their apartment after the travel restrictions had been lifted and they could finally cross the channel and return to Paris. Mildred had reasons apart from seeing her friends to make the trip.

The journey out to the graves had made her think of her British boys. She wondered how they were:

> I was in Paris for Christmas – not because I wanted to go, but because the few friends I have left there felt that I needed a change, and clinched the matter by thinking that they needed me. Besides I wanted to get packages to the English boys who were here in September, and it was easier to do it from Paris than from [La Creste].

Mildred also recognised that it was her duty to make sure the bravery and sacrifice of the British troops did not go unnoticed by the French. At every opportunity, be that whilst on the train to Paris, or sitting in a street café, she would heap praise on the British boys. 'It is a moral duty,' she announced to anyone who would listen, 'to let the French people get a glimpse of the wonderful fighting quality of the boys under the Union Jack.' (To be strictly accurate, they were fighting under the Union Flag, as the Union Jack is actually associated with naval activity and not land forces.) This did not detract from her sincerity – few people know the difference anyway.

Everywhere Mildred went she seemed to meet women who had lost husbands and sons in the war. These bereaved women, especially the mothers of just one son, were inconsolable and carried grey, haunted looks. They seemed to see no future ahead, just long years of bitter regret. As much as Mildred sympathised with these women in their raw grief, she found it affected her own mood and began to drag her down. It could explain why she preferred to see the death of these young men as a sacrifice they were willing to make for their country. The weather did little to help lift the gloom:

> I did not do anything interesting in Paris. It was cold and grey and sad. I got my packages off to the front. They went through quickly, especially those sent by the English branch post-office, near the Etoile, and when I got home, I found the letters of thanks from the boys awaiting me.

One of the letters Mildred received bore sad news. 'Among them was one from the little corporal who had been here in September, who wrote in the name of the Bedfordshire Regiment, "I am sorry to tell you that Lieutenant Edwards was badly wounded and sent back to

England, where he died from his wounds."' He was 19 years old. 'That gave me a deep pang,' admitted a bereft Mildred, 'and he was so young but then so mature for his age. It was heartbreaking.'

The winter would not get any better. It would not snow but instead continued very wet and damp: 'nasty and changeable winter,' Mildred recorded in her journal. She described it as the 'most horrid winter' she had thus far experienced in France. Because of the wet, and the unfrozen ground, there was thick mud everywhere. The Marne valley was flooded and resembled a sea rather than a river valley. The distant fighting was still clearly audible in the background – the constant firing and exploding artillery and cannon. Life went on in the little hamlet of Huiry, but that sound reminded Mildred, and everyone of the commune, that the slaughter continued unabated not that far away. Mildred wrote to a friend in the United States:

> As a rule my days have been divided into two parts. In the forenoon I have hovered about the gate watching for the newspaper. In the afternoon I have rechewed the news in the vain endeavour to extract something encouraging between the lines – and failed.

She goes on to report news in a rather detached and unemotional way, perhaps as a result of blunted sensibilities towards death. 'A Zeppelin got to Paris last night. We are sorry, but we'll forget it as soon as the women and children are buried. We are sorry, but it is not important.'

Mildred's curt dismissal of this tragedy could be down to the fact that many feared the war was going badly for the Allies. It had been assumed that the war would finish quickly once the Germans were halted, but that expectation did not come to pass. This would have had a shattering effect on morale generally, added to which were the deprivations suffered by civilians. Food and fuel were scarce and hard to come by, even if the money was available to purchase them. By the end of March 1915, Mildred recorded in her journal:

> Things are a bit livened up here. Day before yesterday a regiment of dragoons arrived. They are billeted [here] for three months … they have been well received, and their presence does liven up the place. This morning before I was up, I heard the horses trotting by for their morning exercise, and got out of bed to watch them going along the hill.

By May the weather had improved slightly and warmer, sunnier days were starting to replace the dark, damp, gloomy ones. There had also been much activity and fighting in the far distance and this had convinced everyone that something important was taking place at the front. Aside from this, Mildred was to discover more shattering news on all fronts. Mildred wrote to Stein on 18 May 1915:

> All through the month of April I intended to write, but I had not the courage. All our eyes were turned to the north where, from April 22 to Thursday, May 13 – five days ago – we knew the second awful battle at Ypres was going on. It seems to be over now. What with the new war deviltry, asphyxiating gas – with which the battle began, and which beat back the line for miles by the terror of its surprise – and the destruction of the *Lusitania* on 7th, it has been a hard month. It has been a month which has seen a strange change of spirit here.

Mildred's fury and bitterness at these appalling events knew no bounds and she didn't hesitate to vent that anger through her writing. She wrote to a friend:

> I have tried to impress on you, from the beginning, that odd sort of optimism which has ruled all the people about me, even under the most trying episodes of the war. Up to now, the hatred of the Germans has been, in a certain sense, impersonal. It has been a racial hatred of a natural foe, an accepted evil, just as an uncalled-for war was [...] But, on the day, three weeks ago, when the news came of the first gas attack, before which [soldiers] fled with blackened faces and frothing lips, leaving hundreds of their companions dead and disfigured on the road to Langemarck, there arose the first signs of awful hatred that I had seen ... Germany is the most absolute synonym of evil that history has ever seen. Having stated that fact, it does not seem to me that I need say anything further on the subject.

The sinking of the *Lusitania*, an American liner, by a U-boat off the coast of Ireland, with the great loss of life involved in that tragedy, did little to make Mildred change her mind. She felt embarrassed and bewildered, as she had expected the United States to declare war on Germany within twenty-four hours of what was seen as unprovoked aggression on innocent women and children. That it didn't happen made her feel confused. She noticed how her neighbours seemed to look at her oddly as time passed and nothing happened. For the first time in her life she felt ashamed to be American. Her next thought was 'what can I do about it?'

> My neighbours who passed the gate looked at me curiously as they greeted me, and with less cordiality as the days went by [as no declaration of war against Germany came from the USA after *Lusitania*]. It was as if they pitied me, and yet did not want to be hard on me, or hold me responsible.

Mildred wrote to Stein in Paris. 'You know well enough how I feel about these things. I have no sentimentality about the war. A person who had that, and tried to live here so near it, would be on the straight road to madness.'

It was around this time in the spring of 1915 that General Joffre finally realised that Sir John French of the BEF was not ignoring his orders, but had been instructed by Kitchener and the War Office in London not to act on any orders from Joffre or French headquarters. For all these months Joffre had assumed that Sir John was arrogant and was ignoring his orders deliberately because he didn't like him, and that the War Office and government in London were weak and unable to make him follow those orders. It was a rude awakening for Joffre and the French command. It was a miracle that they had managed to avert the German capture of Paris with such bad communication between the upper echelons of the respective armies. However, the very survival of France and Great Britain still lay in the hands of these men.

'All these things are but incidents,' declared Mildred at this unfortunate situation, 'and will have no effect on the final result. A nation is not defeated while its army is still standing up in its boots, so it is folly to bother over details.' She ended on a more thoughtful note. 'Do you ever wonder what the poets of the future will do with this war? Is it too stupendous for them, or, when they get it in perspective, can they find the inspiration for words where now we have only tightened throats ...'

10

THE LONG ROAD TO 1918

The Stars and Stripes are flying at my gate, and they are flying all
over France. What is more they will be flying – if they are not already
– over Westminster, for the first time in history.

Mildred Aldrich.
On hearing the USA was entering the war, 8 April 1917

Mildred's frustration and annoyance at her country's reluctance to enter
the war and help defeat the Germans was like a constant weeping sore
in her heart. She couldn't understand the reluctance and seeming indif-
ference of the government in Washington. They did not want to become
embroiled in this European war, so she decided she must take action to
make them change their mind. But how? Sending a letter to the White
House seemed pointless – and she could imagine it being lost in a sea
of mail and ending up in some filing cabinet unanswered. It was at this
point that Mildred began to plan a way to publish her letters as a book
that would show her fellow Americans, on the other side of the Atlantic, what the reality was in Europe and why they needed to help

In the meantime the war continued and Mildred's life settled into
what could pass as a normal routine from day to day. The troops would
pass through, marching to relieve and reinforce those at the front, and
those that were exhausted or wounded were transported back to hospitals or on leave. Those returning for respite looked haunted and pale,
their voices shocked into silence by what they had seen and experienced in the trenches at the front:

During the war all my plans to live alone and to myself disappeared; life goes on as naturally as it does in times of peace. One lives and sleeps – when one can – one keeps tidy and eats – what one can. The strange thing is life becomes more interesting because [it is] more intense. Otherwise nothing seems changed but the stage setting.

There were of course differences and she recalled that 'there is death in the air – but so there is always'. This of course is true but in time of war, as experienced by Mildred, and especially the brutal trench warfare of the First World War, the smell of death, and unwashed male bodies, permeated the atmosphere depending on the direction the wind blew. 'One goes on instinctively with a life which one tries to make normal,' she continued. 'Day after day one hears the cannons.'

Mildred was also becoming more disillusioned with what she perceived to be shoddy journalism, a subject close to her heart because of her own ambitions and experiences in that career:

Day after day one reads things in sheets that call themselves newspapers and knows that the truth is not there, and while politics – the curse of the modern world – are messing things up, wishes one had the courage not to read the papers. It used to seem sometimes that it was wicked to find it all so interesting ...

There were more urgent matters that needed attention close to her own hearth – quite literally! Once again Mildred found herself in the position where she had to give up a part of her independence. Living alone suited her and, once the immediate danger from the Germans had passed, Amélie had returned to her little house and Abelard, her husband, had also returned from Paris. In the days that followed, because of the shortages of food and fuel, it became harder and harder to keep the house warm and to cook food in her small kitchen:

Amélie and I found that it was [again] wise to unite our forces. So once again, in spite of myself, I found myself at the head of a household. She had a little wood, I had a little coal still when the fuel question became hard. It seemed folly to try and run two kitchens when neither one nor the other could be properly provisioned. So the kitchen in my house did for us both. She and her husband had vegetables [stored] in their cellar. I had none [apart from those growing in the garden patch] and no one here had any to sell. I had money enough to buy the little meat we needed after we had eaten up Amélie's chickens and rabbits. So the two households were united and Amélie and [Abelard] ate in my kitchen, and their lives became [even more] part of mine. In the end it was a blessing from every point of view. But it was all the same a rude jostling of all my original scheme.

Meanwhile nearer the front line Haig was recording in his diary events after the Second Battle of Ypres. 'I recommended,' he wrote matter of factly, 'that 3 men of the Loyal North Lancs who had deserted deliberately (one found in Paris) and after being arrested again, should be shot. The state of discipline in this battalion is not very satisfactory.' He went on to record how 'Sir John French came to see me to tell me the situation generally and to ask my opinion regarding the withdrawal from the Ypres salient …'

The Germans were using poison gas regularly and as a result there was pressure to withdraw to a new and presumably safer position until a suitable strategy could be put in place to deal with this new and devastating weapon. Sir John and his commanders bickered as soldiers died horrendous deaths in the gas attacks. Haig also commented on the manipulation of the press and supported Mildred's theory that it could not be relied upon to report facts accurately. On 26 May 1915 he records in his diary a note about a letter he had received from a Major Wigram:

He states that there was an organised conspiracy in the press controlled by Lord Northcliffe against Lord Kitchener; and that Sir J. French's personal Staff are mixed up in it. Fitzgerald and Moore [Army Staff], the American (with whom Sir J lives when in London) approached the editors of the daily press and asked them to write up Sir J. and blackguard Kitchener … A most disgraceful state of affairs. Wigram thinks I have influence with Sir J. and can keep him from quarrelling with Kitchener! I have always put in a word, when I get the chance, advising that we all […] should pull together, and think about nothing but beating the Enemy! I fear such advice from me had no effect. The truth is that Sir J. is of a very jealous disposition.

Lord Northcliffe's *Daily Mail* and other papers had begun to call into question Kitchener's handling of the armed forces since the war had continued past Christmas and also because the stalemate on the Western Front seemed impossible to break. When travel restrictions were lifted, Northcliffe sent reporters to the front, and he also recruited soldiers on leave in London to report back the real conditions. Many soldiers and officers were constantly frustrated by, and happy to talk about, the lack of artillery shells and ammunition available. They were running perilously short of ammunition, which exposed British troops to German bombardment and left them nothing to fight back with. Kitchener, the government and the War Office found it impossible to censor this information, and Northcliffe's newspapers had blaring headlines about the inadequate armament supplies. Haig records in his diary: 'Sir John considered my estimate for ammunition for the attack on Rue d'Ourvert excessive,' and observations such as, 'This based on several objectives, and the number of rounds calculated as necessary for destroying certain houses, blocking communications, for counter-batteries, etc.'

It must have been an intolerable position for the commanders on the ground to have their munitions for artillery and rifles rationed to the point where it affected their ability to take full advantage of offensive operations. It was a situation that would not last. For all its faults, Northcliffe's campaign did in the end succeed and more munitions were manufactured in the United Kingdom to properly supply troops at the front. The Rt Hon. Lloyd George MP was made Minister for Munitions.

Haig recorded in his diary that over lunch he and Lloyd George:

... discussed the nature of guns and ammunition most required ... I said large numbers of heavy guns because the Enemy's defences had become so strong. We ought to aim at having enough heavy guns to engage enemy on a front of 25 to 30 miles, while retaining a strong central reserve ... a lighter machine gun, with tripod and gun in one part is a necessity. Mobility is most important ... Daggers or short bayonet for use in trenches.

Whilst these power struggles and bickering between the British commanders and politicians took place, Mildred was having problems with a power struggle of her own – one which created a lighter moment for her in the endless speculation, hardships and propaganda of the war.

Ninette, the ever-faithful donkey, held a special place in Mildred's affections:

> She was a sweet old thing ... it was behind her [in a rickety carriage] ... going to and fro from our little hospital at Quincy, and up and down the hill to Couilly, where we had a railway station, – when the little narrow gauge [track] had a service. I used to go alone in the early days even to Esbly, five miles away, which was a station [now] on the main military line to the front.

Mildred did her best to help with the livestock, and another donkey in the neighbourhood had captured her attention along with the twinkle in its eye:

> He was very young and pretty, a sort of dappled creature with slim legs, and quite tall for a donkey. He belonged to a neighbour of Amélie's, and his name was Sadi-Carnot. His owner was old and a bit timid. Sadi-Carnot was a young stallion and frisky, and so while he was being broken, Amélie and I used to drive him whenever we went to Meaux, which was five miles away.
>
> I got fond of this pretty donkey and always had a pocket full of sugar for him. One morning about four o'clock in the second war summer, I was in the garden alone. Amélie and Abelard were already in the field to turn the grass which had been cut the day before. It was a lovely morning – the prelude to a hot day. Except for the birds and the distant sound of a reaper in the field, I seemed to be alone in the world.
>
> Suddenly I heard the sound of trotting feet in the road and Sadi-Carnot appeared at the gate. He had somehow escaped from his little stall and had come to take a walk himself. He was naked – not even a halter. I went to the gate. I thought to myself that I must lead him home, or he would go too far and be hard to find. He knew me, so of course I expected he would let me catch him and lead him home by the mane. I opened the gate and said: 'Good-morning, Sadi-Carnot. Walk in.'
>
> He walked in.
>
> But when I put up my hand to take hold of his mane, he danced away, and all my efforts to catch him were in vain.

Mildred decided to outwit the donkey and lead him home by using sugar lumps instead of a carrot on a stick. His ears pricked up as soon as she said the word 'sugar' so it seemed a sensible ploy to get the donkey back in his stall:

He followed me to the kitchen door – he pursued me into the kitchen, where I filled my apron pocket with sugar – not an easy task – as I had to keep his mouth full to be able to close the box and put it into its place. That done he followed me to the gate and out into the road, and we started gaily down the hill. Every time I gave him a lump of sugar I tried to run a few steps to get over the ground. But he immediately dashed at me and tried to help himself out of my apron pocket, and I was not half way down the hill before he had eaten all the sugar from both pockets and was insisting on more.

Then Sadi-Carnot's fun began. He did not believe there was no more sugar. He danced around me, nosing my pockets, and pushing me – he was perfectly amiable – I suspected that he was laughing – and he had the right. I looked back at the gate up the hill. I wished I had brought the sugar box. I wondered if he would let me make a dash for it. Then it was my turn to laugh. I could not even run down the hill to save my life – and up the hill would mean a fall sure. One thing was certain, I was going, I was sure, to take measure of an undug grave at any moment, and as a precaution I made a move toward the high grass-grown bank which bordered the road. As I reached it, Sadi-Carnot gave me a push and down I rolled, and he deliberately turned me over with his nose and tried to chew my pocket where the sugar had been. The one thing I was afraid of was his hoofs. I found the fooling of a donkey a bit more 'rough house' than was to my taste.

I always wondered what would have happened if a farm wagon with two [elderly] men in it had not come in sight, when the donkey simply leaped over me and dashed up the hill, and then I sat up and watched the beginning of a chase which lasted an hour … And I thought we were friends – Sadi-Carnot and I – and that I was going to lead him back to captivity with kind words and sugar … I had learned a lot about donkeys. Luckily I never had to learn the same lesson twice.

Mildred would often think of that afternoon with a smile and liken Sadi-Carnot's wilful stubbornness to that of her United States Government for refusing to declare war on Germany and help bring about a victory for the Allies in Europe. Maybe she could help persuade them by using her writing skills as sugar lumps to change public opinion and put pressure on the White House and the president. With these thoughts a plan of action was finally shaping in her mind, one she would put into practice as soon as possible. The arrival of a letter made her more determined than ever to do something to influence and persuade her country it must help and not sit on the fence.

The letter shook Mildred to her core. She retired to her library and just closed herself away for a few hours. She wept silently to herself and could not understand why she should feel so heartbroken at the news; especially considering all the officers and men that had passed through her hands since this terrible war had started. Maybe it was because Captain John Simpson had been the first officer who had shown her such kindness in those first awful days of September 1914.

Captain Simpson's men respected him unconditionally. One of them had written to inform Mildred that he had been killed in action on 31 October 1914 – he was responding to a letter she had sent months previously to Simpson to ask how he was, and to call and see her again if he could. Simpson had been leading his men in an attack at Messines, was 'shot through the chest and killed instantly'. He was also mentioned by Sir John French's despatches on 8 October for 'his gallant and distinguished service in the field'. He was 41 years old.

'I had written to Captain Simpson to let him know that "all was well at Huiry – that we had escaped, and were still all grateful for all the trouble he had taken".' The officer who had promised to pass it on, whose name she could not recall, had instructed her to seal it unread by him for censorship reasons. 'He watched me seal my letter and then wrote "read and approved" on the envelope before handing it to his orderly to send in the military post.'

Mildred couldn't help remembering the day she and Amélie had travelled out to the various battlefields beyond Meaux. Messines had been in the vicinity. She remembered all the countless little flags fluttering in the breeze as far as the eye could see, to mark the spot where soldiers had been buried in the fields and woods where they fell. It seemed incomprehensible to her that Captain Simpson had been out there somewhere amongst the fallen:

I remembered his stern, bronzed, but kindly face, which lighted up so with a smile, as he sat with me at tea on that memorable Wednesday afternoon, and of all that he did so simply to relieve the strain on our nerves that trying day. I know nothing about him – who he was – what he had for family – he was just a brave, kindly, human being, who had met me for a few hours, passed on – passed out [of life]. He is only one of thousands, but he is the one whose sympathetic voice I had heard and who, in all the hurry and fatigue of those hard days, had time to stop and console us here, and whom I had hoped to see again; and I grieved with his men for him.

It transpired that Captain Simpson's brother, Captain Lancelot Simpson, whom he believed to have been killed, had in fact been injured and taken prisoner by the Germans, and was in a prisoner-of-war camp. There was, with that information, some consolation for the family back in London.

The arrival of Gertrude Stein and Alice Toklas at La Creste always shook Mildred out of herself and she always enjoyed their company for a few days. They would muck in and help with the daily chores, but also keep Mildred updated with all the news from Paris and of various friends scattered around the world. It was during one such visit that Mildred discussed with Stein the idea of compiling a small book of letters she had sent to friends in those early days of September 1914, during the Battle of the Marne. It would, she hoped, if it could be published in America, make the public there realise the enormity of what was happening in Europe and help change public opinion. She proposed to call it *A Hilltop on the Marne* and also hoped it might put pressure on the White House to do something. Stein thought it was a brilliant idea and suggested that Mildred start to compile the letters for inclusion in the book immediately as there was no time to lose. Once they had departed for Paris, Mildred began to put her letters together and edit them into a small volume in chronological order. It would help her to keep busy during the long evening hours of the coming winter.

'My garden, my animals – the soldiers cantoned among us ... occupied me easily during the hours of daylight,' wrote Mildred in her journal. This reference to 'animals' included the many cats that chose La Creste's outbuildings and barn as their home with no invitation from Mildred:

During those hours life had to go on as nearly normal as possible. The sun rose and set at the same hour it had always done. The moon increased and diminished as usual, in spite of the scenes she looked on. Grass grew green and withered. The trees leaved and became bare seasonably. The birds sang as always. The swallows came and departed on their fixed dates. It was up to us all to follow their example, and we tried to do it.

Amélie and Abelard had decided to sleep in their own cottage along the lane but continued to share the kitchen and have meals with Mildred at La Creste during the day. This suited Mildred as she could have some hours of peace to read and work on her volume of letters. However, it was not all she thought it would be, especially in the winter months. Accompanied always by the eerie sound of artillery explosions in the far distance; the volume dictated by the direction the wind blew from the front:

It was the dark hours that were hardest – the winter days when it was dark from four in the afternoon until nearly eight in the morning – sixteen hours of blackness. To be absolutely alone in peace here had been lovely at first, but I had no winter here before the war, and when the [Zeppelin] air raids began I could leave no window unshuttered or uncurtained after the lamps were lighted.

We had never a street light of any kind here. If we had had it could not have been lighted. The distance from my house to Amélie's was not long, but on the black nights we needed a lantern, and were forbidden to use one. I had never been in the country in winter. I did not know how black a cold, moonless night could be. I never made but one attempt to get from my house to Amélie's in the evening. I had both lanterns and a little electric lamp, but I could not use either. I went out, closed the door carefully behind me, and started out. I could not see my hand before my face, and I had no sense of direction. I managed to get into the road, and started up it. But I soon ran into a wall, and I could not find out what wall it was. In the end I had to scream for aid, as I could not find my way back, and when after some time I was finally rescued I was some distance up the hill, as far from Amélie's house as from my own. After that I stayed in my shut-up house. It was … little use to hope to sleep until eleven – I was always listening for an air raid.

During these long, dark winter nights Mildred edited and formatted the letters she had decided to include in *A Hilltop on the Marne* before sending them to her friend in Boston, who had agreed to try and secure a suitable publisher. In between her work she began to rediscover books she had long since put aside from lack of time and found they helped to fill the long, lonely nights at La Creste.

'Reading was, of course, my salvation. I had always said that no one who loved to read was ever lonely. But I rarely saw a new book. It was then that I began my last phase of theatre going.' The kind of theatre going she referred to was the kind that occurred in one's mind – her imagination easily brought to life the pre-war Paris theatre days she had enjoyed so much. 'It was a return to my old habits that I thought I had left behind forever. For many months I went to the theatre every night [in her mind] – sometimes twice a night.'

Her library was full of books and plays she had collected over the years and had derived so much pleasure from – to read but also when she saw productions of them on the London, Paris or New York stage, in that life she had lived before coming to the hilltop:

> My little library was full of plays. I had several editions of Shakespeare and a large number of Elizabethan dramatists; Congreve and some of the best of Restoration dramas; a large number of French plays from the 1830 period down to 1914; all of Ibsen and Bjornson, Tolstoi; all of Pinero and Shaw and such modern English drama as had been published then, as well as Hauptmann and Sudermann and Tcherkov [sic].
>
> It was a decent outfit, for an elderly lady who had abandoned, as she supposed forever, all interest in the theatre, and had religiously refrained from even reading theatre advertisements, or any announcement whatsoever concerning the theatre or theatre people.

It would seem that for all her protestations to the contrary, Mildred did miss some aspects of the life she had enjoyed in Paris, especially the theatre and the plays she had so enjoyed. That she could relive those ties through the play texts did much to help her endure the bleakness of the dark winter months: 'I must confess that in those hard days, when I needed distraction,' she recalled, 'I had good reason to bless the training the theatre had given me.'

Sitting alone in the evening by her meagre fire, she would wrap a shawl over her legs and put her feet on a heated brick. The bricks were Amélie's invention. She placed three in the oven and let them absorb the heat from the range. She would wrap two in cloths and put them in Mildred's bed, the other Mildred would put her feet on to keep warm whilst sitting by her fire to read:

I had to make no effort – that is to say, no physical effort – to get the curtain up. I had to buy no ticket – make no toilette – hunt for no cab – take no note of the hour. I had all the space I wanted – suffered from no bad air. I cannot recall that I missed the crowd or the footlights, or the applause. I suppose the long habit and my imagination supplied that – or was it the spirit of resignation to the inevitable?

Mildred had a wonderful selection of plays to pass the time with. Many she had seen performed by the finest actors and actresses of the time. They still had a life so vivid as to be almost touchable for her. Most importantly it gave her a focus and a release for her creative spirit, the colour and gaiety of the theatre lifting the black and grey confines of her wintry existence:

Of course with many of the plays with which I was most familiar the actors I had known in the roles simply stepped onto the scene and played the roles out. Sometimes the actors who appeared surprised me. I remember that the night I read *Hamlet* I was surprised to find Henry Irving moving across the page. I had opened the book, with which I was so familiar, without casting the play at all. I don't know what would have been the result if I had chosen the star that night. But to me in that case 'the play was the thing', and Irving's appearance was a surprise, and once he played the play out just as I had seen him do in Boston at least twenty years before.

Mildred found herself wondering about her past collaborator Maeterlinck, for whom she had translated *The Blue Bird* into English, and remember him telling her how 'it was torture for him to see one of his plays acted out,' and that he objected more to the 'physical form, the voice of the actor coming into the picture his imagination had created,' which upset him terribly because they were 'so unlike what he had conceived that he actually suffered.'

For Mildred the plays were a blessing and helped keep her imagination fertile. It also helped to inspire her to write more herself and not just content herself with the numerous letters she wrote to friends and soldiers of her acquaintance. Perhaps there was a creative possibility for her, an important one at that. 'I had seen the days when I bitterly regretted,' she remarked philosophically, 'that a long life given up to play going had made me instinctively see so much of life and its movement for its theatre value. I felt strangely different after those hard days when play reading added so much to my life by its capacity to amuse and uphold me.'

By the spring of 1915 Mildred had completed *A Hilltop on the Marne*. It was published in the United States that year and sold well enough to be considered for another edition and print run. Because of this success she started on another book, *On the Edge of the War Zone*. She sent the manuscript to her friend in Boston after Gertrude Stein had suggested alterations and additions. Stein was pleased to see that Mildred had included several of the letters she had sent to her in both of these projects. Stein enjoyed staying with Mildred and did so frequently – at least a few days every couple of months. Mildred also occasionally went to Paris and stayed with Stein, but less frequently. She felt more and more out of place during those visits to the city. Stein said Mildred's appearance suggested she was in fact turning into a French peasant woman. Indeed, Stein declared, she had begun to resemble one with edges of a New Englander, with 'George Washington' features, and steely grey hair. Stein also marvelled that Mildred could live in a French peasant house, with French furniture and still manage to make her interior decoration have a very American feel.

Mildred, as was her nature, accommodated and amused her friend and was always happy to see her however trying she could sometimes be. Mildred always felt that Stein was not valued and appreciated enough for her intellectual talents and her writings – there were dozens of unpublished manuscripts languishing in her Paris apartment. Stein seemed indifferent, but underneath, Mildred felt, she was frustrated by those who saw her as a writer of little substance. Mildred fought for many years to get Stein included in the American *Who's Who* but to no avail. It was an omission that infuriated Mildred for many years – at least according to Stein, with her tongue set firmly against her cheek.

By the May 1916 General Douglas Haig had replaced Sir John French as commander of the British Army in France. He was then embroiled in frustrating discussions with Joffre, and one of his commanders Foch, about the planned summer offensive by French and British troops in a joint operation to try to unseat the Germans and push them back. It was clear that the Russians would be of little help as the Tsar's internal struggles had taken his attention and there was little coordination where his troops were concerned as a result of this turmoil. Haig was determined he would not be pushed into any hasty plans and felt any major offensive needed careful planning to ensure maximum impact and progress. Even the French were concerned. Clemenceau, chair of the Military Committee, held a meeting with Haig that he recorded in his diary on 4 May:

> His object in coming to see me was to get me to exercise a restraining hand on General Joffre, and prevent any offensive on a large scale from being made until all is ready, and we are at our maximum strength. We cannot expect that Russia will be able to do much towards the defeat of Germany, so we must rely on ourselves. If we attack and fail, then there will be a number of people in France who will say that the time has arrived to make terms ... the French people are in good heart, but if there was a failure, after a big effort, it is difficult to say what the result on their feelings might be.

Haig was certainly cautious and also mindful of the difficult position he was in with his French allies. 'I assured him,' Haig recorded in his diary, 'that I had no intention of taking part prematurely in a great battle, but, of course, I was making ready to attack to support the French in case anything in the nature of a catastrophe were to happen.' The Battle of the Somme was destined to start on 1 July 1916, and not in August as Haig had originally hoped. Haig was adamant that whatever happened there would be no situation where making 'terms' for peace with the Germans would occur. That line had been passed long ago.

Back at Huiry, Mildred had noticed an increase in the number of troops passing through. As a result she found herself a compulsory hostess to officers billeted in her spare room. She would also have found any suggestion of peace terms with the Germans an outrage to decency. As far as Mildred was concerned this war had been deliberately brought to bear on the civilised world because of the Germans' lust to conquer and control. There were no 'terms' that they could demand of anyone.

In early May Mildred was writing to friends about the changeable and unpredictable weather. She also fretted at the news of the Battle of Verdun. 'I have lived through such nerve-trying days lately,' she declared with frustration, 'that I rarely feel in the humour to write a letter.' Thankfully she soon overcame such reluctance and continued to record the events she witnessed and the news from her unique position:

The spring has been as changeable as even that which New England knows. We had four fairly heavy snowstorms in the first fortnight of the awful fighting at Verdun. Then we had wet, and then unexpected heat – the sort of weather in which everyone takes cold. I get up in the morning and dress like a polar bear for a drive, and before I get back the sun is so hot I feel like stripping.

She goes on to give her impression of the battle at Verdun:

There is nothing for anyone to do but wait for news from the front. It is the same old story – they are see-sawing at Verdun, with the Germans much nearer than at the beginning – and still we have the firm faith that they will never get there. Doesn't it seem to prove that had Germany fought an honest war she could never have invaded France?

The Germans had attacked the French at Verdun on 21 February and it had turned into another stalemate, frustrating the long-term plans for a major offensive coordinated between the British and the French. Verdun was eating up French troops and exhausting the reserves. Haig had a meeting with Kitchener in London around 25 February to discuss the options:

I told him that I thought we ought to be prepared for one of three situations arising as a result of the fighting at Verdun.

A kind of stalemate. Both sides having lost very heavily, and the French (owing to lack of reserves of men and ammunition) unable and unwilling to carry out a vigorous offensive again.

In my opinion, our action should then be to ask the French to take over some of the front from us so as to set free as many troops of ours as possible for a large offensive. In this case, our attack should be on the front from Ypres to Armentières in the direction of the Dutch frontier north of Lys. ... If, however, the French have sufficient troops left for the general attack, then we should make our attack alongside theirs, say, astride the Somme ...

In the case of success. We must attack at once on the front of the Third Army. The enemy will probably have had to reduce the numbers of his troops holding the front if he has suffered a check at Verdun.

In the case of disaster. We must counter-attack at once close to the French. I do not think an attack on the front of our Third Army in such case would do any good. This attack cannot be ready to start at once because there must be a delay in preparing for it, which people will attribute to a determination to do nothing! Also the German line would not have been weakened, as would most likely be the case in the event of the Germans receiving a [battle] check.

The problems and stalemate caused at Verdun dragged on and caused Mildred to complain that there was no progress, which added to the frustration experienced by the civilian population and the Allied military. There was always the hope in Huiry that the next big attack would bring the war to a swift conclusion. But there had been too many times when hopes were raised and as quickly dashed. Verdun had been no different. But worse was yet to come.

Joffre had told Haig by late May 1916 that 'the French had supported for three months alone the whole weight of the German attacks at Verdun'. He made it clear that if this continued the French army 'would be ruined'. He went on to say that the latest date for the planned joint offensive should be 1 July 1916. Haig was still procrastinating, mainly because he wanted to be sure that it was the right time and that thorough planning was carried out to ensure success. In comparison to Sir John French, Haig improved the working relationship with Joffre and his generals, but it was still difficult. Haig's next shock was the death of Lord Kitchener in early June 1916. Kitchener was lost at sea when the ship he was travelling on sank in the North Sea.

The news of Kitchener's sudden and unexpected death reached Mildred at Huiry, and cast a gloom over the small community. It seemed that as soon as progress was made something happened to set everyone back. This all prompted Mildred to declare, 'the affairs of the whole world are in a mess'. In a letter to a friend in Boston she revealed her thoughts on how the women were coping with the war and the absence of men:

There are many aspects of the war which would interest you if you were sitting down on my hilltop with me – conditions which may seem more significant than they are. For example, the Government has sent back from the front a certain number of men to aid in the farm work until the planting is done. Our commune [Huiry] does not get many of these. Our old men and boys and women do the work fairly well, with the aid of a few territorials, who guard the railway two hours each night and work in the fields in the daytime.

The women here are used to doing field work, and don't mind doing more than their usual stunt.

Mildred had always been a feminist in as much as she believed that women should be equal to men in all aspects of life – including employment. She knew first hand the frustration of a woman attempting to have a career in a male-dominated world. She was impressed that the lack of men had not hindered the women at all in coping with the hard farm labour they took on as the younger men were called up into the army:

> I often wonder if some of the women are not better off than in the days before the war. They do about the same work, only they are not bothered by their men. In the days before the war the men worked in the fields ... it was a hard life, and most of them drank a little ...

Mildred also touches on the politics of the farm workers and how as a result they were predisposed to be against the government of the day:

> Of course, being Socialists and French, they simply had to talk it all over. The café was the proper place to do that – the provincial café being the working men's club. Of course, the man never dreamed of quitting until legal closing hour, and when he got home, if wife objected, why he just hit her a clip, – it was, of course, for her good ...

It seems unbelievable more than a century later that such domestic violence was written about with such matter of factness. Such behaviour was anathema to Mildred and she would not have condoned it had she witnessed it, or knew such violence was being inflicted on anyone she knew, such as Amélie. That said, she was simply passing on information about daily life in a tiny French hamlet where things hadn't changed much for centuries. It gives a glimpse into a lost world, a moment in history:

> Almost always in these provincial towns it is the woman who is thrifty, and often she sees but little of her man's earnings. Still, she is, in her way, fond of him, tenacious in her possession of him, and Sundays and fete days they get on together very handsomely ... All the women here, married or not, have always worked, and worked hard.

There was another dramatic distraction in those weeks prior to the Battle of the Somme in July 1916. Mildred knew that there was a big offensive coming up, but she didn't know the details and wouldn't until much later. But she was aware of troops and equipment moving towards the front – and the sense of anticipation in the atmosphere. She also remarked how the fighting, artillery and explosion from the front were affecting the weather and making it unseasonal, even hailstorms, and very unsettled. This theory was discussed endlessly; especially by the elderly of the commune. 'It has knocked all the buds off the fruit-trees,' declared Mildred tartly, 'so, in addition to other annoyances, we shall have no fruit this year.'

The other drama concerned General Foch, who was in the hospital at Meaux:

No one knows it, not a word has appeared in the newspapers. It was the result of a stupid, but unavoidable, automobile accident. To avoid running over a woman and a child on a road near here, the automobile, in which he was travelling rapidly in company with his son-in-law, ran against a tree and smashed. Luckily he was not seriously hurt, though his head got damaged ... It was a lucky escape for Foch. He would have hated to die during this war of a simple, unmilitary automobile accident, and the army could ill afford just now to lose one of the heroes of the Marne. Carefully as the fact has been concealed, we knew it here through our ambulance [hospital], which is a branch of that at Meaux, where he is being nursed.

Three months since the battle at Verdun began, and it is still going on, with the Germans hardly more than four miles from the city, and yet it begins to look as if they knew themselves that the battle – the most terrible the world has ever seen – was a failure. I begin to believe that had Germany centred all her forces on that frontier in August, 1914, when her first-line troops were available, and their hopes high, she would probably have passed.

Perhaps Mildred's analysis would have proved accurate, but it was all academic by this stage. The Germans chose another plan and it had resulted in the stalemate of trench warfare, causing the slaughter of millions of men. The Battle of the Somme began on 1 July 1916. Civilians like Mildred a few miles back from the front heard the artillery fire and explosions as the British hammered the German trench lines as a prelude to the soldiers going over the top to attack and finish off the German troops in their trenches. It was hoped this would be a turning point and enable the British and French to force an early end to the war. What the Allies didn't know was that the Germans had dug their defences deep underground, using sophisticated trench construction. As the artillery barrage rained down they were mostly safe in underground bunkers. Once the artillery stopped, they emerged to man their machine guns and easily mowed down the British and French troops as they responded to the officers' whistles – the signal for them to go over the top and into no-man's-land between the trench lines. It was wholesale slaughter and a disaster for the British. On that one day the British suffered 57,000 casualties – nearly 20,000 of them killed. Haig recorded in his dairy the early morning conditions prior to the artillery barrage beginning:

A fine sunny morning with gentle breeze from the west and southwest. At first some mist in the hollows. This is very favourable because it concealed the concentration of our troops. The bombardment was carried out as usual … but at 7.30 a.m. the artillery increased their range and the infantry followed the barrage [over the top].

Mildred wrote to a friend in the United States on 4 August 1916. She reflected on the current news and an article sent to her, and also how things were perceived more than a month after that first disastrous day of the Battle of the Somme:

Well, here we are in the third year of the war, as Kitchener foresaw, and still with a long way to go to the frontier. Thanks, by the way, for the article about Kitchener. After all, what can one say of such an end for such a man, after such a career, in which so many times he might have found a soldier's death – then to be drowned like a rat, doing his duty? It leaves one simply speechless. I was, you see. I hadn't a comment to throw at you.

She continues to describe how the weather has improved and at last she can manage without lighting a fire in the evening. She also describes how the harvest is generally poor because of the erratic, wet weather which caused much root damage to crops. All this added to food shortages, which was a greater difficulty than normal because the food was so desperately needed by the civilians to survive:

> It is hot at last, I'm thankful to say, and equally thankful that the news from the front is good. It's nothing to throw one's hat in the air about, but every inch in the right direction is at least prophetic ... I do nothing but read my paper, fuss in the garden ... write a few letters, and drive about, at sundown, in my perambulator. If that is not an absurd life for a lady in the war zone in these days, I'd like to know what is. I hope this weather will last. It is good for the war and good for the crops. But I am afraid I shall hope in vain.

The Battle of the Somme continued and by 22 August, Haig was recording his thoughts on the current situation – it had also been accepted that the initial gains had been limited and short-lived. Haig had requested an intelligence report on the situation and the German troops in particular:

> A return compiled by my Intelligence Branch shows that whereas a German Division is worn out in 4½ days opposite the British, opposite the French they last very much longer, sometimes 3 weeks! This clearly shows how regular and persistent is the pressure by the British.

Haig seemed to be suggesting, probably for his own purposes and propaganda, that the problems experienced on the Somme were more to do with an inadequacy in the aggressiveness of the French troops. The British troops were, he seemed to suggest, being burdened by this but holding things together with their superiority. It was perhaps a way for Haig to justify the disaster and loss of life, the details of which had trickled back to the United Kingdom.

'The number of German Divisions engaged on the Somme front amounts to 42,' Haig continued to record in his diary, 'and possibly 45 because it is thought that 3 more are in process of being relieved. Since 30 July 12 divisions have been exhausted on the north of the Somme; of them the British have dealt with 9. The French 3.'

Haig's relationship with Foch and Joffre still seemed to be strained. Little wonder that Haig described the French as less than effective in some of his diary entries. Some of their suggestions he dismissed as 'doomed to failure':

> Joffre has ordered the Tenth Army to attack south of the Somme in the first week September or thereabouts. He wishes the British to put in a big attack then instead of waiting till the middle of September. I said that I would do what was possible to meet General Joffre's wishes, but I could not attack northwards until I had established my flank eastwards of Ginchy in conjunction with the French.

Haig was still unsure about the plans and was unhappy with Joffre's inclination to rush things and not plan properly. By 25 August, Haig entered in his diary another meeting with his Allies:

> After I left Foch's HQ I was handed a letter from General Joffre in which, after expatiating on what the French Army had done at Verdun and on the Somme etc., I was asked to attack in force on 6 September latest ... I presume that Joffre has pledged himself to this owing to pressure from Russia, but before fixing the date, he should have ascertained what the British Army can do!

The lack of communication seems clear and the antipathy, bordering on outright hostility, is tangible. This went on as thousands of men died on the front line. Haig made an entry in his diary, dated 26 August 1916, which is important for the new machine it introduced into warfare:

> At 3 p.m. I was present at a demonstration in the use of 'Tanks'. A battalion of infantry and 5 Tanks operated together. Three lines of trenches were assaulted. The Tanks crossed the several lines with the greatest ease, and one entered a wood, which represented a 'strong point' and easily walked over fair sized trees of 6 inches through! Altogether the demonstration was quite encouraging, but we require to clear our ideas as to the tactical handling of these machines ...

The invention and introduction of the tank into modern warfare was one of the 'killing machines never before imagined' that Mildred had predicted would be unleashed on the world. She was still blissfully unaware of tanks. She had yet to read about them, or see them in action, and thankfully she would be spared seeing any of these killing machines roaring up the hill at Huiry and through her garden at La Creste. As Haig and his French allies tried to unscramble the mess on the Somme, Mildred became aware of the dynastic and political implosion of Russia. On 30 September 1916 she wrote to Getrude Stein:

> What a disappointment poor Russia has been to the big world, which knew nothing about her except that she could put fifteen millions of men in the field [of war]. However, as we say, 'all that is only detail'. We are learning things every day. Nothing has opened our eyes more than seeing set at naught our conviction that, once the Rumanian frontier was opened to the Russians, they would be on the Danube in no time.

She continued by reflecting back to the early thoughts and anticipated contribution this great bear of a nation could contribute as an ally:

> Do you remember how glibly we talked of the 'Russian steam-roller', in September, 1914? I remember that, at that time, I had a letter from a very clever chap who told me that 'expert military men' looked to see the final battle on our front, somewhere near Waterloo, before the end of October, and that even 'before that, the Russian steam-roller would be crushing its way to Berlin'. How much expert military men have learned since then!

The French had imposed some strict rules on the civilian population inside the war zone by this time and Mildred found herself restricted quite severely. Her French neighbours seemed more upset by this than she was; Mildred took it as a necessary inconvenience to ensure security and safety. Everyone had to have their photograph taken, much to the horror of older residents who had never seen a camera, by order of the military and local police, and everyone had to apply for, and keep possession of, their residents' permit papers – to be produced on demand with a penalty of imprisonment should one be caught without them. As an American citizen, Mildred had to be interviewed and given permission to remain inside the zone – a condition being that she remained within her hamlet and in the immediate vicinity unless permission was given to travel further afield or into Paris.

The reason for this strict imposition became clear in early November 1916 when Mildred reported some unusual activity in the hamlet:

Last Wednesday we had a little excitement here, because sixteen German prisoners, who were working on a farm at Vereddes, escaped – some of them disguised as women. I wasn't a bit alarmed, as it hardly seemed possible that they would venture near houses in the district, but [Abelard] was very nervous, and every time the dog barked he was out in the road to make sure that I was all right ... If they caught them, they [didn't tell] but we have been ordered to harbour no strangers.

By the end of November Mildred was remarking bitterly on the death of Franz Josef, emperor of the Austro-Hungarians:

In the meantime I am sorry that Franz Josef did not live to see this war of his out and take his punishment. I used to be so sorry for him in the old days, when it seemed as if Fate showered disasters on the heads of the Hapsburgs. I wasted my pity. The blows killed everyone in the family but the father. The way he stood it and never learned to be kind or wise proved how little he needed pity.

The war had taken its toll on everyone, even Mildred, and her anger at the waste of life and the futility of it all bore down on her spirit as another bleak, dark winter approached. Her feelings and thoughts towards Kaiser Wilhelm were, not surprisingly, even more bitter. The rain and the cold duly arrived. The bitter winds, Mildred decided, never went round her when they could cut right through her and chill her bones. By the middle of December Mildred was glad another regiment had arrived on the hilltop to be looked after until they marched to the front. It gave her a purpose and distracted her from the cold.

Because of the success of *A Hilltop on the Marne* Mildred had decided to compile another book of letters and stories and planned to publish it in 1917 under the title *On the Edge of the War Zone*. She had been busily putting together a collection of letters for inclusion. This would, at least, give her a purpose during those endless winter nights to come. The success of the first publication had given her heart and made her feel she was doing something to encourage the United States to enter the war and help the Allies. She had received many letters from the other side of the Atlantic supporting her, and *A Hilltop on the Marne* had also received favourable reviews in the New York press.

Mildred remained optimistic, but she would still admit to anyone who would listen her utter frustration that the United States seemed determined to ignore the dire situation in Europe – she feared it would have a lasting impact on world peace in the future. She had also decided that any money earned from the books in royalties she would donate to those who had lost their homes and families since 1914. In her small way, she was determined to help however she could. As these thoughts went through her mind, a sharp knocking at her front door interrupted her:

> It was just after lunch on Sunday, a grey, cold day, which had dawned on a world covered with frost ... I opened [the door] and there stood a soldier, with his heels together, and his hand at salute, who said: '*Bonjour madame, avez-vouz un lit pour un soldat?*' Of course I had a bed for a soldier, and said so at once.

The French soldiers of the 23rd Dragoons joined Mildred on the hill-top – an infantry regiment on active service for the front line in the trenches at 'Tracy-le-Val, in the Forêt de Laigue, the nearest point to Paris in the battle-front'. Amid the hustle and bustle of pitching tents and organising horses in stables, Mildred decided it to be tremendously interesting, more so than anything which had happened since the Battle of the Marne.

The new arrivals allowed Mildred to focus her energies on being useful again and helped her forget her frustrations at the lack of food and fuel. Warmth seemed a distant memory and the lack of fuel would ensure it remained so. Mildred was the first to admit that she had a preference for the British soldiers – they were less serious and more inclined to see the positive side of things, whereas the French seemed overly serious and rather glum at times. However, Mildred was thrilled that new soldiers were on the hilltop and she was determined to make the most of it and assist in any way possible:

> You see it is all polite and formal, but if there is a corner in the house which can serve the army the army has the right to it. Everyone is offered the privilege of being prettily gracious about it, and of letting it appear as if a favour were being extended to the army, but, in case one does not yield willingly, along comes a superior officer and imposes a guest on the house.

However, that sort of thing never happened here. In our commune the soldiers are loved. The army is, for that matter, loved all over France. No matter what else ... the crowd never fails to cry '*Vive l'Armée!*' Although there are places where the soldier is not loved as a visitor [because of the disruption these cause].

I asked the adjutant in, and showed him the [guest] room. He wrote it down in his book, saluted me again with a smiling, '*Merci bien, madame,*' and went on to make the rounds of the hamlet, and examine the resources of Voisins, Joncheroy, and Quincy. The non-commissioned officers, who arrange the *cantonnements*, are very clever about it. They seem to know, by instinct, just what sort of a man to put in each house, and they rarely blunder.

All that Sunday afternoon they were running around in the mud and the cold drizzle that was beginning to fall, arranging, not only quarters for the men, but finding shelter for three times as many horses, and that was not easy, although every old grange on the hilltop was cleaned out and put in order.

Mildred was amused to discover that one such officer, in charge of finding suitable stabling for several horses, decided that her grange on the north side of the house would easily fit four horses. Mildred attempted to explain that, as much as she would be more than happy for this to happen, she feared that four horses in such a confined space would result in the collapse of the grange if the horses became unsettled. Although she had confidence in her stable, she was far less confident of the rotten timbers in the old unused grange, which was used only for dry storage.

Eventually the officer relented when Mildred declared with concern how 'I'd hate to have handsome army horses killed like that on my premises.' On Mildred's suggestion, the officer went to see Amélie, to see if any more room could be made in her barn for the horses. 'By sundown,' Mildred recorded for posterity, 'everything was arranged – four hundred horses along the hilltop and, they tell us, over fifteen thousand along the valley.' It would seem that the smell of unwashed male bodies was now punctuated with the odour of several thousand horses. At least it was winter.

It did not take long for the men to realise that they could always find hot water and refreshments at La Creste:

They were welcome to it if they could keep the kettle filled, and that I did not mind their coming and going – and I don't, for a nicer crowd of men I never saw. They are not only ready, they are anxious, to do all sorts of odd jobs, from hauling coal and putting it in, to cleaning the chimneys and sweeping the terrace. When they groom the horses they always groom Gamin, our dapple-grey pony, and Ninette, which were never so well taken care of in their lives – so brushed and clipped that they are both handsomer than I knew.

During the course of the past few years Mildred had met and befriended hundreds, if not thousands, of British and French soldiers as they passed to and from the front line. Some she received letters from, and if she could she would write to those who formed a special bond with her on the hilltop. When those letters arrived she would sit quietly in her library and give them her full attention. One such letter from a French officer, who had recently departed, arrived in February 1917:

Dear Madame,
Bravo for the pretty idea you had in flinging to the winter breezes the tri-coloured flag in honour of our departure. All the soldiers marching out of Voisins saw the colours and were deeply touched. Let me bear witness to their gratitude.

How I regret La Creste. One never knows how happy he is until afterward. I am far from comfortably installed here. I am lodged in an old deserted chateau. There are no fires, and we are literally refrigerated. However, we shall not stay long, as I am returning to the trenches in a day or two. It will hardly be warm there, but I shall have less time to remember how much more than comfortable I was at Huiry.

We made a fairly decent trip to this place, but I assure you that, in spite of my 'extreme youth', I was near to being frozen en route. We were so cold that finally the whole regiment had to dismount and proceed on foot in the hope of warming up a bit. We were all, in the end, sad, cross, and grumbly. You had spoiled us all at Huiry and Voisins. For my part I longed to curse someone for having ordered such a change of base as this, in such weather. Wasn't I well enough off where I was, toasting myself before your nice fire, and drinking my tea comfortably every afternoon?

However, we are working tremendously for the coming offensive. And I hope it will be the final one, for the Germans are beginning to show signs of fatigue. News comes to us from the interior, from a reliable source, which indicates that the situation on the other side of the Rhine is anything but calm. More than ever now must we hang on, for the victory is almost within our clutch

Accept, madame, the assurance of my most respectful homage.

A – B [French soldier's name blacked out for censorship]

The new year, 1917, was to be pivotal for the war. The French, under General Nivelle, who had replaced Joffre, were pressing the British to support them with a new offensive – the Second Battle of the Aisne – the one mentioned by the French soldier in the letter to Mildred. Haig was having problems of his own. December 1916 had seen the election of David Lloyd George as prime minister. Haig felt Lloyd George was not wholly supportive of him and he feared that Lloyd George would attempt to put the BEF under the direct orders of Nivelle and the French military. This did not come to pass, but Lloyd George was certainly not averse to putting British troops under French command, for he maintained that the 1916 Battle of the Somme had been a mismanaged disaster and an appalling loss of life. As a result the relationship between Haig and Lloyd George remained strained and full of suspicions.

Nivelle's planned offensive never achieved what he had hoped, mainly because the Germans had continued to retreat and entrenched the fortifications of the Hindenburg Line – making the plans worthless. Haig, for his part, felt the French were tired and incapable of inflicting any serious harm to the German lines. Plans were now fully implemented for the Battle of Arras (9–4 May 1917) and the Third Battle of Ypres and Flanders (31 July–6 November 1917), culminating at the Battle of Passchendaele Ridge on 6 November 1917. November would also see the first Allied tank attack at Cambrai.

In Huiry, Mildred was busy with yet more French and British infantry. 'Well, the 118th has settled down to what looks like a long *cantonnement*. It is surely the liveliest as well as the biggest we ever had here, and every little town and village is crowded between here and Coulommier.' Mildred was shocked at the sheer numbers arriving, and found it hard to suppress her enthusiasm and suspicion it meant good news:

Not only are there five thousand infantry billeted along the hills and in the valleys, but there are big divisions of artillery also. The little square in front of our railway station at Couilly is full of grey cannon and ammunition wagons, and there are military kitchens and all sorts of commissary wagons along all the roadsides between here and Crecy-en-Brie, which is the distributing headquarters for all sorts of material.

Unbeknown to Mildred, the Allies had been meeting and planning and usually disagreeing on whether to support each other's proposed offensives. Haig was still unsure of the support he was getting from the prime minister and Nivelle seemed hell bent on making his mark. The Germans had removed all agreements on shipping and had declared that any British ship, civilian or otherwise, was a fair target for its U-boats to sink without warning. The Allies were preparing for another major offensive, but Mildred's hopes it would bring a swift end would be dashed. However, she concentrated on the military activity and troops building up in her immediate area:

As the weather has been intolerably cold, though it is dry and often sunny, the soldiers are billeted in big groups of fifty or sixty in a room or grange, where they sleep in straw, rolled in their blankets, packed like sardines to keep warm ... They came in nearly frozen, but they thawed out quickly, and now they don't mind the weather at all.

A few days later she had gone for a walk when she came across an inspiring sight:

It was a sunny afternoon. I was walking in the road, when, just at the turn above my house, two officers rode round the corner, saluted me, and asked if the road led to Quincy. I told them the road to the right at the foot of the hill, through Voisins, would take them to Quincy. They thanked me, wheeled their horses across the road and stood there. I waited to see what was going to happen – small events are interesting here. After a bit one of them said that perhaps I would be wise to step out of the road, which was narrow, as the regiment was coming.

So I sauntered back to my garden, and down to the corner by the hedge, where I was high above the road, and could see in both directions. I had hardly got there when the head of the line came round the corner. In columns of four, knapsacks on their backs, guns on their shoulders, swinging at an easy gait, all looked so brown, so hardy, so clear-eyed, the men from Verdun marched by.

I had thought it cold in spite of the sun, and was well wrapped up, with my hands thrust in a big muff, but these men had beads of perspiration standing on their bronzed faces under their steel helmets.

Mildred watched as they marched by, so well disciplined and so heart-breaking. She could not but wonder how many of these brave young souls would survive. Not many she feared, especially going on the events of the past years. In spite of the terrible casualties, they still proudly marched to the colours, determined not to let the Germans destroy their freedoms – or the freedoms of the world. It brought a lump to her throat and tears to her eyes. Watching those young men march that day seemed to intensify her experience and her steely reserve was for once allowed to slip. Then, just as quickly, her emotions in check, she could appreciate what happened next:

Before the head of the line reached the turn into Voisins, a long shrill whistle sounded. The line stopped. Someone said: 'At last! My, but this has been a hot march,' and in a second every man had slipped off his knapsack and had a cigarette in his mouth. Almost all of them dropped to the ground, or lay against the bank. A few enterprising ones climbed the bank, to the field in front of my lawn, to get a glimpse of the view, and they all said what everyone says: 'I say, this is the best point to see it.' But that is not what gave me my thrill. The rest [for the men] was a short one. Two sharp whistles sounded down the hill. Instantly everyone slipped on his Knapsack, shouldered his gun, and at that minute, down at the corner, the military band struck up … Every hair on my head stood up. It is the first time I have heard a band since the war broke out, and as the regiment swung down the hill to the blare of brass … it cut the air that sunny afternoon.

Mildred could not help but reminisce and think of all those who had marched past her little house upon the hilltop. Some she would never see again, the fate of others would remain forever unknown, but all of them held a place in her life and her memory and always would:

I had so often seen those long lines marching in silence, as the English and the French did to the Battle of the Marne, as all our previous regiments have come and gone on the hillside, and never seen a band or heard military music with the soldiers, although I knew the bands played in the battles and the bugle calls were a part of it.

Gertrude Stein sent Mildred a letter and mentioned a letter Mildred had sent her in late 1914, where she had remarked 'the annoying thing is, that, after this is over, Germany will console herself with the reflection that it took the world to beat her.' It caused a chill to run down Mildred's spine. She was surprised she had been so prophetic, but she could see that her prophecy would become a truth yet. There was hope that America would finally join the war against Germany, which heartened her.

On 8 April 1917, Mildred was jubilant. The Germans had managed to provoke fury in the United States by attempting to coerce Mexico and Japan into declaring war. A telegram intercepted by the British, sent by Arthur Zimmerman on behalf of the Imperial German Government, read thus:

We intend to begin on the first of February unrestricted submarine warfare. We shall endeavor in spite of this to keep the United States of America neutral. In the event of this not succeeding, we make Mexico a proposal of alliance on the following basis: make war together, make peace together, generous financial support and an understanding on our part that Mexico is to reconquer the lost territory in Texas, New Mexico, and Arizona. The settlement in detail left to you. You will inform the President [of Mexico] of the above most secretly as soon as the outbreak of war with the United States of America is certain and add the suggestion that he should, on his own initiative, invite Japan to immediate adherence and at the same time mediate between Japan and ourselves. Please call the President's attention to the fact that the ruthless employment of our submarines now offers the prospect of compelling England in a few months to make peace.

In late 1916 President Wilson had taken a harder stance against the Germans – although they had been assisting the British through the war. He had also increased the size of the military and issued a warning to Germany regarding its use of submarines to destroy civilian ships. President Wilson's warning shot was thus:

Unless the Imperial Government should now immediately declare and effect an abandonment of its present methods of submarine warfare against passenger and freight-carrying vessels, the Government of the United Sates can have no choice but to sever diplomatic relations with the German Empire altogether.

The Germans had responded by ceasing submarine operations. By 1917 the German ambassador announced Germany was recommencing submarine warfare and he broke off diplomatic relations with the United States. It was a slippery slope and as a result of these actions President Wilson, on 6 April 1917, formerly asked Congress if it would give him permission to go to war. Wilson's rallying call was the duty to 'make the world safe for democracy'. The state of war became official on 8 April 1917.

Mildred was beside herself with joy:

The sun shines, and my heart is high, this is a great day. The Stars and Stripes are flying at my gate, and they are flying over all France. What is more they will soon be flying – if they are not already – over Westminster, for the first time in history. The mighty, unruly child, who could never quite forgive the parent it defied, and never has been wholly pardoned, is to come back to the family table, if only long enough to settle the future manners of the nations about the board, put in, I suppose, a few 'don'ts,' like 'don't grab'; 'don't take a bigger mouthful than you can becomingly chew'; 'don't jab your knife into your neighbour – it is not for that purpose'; 'don't eat out of your neighbours plate – you have one of your own' – in fact, 'Thou shalt not – even though thou art a Kaiser – take the name of the Lord thy God in vain'; 'thou shalt not steal'; 'thou shalt not kill'; 'thou shalt not covet', and so on. Trite, I know, but in thousands of years we have not improved on it.

So the Stars and Stripes are flying over France to greet the long delayed and ardently awaited, long ago inevitable declaration which puts the States shoulder to shoulder with the other great nations in the Defence of the Rights of Man, the Sacredness of Property, the Honor of Humanity, and the news has been received with such enthusiasm as has not been seen in France since war broke out.

Mildred was understandably delighted at the news. It gave her fresh hope that now the USA had entered the war there was no chance of the Germans being able to dominate Europe. The Kaiser, all his army and his allies would now face the consequences of their actions. Mildred was a patriot and her patriotism knew no bounds at this remarkable event:

> It is not, I know, today or tomorrow that it will all end; it is not next year, or in many years, that poor Poland's three mutilated parts can be joined and healed in harmony; and oh! How long it is going to be before all the sorrow and hatred that Germany has brought on the world can be either comforted or forgotten! But at least we are sure now of the course the treatment is going to take – so the sun shines and my heart is high, and I do believe that though joy may lead nowhere, sorrow is never in vain.

These are the words Mildred used to complete her second volume of letters, *On the Edge of the War Zone*. The book generated more royalties, enabling her to help those who had lost everything because of the war. There would be more slaughter and heartache to come, for 1918 had still to dawn on the world. But Mildred would hold firm and help in any way she could, as she had done since that first day in 1914. There was still work to be done. It was far from over yet but complacency was never welcome at Mildred's door.

11

THE END GAME

What joy it was for us of the Cavalry to pass over the trenches and fly
across the plains in the pursuit of the Germans ...
French officer in a letter to Mildred Aldrich.

'I am feeling today,' wrote Mildred, 'as if it were no matter that the
winter had been so hard; that we have no fuel but twigs; that the
winter wheat was frozen; that we have eaten part of our seed potatoes
and that another part of them was frost-bitten; that butter is a dollar a
pound (and none to be had, even at that price, for days at a time); that
wood alcohol is sixty-five cents a litre, and so on and so forth.'

In spite of her jubilation, the war was not over. There were hard
times to endure and everyone still had to eat something and keep
warm somehow. Mildred declared to Amélie, for perhaps the first
time openly, that she was very, very tired. This tiredness was not just
physical, it was also a mental tiredness that caused her to even leave
her books unread. Books that had for so many years given her such
joy and revealed new information at each reading, now seemed to be
as heavy and lethargic as Mildred's bones. In 1918 Mildred would
be 64, but she felt 164 at times, especially when she had to manoeuvre her weary bones from bed in the morning. Her joints seemed
to set during the night and no amount of rubbing or Amélie's spe-
cially prepared liniments would persuade them to ease up a little.
Only her sense of humour kept her going at these times – aided by
Amélie's giggles as she tried to assist. Mildred thanked God for Amélie –

she would never have managed on this hilltop without her or her husband, Abelard. Indeed, everyone of the commune was remarkable and kind.

Mildred was delighted to receive another letter from her French officer friend, from his base camp at the front. His main objective was to share his joy at the recent developments, as well as letting her know he was well and what progress his cavalry regiment had made since he last wrote some months before:

Dear Madame,

It has been a long time since I sent you my news. The neglect has not been my fault, but due to the exceptional circumstances of the war.

At last we have advanced, and this time as real cavalry. We have had the satisfaction of pursuing the Boches [Germans] – keeping on their flying heels until we drove them into St. Quentin. From 18 to the 28 of March the war became once more a battle in the open, which was a great relief to the soldiers and permitted them to once more demonstrate their real military qualities. I lived through a dozen days filled to overflowing with emotions – sorrow, joy, enthusiasm. At last I have really known what war is – with all its misery and all its beauty. What joy it was for us of the cavalry to pass over the trenches and fly across the plains in the pursuit of the Germans! The first few days everything went off wonderfully. The Boches fled before us, not daring to turn and face us. But our advance was so rapid, our impetuosity such, that, long before they expected us, we overtook the main body of the enemy. They were visibly amazed at being caught before they could cross the canal at St. Quentin, as was their plan, and they were obliged to turn and attempt to check our advance, in order to gain sufficient time to permit their artillery to cross the canal and escape complete disaster.

It was there that we fought, forcing them across the canal to entrench themselves hastily in unprepared positions, from which, at the hour I write, our wonderful infantry and our heavy artillery, in collaboration with the British, are dislodging them.

Alas! The battles were costly, and many of our comrades paid with their lives for our audacious advance. Be sure that we avenged them, and cruel as are our losses they were not in vain. They are more than compensated by the results of the sacrifice – the strip of our native soil snatched from the enemy. They died like heroes, and for a noble cause.

Since then we have been resting, but waiting impatiently to advance and pursue them again, until we can finally push them over their own frontier. Today's paper brings us great and comforting news. At last, dear madame! With a full heart I present to you my heartiest congratulations. At last Wilson understands, and the American people – so noble, and always so generous – will no longer hesitate to support us with all their resources. How wonderfully this is going to aid us to obtain the decisive victory we must have, and perhaps to shorten the war.

Here, in the army, the joy is tremendous at the idea that we have behind us the support of a nation so great, and all our admiration, all our gratitude goes out to your compatriots …

My greetings to Amélie and Papa [Abelard]: a caress for Khaki and Didine [Mildred's cats] … Receive, madame, the assurance of my most respectful homage.

A – B – [Name blacked out by censor]

As time passed and 1918 progressed, it became clear that the Germans were attempting to create chaos between the French and British before the United Sates army had time to mobilise on the Western Front. The Germans had in fact overstretched themselves and found it impossible to keep their troops adequately fed and equipped with supplies and ammunition. There would be significant battles in the Germans' spring offensive. The Second Battle of the Somme (March – April), the Battle of Lys (April), the Third Battle of Aisne (May – June), culminating in the Second Battle of the Marne in July and August. The latter would once again cause Mildred sleepless nights at Huiry, as she wondered if the battle meant a repeat of the German offensive on Paris they had endured in 1914.

The Second Battle of the Marne was in fact the final German offensive of the war and, unbeknown to Mildred, a desperate effort to deflect attention away from the Flanders fields in the hope the Allies would divert troops from that area. The German commander, Ludendorff, had planned to then break the front line on the Western Front. His attempt to cross the Marne River at Rheims was successful from the west, but the French, east of Rheims, blocked his troops on the first day. The lack of initial artillery explosions caused some confusion at Huiry:

The only explanation seemed to us was that the attack was, after all, not here but on a part of the line farther north – perhaps again in Picardy where the attack of March had carried the Germans nearer the sea and nearer still to the railroad communications so important to the British. So you can imagine our surprise when the news came that the attack, which had begun at three o'clock in the morning, was against the line in front of us from Montdidier in the west, with Compiègne and the route to Paris down the Oise valley, Château-Thierry and the route down the Marne, Reims and Chalons, as objectives.

The British, French, American and Italian troops managed, as a combined effort, to push the Germans back. As a result of this defeat, the planned surprise attack at Flanders was called off by the German generals. It proved to be the start of a gradual retreat by the Germans, who never recovered from this disaster, and marked the beginning of the end as November 1918 approached.

'Apparently, without any definite facts to go on,' recorded Haig in his diary in July 1918, 'Foch has made up his mind that the enemy's main attack is about to fall on the French in the east of Rheims ... as a result a second British Division was moved south of the Somme as a reserve to the left of the French.'

Mildred was frustrated with the lack of news; sometimes the news they did get was infuriating in its criticism of those doing their best in a difficult job. She admitted, 'I am beginning to feel as Amélie does.' Amélie had taken exception to the bad press Haig was getting at home:

The other day there was a criticism of a military operation in the English parliament, and she said, impatiently: 'Well, if I were Haig I would simply reply, If you don't like the way I am doing this thing, just get down off your cushioned seats, and come out and face the guns yourselves.' She does not know whether the benches in the House of Commons are cushioned or not. For that matter, neither do I ...

Haig was concerned and by the 15 July the Second Battle of the Marne was underway. Haig recorded in his diary his feelings after various meetings with Foch and also an instruction to use his judgment to protect British interests:

Foch was in the best of spirits. He told me that after three hours' bombardment, the Enemy had attacked at 4 a.m. this morning on two fronts east and west of Rheims. East of Rheims on a front of 26 miles, and west of Rheims on a front of 29 miles. A front of 16 miles about Rheims itself was not attacked. The total front attacked seems therefore to be about 55 miles.

Mildred was very aware the Germans were once again marching towards the Marne and the ever-present sound of artillery bombardments and explosions once again drew nearer than comfort could bear. Thankfully the reports seemed to almost immediately confirm the German offensive on the Marne had been crushed almost before it had begun, although there were rumours that the Germans had managed to cross the Marne River at Rheims:

On Saturday came word that Foch had launched his counter-attack and that it looked brilliantly successful. By Sunday morning we knew that the Germans had crossed the Marne at Dormans, just south-east of Château-Thierry, hotly pursued by the Americans [plus the British, French & Italians] – not a live German, unless he was a prisoner, left on the south bank of the river. Every day since then the Germans have retreated. It is slow, but it is hopeful … they [the Germans] advanced thirty miles in six days. It has taken us nearly a week to push them back, mile by mile, a third of the way, so our relief is great …

The Americans finally entering the war had been welcomed, but at times Mildred became almost evangelical in her statements as to their capabilities and the fact they would resolve all and save the world. There were those who felt that it had been a long-overdue decision and that the rest of the Allies had been fighting and sacrificing their young men by the millions whilst America dithered. Besides, once America entered the war, it did so as an independent authority and not as part of the Allies .Many felt this was an insult and demonstrated that America had only its own financial and economic interests at heart. It left a bad taste in the mouth of some of the Allied nations, but in spite of this they were glad to have the Americans fighting beside them. One of the outward signs of the Americans entering the war was the eventual arrival of soldiers in Paris on their way to the front or on their return:

The streets of Paris are full of American boys in khaki, sombreros, and new tan gaiters, and all behaving as if they were here for a sort of glorification. In a sense it is a big adventure for them … to come over the sea, all dressed up in new uniforms, to walk about the streets of Paris before going on 'out there'. No one blames them for enjoying it, any more than anyone blames them for looking rather like the supers in a Charles Froham border drama.

One young American officer who struck up a conversation with Mildred explained his feelings since arriving in France. 'It is odd,' he declared, 'these people do not look a bit like us. They don't speak our language. I speak very little of theirs. But somehow they are like us. I felt at home with them at once, and every day I feel more at home. I don't know why it is – can't explain it.'

Following the arrival of Americans in Paris the Germans started bombing the city at night. Mildred had known of several air raids on London, but Paris had been left in peace, more or less. Bombing from the air was a new form of warfare and it was frightening to experience a raid, especially in the pitch blackness of a night made darker by the blackout orders. Mildred recalled one such attack on Paris in 1918:

On Wednesday night I went to bed early. I must have got to sleep about eleven. If I do not sleep before midnight there is a strong possibility of my not sleeping at all, one of my old-age habits. My first sleep is very sound.

I wakened suddenly with the impression that I heard someone running along the terrace under my window. I sat up and listened, half believing that I had been dreaming, when I saw a ray of light in the staircase – my door was open.

I called out, '*Qui est la?*'

Amélie's trembling voice replied, '*C'est moi, Madame,*' and I had the sudden wide vision of possibilities, which I am told is like that of a drowning man, for I realised that she was not coming to me in the middle of the night for nothing, when she appeared in the doorway, all dressed, even to her hood, and with a lighted candle in her hand.

'Oh, *Madame,*' she exclaimed, 'you were sleeping? You heard nothing?' And at that moment I heard the cannon. 'Oh, *mon Dieu, Madame,* what is happening out at the front? It is something terrible, and you slept!'

'That is not the front, Amélie,' I exclaimed. 'It is much nearer, in the direction of Paris. It's the guns of the forts.' At that moment a bomb exploded, and I knew at once. 'It's the Gothas [aircraft], Amélie.'

It took me less than ten minutes to dress – it was bitterly cold – and I wrapped myself in my big military cloak, put a cap over my tumbled hair, and a big fur round my neck, grabbed my field glasses, and went out into the orchard, which looks directly across the fort at Chelles in the direction of Paris.

Mildred, Amélie and Abelard, stood in the garden of La Creste and looked towards Paris as the bombardment took place. They could see little but the flashes of explosions and the eerie sound of motors whirring above them as the aircraft came and went on their deadly missions:

It was our first experience, and I assure you it was weird. At times it seemed as if one of three things was happening – either that we were destroying the fleet in the air, or they were destroying us, or that Paris was being wiped out … as the long minutes crept by, we began to notice details – for instance, that the air battle moved in waves, and we easily understood that meant several squadrons of German machines, and we could finally, though we could see nothing distinctly, realise by the firing that they approached, met the guns of the forts – passed over or through the barrage curtain, or retired, and tried again, then, having dropped their bombs swept more to the west, and gave place to another attacking squadron.

In the blackness, the dull glow on the horizon towards Paris, and the explosions, were the only visible signs of the devastation the bombing raid caused. It was a frightening and surreal experience, one which brought home to Mildred how vulnerable they all were. If the Germans could drop bombs on Paris, then they could be dropped anywhere – even on her home. They eagerly awaited the arrival of the newspapers:

They contained nothing but the mere fact that Paris had been bombed by Gothas. There had been victims and damage, but in comparison with the effort, the result had been unimportant. Out of the twenty-eight German machines which had taken part in the attack, only one had been brought down – that fell near Vaires, not far from Chelles … The big gun, which had begun to bombard Paris at half-past six in

the morning, was still firing at half-past six at night, and at half-past
ten at night there was [another] air raid which lasted about an hour
and a quarter.

Fortunately they did not have to endure too many of these frightening
night-time attacks. As the months passed the Germans were more pre-
occupied with holding out on the front than worrying about attacking
Paris with primitive air raids. The sound of the infamous cannon had
also ceased, much to everyone's relief.

'The French and British are well across the Hindenburg line in the
north, and at the centre they are again approaching the tragic, desolate, bomb torn Chemin des Dames,' reported Mildred as the summer
of 1918 progressed as fast as the ground taken by the Allies:

> The Big Bertha has not fired for over four weeks. We still speak
> of it, but always with the conviction that it has had to retreat so
> far that Paris is out of range. No Gotha [aircraft] has visited Paris
> since June 27 – ten weeks. We still wonder what desperate attempt
> the chronic spirit of wilful destruction may inspire the Bosches
> [Germans] to bring off before they give up ...

Aside from these steps forward that gave everyone hope, there were
other distractions. One hot afternoon, Mildred saw a young American
soldier standing by her gate. She spoke to him and he was very friendly
and amiable, although he seemed a little vague about why he was still
in the neighbourhood and seemed unconcerned about having to report
back or move on to his regiment:

> He did not seem to be making much conversation, so, to keep it up
> [the conversation], I asked him some more questions. The first was,
> unfortunately, indiscreet – I asked him what he was doing here all
> alone. The instant the question was out of my mouth I knew that
> I had no business to ask it. So I was not surprised when, instead of
> answering, he lighted a match and took another cigarette. Under
> cover of which, and to conceal my confusion, I asked his name.

Mildred was no fool and she began to realise that this young American
was most likely a deserter. It started to make her feel a little uneasy,
but she could not help feeling sorry for him as he seemed confused and

rather dazed – as if he had woken up and found himself in a strange, hazy dream. Mildred began to feel she had joined him in that strange dream world:

> He replied without hesitation that his name was Robert, and volunteered the information that his father was at the head of some big oil wells ... To my question as to what he did in civil life, he said that he was a chauffeur, 'That is to say,' he said, 'I own several big cars and take rich people out on long joy rides.' That sounded all right, and he looked the job. He was tall, straight, well set-up lad, in, I judged, his early twenties. I couldn't be quite sure of his class – I often can't with Americans.

The meeting was surreal and Mildred, although her mind was working overtime trying to figure this enigmatic man out, outwardly remained calm. The fact he was so calm made her feel he could be exactly the opposite if provoked. Mildred noticed obvious differences immediately:

> While he seemed perfectly frank, and was absolutely at his ease, he was not as talkative as most of the boys from home whom I have run across over here. I thought instinctively of the Marines I saw here, who, in two minutes, had told me all about home and family, their school days, their careers and their girls. He answered my questions with perfect ease and good nature, but I could not call him expansive.

As time passed, and after she had given him some refreshment and as he relaxed in her garden, Mildred found herself growing increasingly uneasy. She considered that as an old woman, American, with steel-grey hair and old enough to be his grandmother, the soldier would most probably not do her any harm. At least that was her hope. Summoning all her courage she decided to question him more:

> With no reason which I could explain I felt nervous, and disliked myself for it. It did not seem right ... that a boy of his age, belonging to the Flying Corps, with no flying insignia on his collar or his cap, should be roaming about alone in the war zone. So I put to him what seemed to me the crucial question: 'Of course you have reported to the military post?'

'Oh, yes,' he replied, 'and I have an appointment with a French officer down there,' and he indicated the direction of Voisins, from which he was coming when I first saw him.

'But,' I said, 'there is no military post at Voisins.'

'All I know,' he replied, 'is that I am to meet an officer there who speaks English, at nine o'clock.'

It was at that time eight. I dismissed my doubts from my mind. What did I know about military matters, or secret missions or the habits of the Flying Corps? So, when he said to me: 'I wonder if you know where I could get a bed for the night?' adding 'I can't get away until morning, and there seems to be no hotel about here,' though, instinctively, I did not care to have him here, I said that my housekeeper could put him up, and I led him to Amélie's.

Amélie sorted out a room for him and he was happy with the accommodation. He then came back to Mildred's garden and sat there in the twilight and chatted away to her 'quietly, talking, practically about nothing'. Afterwards she could not remember anything he had said apart from how pretty the view was. At a quarter to nine he got up to leave:

He bade me 'good night' and strolled down the hill to Voisins. As I looked after him, I noticed that he walked close to the hedge as he had done in coming up the hill. I came into the house, and, oddly enough, at once forgot all about him, nor did I again think of him until Amélie came in the morning when she volunteered the information that he had come in at midnight, that he had taken a 'big bath', and she had left him over his coffee, and he had a hearty appetite, and after a moment, she added: 'I am afraid, *Madame*, that he had no dinner last night. Do you know the poor lad has not a sou? He made me understand that when I showed him his breakfast tray – he emptied his pockets, nothing in them. He has not even got a revolver. I made him understand that he was to eat – I did not want his money. But isn't it a bit queer for an aviator like that to be flying around without a sou in his pocket.'

The soldier appeared in Mildred's garden again. He smiled and shook her hand and thanked her and Amélie for their kindness and hospitality. He then walked off down the hill toward Voisins – they watched as he vanished from sight. One of Mildred's neighbours had also seen him departing and asked who he was. Mildred said he was an aviator and was going back to his unit. She made a typical French gesture followed by a shrug and said: 'Not much, he isn't!' Mildred asked her what she meant and she replied sincerely:

No *avion* has landed at Quincy for weeks. Why that chap has been hanging around here for almost a week. He doesn't care much to be seen – except by the women. I've been watching him, and I notice that whenever a soldier is in sight, or an automobile, he hides. I've seen him lying in bushes by the roadside. They say he can't speak more than two words of French. He hasn't any money. He has eaten in half a dozen houses – welcome for his … uniform, I suppose. Of course it is a fine thing to be a good looking youngster in an American uniform, I can tell you, in these days, and plenty of the girls down below have been trailing around with that lad in the woods …

Mildred was shocked whilst listening to this diatribe. 'All the suspicions against which I had struggled flashed through my mind with the rapidity of a cinema film.' She also realised that he could have been English, American or, with his blond good looks, even German. It then occurred to her that they had been warned the Germans were landing spies behind the lines. In spite of his American accent she could not help but wonder if she had been truly duped by that mysterious young man.

Mildred immediately went to the military post at Quincy to report the incident and explain fully what had happened. The major listened and thanked her for letting them know. He also said he felt the boy was an American deserter and that he would be picked up eventually. They asked that if he returned, Mildred should put him up and send word and they would come immediately. He was seen once more and ran away across a field – never to be seen again. Mildred often wondered about him and thought of him like a ghost or apparition – he had an unreal quality about him, ethereal, that had both fascinated and disturbed her.

The summer soon turned to autumn and the talk of a German collapse began to occupy everyone's thoughts and conversations. The gossips were out in force and Mildred found the incessant chatter and endless speculations about what might be happening, or not, insufferable. Amélie laughed at her persistent use of her favourite phrase 'stuff and nonsense' when subjected to wild speculations:

Ever since, in June, the American Army [in coordination with British and Allied troops] proved itself on the Marne [second battle] to be a fighting army, Germany has known that she could not win. Naturally she regrets that, but I have seen no sign that she regretted anything but that.

One does not need to be a very keen student of the racial characteristics of Germany to know that she will somehow save her skin – if we let her. It is purely a military victory for the Allies, only made possible so soon after the loyalty of the States in speeding up as they have and the aid of the English ships in making that speeding up possible [to end the war].

Anger and hostility towards the Germans had developed over the past few years as time and again their actions horrified the general populace, what with their disregard for life and the terrible treatment they subjected their enemies to. It seemed unbelievable that the Germans should be allowed to retreat to their homeland and have no punishment inflicted on them equal to their terrible actions:

I only pray that nothing will be done which will permit the Boche to overlook the fact that it is a military victory, or to camouflage it in any way. It was as a military power that Germany made this war, and to her long-perfected military machine she deliberately added every scientific terror, every underhand method of attack, that a trained, money-supplied, biologically cruel race could muster. She has taught the world much. It would be a pity if we could not better her teaching. Her army is going to be beaten to a finish. But her character is hardly likely to change, and that is why we here are praying with all the strength we have that there will be no armistice while there is a chance of the Hun being in condition to take advantage of it.

Mildred's fear was that the Germans, and the Kaiser in particular, would not face the full force and wrath of the Allies, and would, with typical cunning and self-preservation, attempt to manipulate an easy exit. It would be an insult to the millions who had died and an insult to the countries so cruelly invaded and plundered with such merciless aggression. Mildred was clearly beside herself with doubts about any armistice terms:

In an age which proudly calls itself civilised – whatever that may mean
– Germany has waged a war such as even barbarous times never knew.
It has not been a war of legitimate slaughter, which would have been
terrible enough in a world of today's aspirations and pretension. It has
been a war of violating women, abusing children, murdering inoffensive
civilians, a war of rapine and wilful destruction, of breaking every law
of God whom they arrogantly claim, of every law man has made for the
safeguarding of the community, a war of lies and cunning, by people
who claim the whole world, and deliberately deny the right of even
existence to every one not born German, who arrogate to themselves
the right to sin, and deny the right to live to all other races.

By early October Haig recorded in his diary that the German government had resigned, aware that defeat was inevitable. The resulting
chaos with the German command further weakened their chances of
securing any kind of victory at this crucial stage. Haig wrote:

[Foch] had a Paris morning paper opened out on the table in which in
a large type was printed a note from Austria, Germany, and Turkey,
asking for an armistice at once, and stating their readiness to discuss
conditions of peace, 'here [said Foch] is the immediate result of the
British piercing the Hindenburg line. The enemy has asked for an
armistice.' His opinion is that the Enemy should be told to retire to
the Rhine as a guarantee of good faith, before any negotiations are
begun … I remarked [said Haig] that the only difference between his
[Foch's] condition's and a 'general surrender' is that the German Army
is allowed to march back with its rifles, and officers with their swords.
He is evidently of opinion that the Enemy is so desirous of peace that
he will agree to any terms of this nature which we impose …

It is interesting to see that even at this stage of the armistice discussions
Haig was determined that the German soldiers and officers should be
treated with fairness and dignity – perhaps he was attempting to dilute
the total humiliation so many were determined to impose on the Germans as part of any terms of peace.

Mildred had opinions of her own in that regard. She had heard of
the utter disregard the Germans held her beloved France in – and more
recently her discovery of the German officers' orders to soldiers prior to
the ill-fated, and thwarted, Second Battle of the Marne earlier that year:

We are told before the offensive ... was launched [at Marne 1918] the disciplinary laws which have long governed armies were all suspended by order of the German Commander-in-Chief, and that the sack of all France on the hoped-for line of march from St. Quentin to the sea, and from the Chemin des Dames to Paris, was promised the German soldiers as their reward for victory, and what really happened seems to bear out the truth of the abominable statement. From St. Quentin to the Somme, and from Chemin des Dames to the Marne, as well as the time permitted, they accomplished the object. The amount of booty they carried off was tremendous, and if everything did not fall as loot to the army, they at least achieved a destruction as complete as possible.

As the war began to draw to a close and the 11 November ceasefire approached, Mildred had other matters to deal with. Many in her small community had suffered terrible colds and flu-like symptoms. It seemed to be almost like a plague and left the worst sufferers weak and seriously ill. Mildred wondered if it was a result of the mixing of the germs of people from different parts of the world and the lack of soap:

I ask myself if one reason we have so much illness is because it is so difficult for most people to keep clean. We lacked soap here for a long time. It is almost impossible to get any washing done. Luckily I buy soap in rather large quantities. In the end it is an economy ... I have had more occasions to know how rare it is than just not being able to get laundry work done ... we also lack kerosene ... we lack wood alcohol and gasoline also. The other day Amélie was at Voisins, and she saw a military chauffeur washing both hands and his camion with gasoline. She rushed at him, and asked him if he had no shame to be wasting gasoline like that when we had none at all? He replied that he would like to know how he was to clean the grease off his hands since he had no soap. So she piloted him up here, and we gave him hot water and soap, and he filled the little night lamps for us.

The shortages of the basic necessities caused as much consternation and discussion as the terms of the Armistice and collapsing German empire. Many people were exhausted, and no one more so than Mildred. The years of hardship and deprivation had taken their toll even on her indomitable spirit and she was tired – more tired than she could find words to express. She wondered to herself how much more of this she could take. Thankfully she found an escape in her writing and also in reading her favourite books. To her friend in Boston she wrote on 31 October 1918:

> What can I write to you in a letter during these hard days of suspense? We all know that Germany is breaking down, but her internal troubles don't console us at all, and we are indifferent to the royal crowns and ducal coronets rolling about like knocked-down men in the bowling alley of history. We take note that Austria is out, and that it is only a matter of a few days before the order 'Cease Firing' will be given on the Balkan front and Servia [Serbia] will be freed. We hardly seem to have a word to say regarding the fact that where it began it has first stopped.

Mildred's attention was taken by a disaster closer to home – quite literally! The chimney breast in her main salon collapsed at one corner. It seemed impossible that during all the renovation work of a few years earlier this weakness could have been missed. But missed it was. The result was a complete mess and a disruption in her home she could have done without:

> It had to be rebuilt, and the house is in a mess. Whatever else you do, don't ever let the masons in your house while you are in it yourself. My poor little house was arranged with no provisions for this sort of work – main staircase right in the salon, no doors on the ground floor, except into the kitchen. I am living with everything draped with big sheets, with heaps of plaster and stone in the salon through which I have to tramp when I go up and down stairs. It is evident I am not to be driven out whether I like it or not. I don't mind eating my allotted peck of dirt, but I draw the line at plaster.

Mildred decided to visit Stein and Toklas in Paris. Whilst there she purchased some provisions and visited the bank for money, enjoying a more tolerable existence until the work was completed on the new chimney breast. 'I shall come back the instant Amélie telegraphs that the fires can be rebuilt. As things are I might be living out of doors …'

Mildred was back at Huiry by 7 November and pleased to see a fire roaring once again in the new fireplace. Amélie had also cleaned La Creste and there was not a speck of dirt or plaster dust to be found.

The Armistice, when it came, was something of an anti-climax and also seemed unreal. The only noticeable difference was the silencing of the distant guns on the front, sounds that had become part of the normal everyday background. People were seen listening to the silence, as if trying to work out what sound was missing. It was strange and surreal. Mildred began to realise that even silence could have a strange power on the senses:

> Germany has been defeated and her civil population had been showing what we all knew must come – signs that we were facing the worst losers history had ever seen, the most unsportsmanlike nation that, convinced of its superior brute force, ever went to war. When historians of the future study the German mentality what a showing up the Huns will get!

The eleventh hour of the eleventh day of the eleventh month would forever mark the moment to remember all wars. But it was the actual date and time that brought this terrible war to an end. It was a Monday, a day of the week that was usually mundane, the first day back at work after a weekend of rest. For the world, it was the first day back to peace for four years. Millions had lost their lives. It was time to pick up the pieces. The Kaiser and other crowned heads of Europe had fallen and scampered into exile, an exile from which they would never return.

General Haig recorded in his diary for 11 November that it was 'a fine day but cold and dull'. He had also noted, on 9 November 1918, 'The Kaiser has abdicated and the Crown Prince has renounced his claim to the throne.' He went on to write how:

> Foch's HQ state that the meeting with the German delegates (which took place in the Forest of Compiègne, not in Chateau as previously reported) began at 2 a.m. and at 5 a.m. the Armistice was signed. The Germans pointed out that if the rolling stock and supplies of the Army (which have to be handed over by the terms of the Armistice) are given up, then Germany east of the Rhine will starve. Report says Foch was brutal to the German delegates, and replied that that was their affair.

The Maestricht reporter for the *Handelsblad* reported on the Kaiser's eventual arrival in exile:

The ex-Kaiser, accompanied by his wife and a numerous suite, crossed the Dutch frontier on the Vie-Maestricht road at about two o'clock yesterday afternoon [10/11/18]. The party travelled in about a dozen luxurious Imperial motor-cars, which bore signs of having travelled far and fast. Early reports stated that the party included the Crown Prince and Field-Marshal Hindenburg, but it was soon ascertained that this was not so. The suite accompanying the ex-emperor and Empress comprised fourteen members, amongst them being Admiral von Hintze. The motor-cars were driven by Prussian officers ... Immediately after crossing the frontier, the members of the party left the motor-cars and walked to Eyesden Station, the Kaiser leaning heavily on his stick. His hair has become entirely grey, and with his ashen face and drooping figure he presented a pitiful spectacle. He wore the uniform of a Prussian General.

'We heard this morning that the Kaiser is in Holland,' continued Haig. 'If the war had gone against us no doubt our King [George V] would have had to go, and probably our army would have been insubordinate like the German Army! After the conference, we were all taken [to be filmed] on the Cinema [Newsreels].' The guns fell silent at 11 a.m. that morning. Mildred wrote to a friend in Boston on 15 November:

Well, dear old girl, the war is over. I have tried to write every day since Tuesday, but simply could not. My nerves were frazzled. It is hard to be calm enough to talk about it, and it has been impossible to write. I suppose I shall make a mess of it even now. But I know that, in the midst of the first fury of excitement and the enthusiasm which I am sure has arisen in one great shout from the Atlantic to the Pacific, and from the Arctic Sea to the Gulf, to the accompaniment of bells and bands and cannon, you have often thought of me, and wanted to know how we got through the historic 11 November. Can it be that it was only last Monday?

It is bitterly cold, – a damp, penetrating cold. However, our boys are going to be more comfortable, and they have escaped all the misery of winter in the trenches. I expect those who are to guard the occupied country, no matter how long they remain under arms, will live in comparative luxury. That is a comfort.

12

AFTERMATH AND LÉGION D'HONNEUR

But it is the same old world – as much a world of slaves as ever it was in the days when Joseph went to Egypt – perhaps more so ...

Mildred Aldrich

The euphoria that accompanied the Armistice was understandable. The civilian populations of Europe celebrated, but nowhere more than in Belgium, whose territories were invaded in 1914 at the start of the war. A young soldier sent a letter to his British friend, Harold Greenwood of the Lancashire Fusiliers, with whom he had served in France, describing the current deprivations and reminiscing about the atmosphere on Armistice day some months before, and responding to the news in the letter he had received from Harold:

My Dear Friend,

I have received your letter ... [we are] in the best of health, for which I thank you very much, but you write us that your wife and children have been very poorly [most likely victims of the influenza epidemic that broke out in 1918 and killed more people than had died in the entire war], we feel ... very sorry for you and all.

Now my dear friends, excuse us for waiting so long before writing back to you all. Because we are in a difficult position, we haven't our furniture back yet, and at present I have no work yet. We wish that we could come to Blackpool, because we [are] feeling so funny, when we see our big city like Antwerp all dead, we can't describe our feelings, we are not a bit happy.

Now dear friends [remember] when the day of peace was settled, our Belgian soldiers, with English friends and American soldiers together were singing, dancing, drinking and Klikking [flirting] with our girls, and every house was [adorned] with flags, flowers and greenery …

I will close this letter with best love, sincere wishes, and best greetings to all of you and waiting to hear your good news …
Frank De Vos
Number 22, Korte Gathius Straat
Antwerp, Belgium

Frank's letter to Harold clearly shows how the economic and infra-structure damage was taking its toll on the population and causing much distress and not a little unhappiness. That said, the warm regard and camaraderie between the fighting soldiers endured even when they were demobilised.

By 1922 Mildred was writing a journal as preparation for an auto-biography that was never published. She was looking back on the events of the war from 1914 and also the effects of the Armistice of 1918 and the Second Treaty of Versailles. It was clear that once the initial jubilation had subsided, more hardship had to be endured by those who had survived. War debts were rampant. Anger at the leni-ency towards a defeated Germany still rankled among a population that had endured their brutality and destruction:

Years have passed since the ill-considered Armistice – years more trying to support than the four years of actual warfare – years which, at times, appeared devoid of hope or uplift.

It would seem that the great victory had done nothing to improve the lives of the ordinary people who had sacrificed so much over the years of slaughter. The bitterness was palpable in Mildred's writing, and an edge of weary acceptance punctuates her prose. The cause of this despair was politics and economics – the latter creating terrible hardships for ordinary people as the war debts piled up around them, suffocating the economy:

It is strange that one should complain so bitterly, as the result is logical. It is the situation that has, without exception, followed every war, and always will. It is very strange that, even if the death and destruction and misery, which attend the progress of war, do nothing to prevent its recurrence, that the aftermath should not. It is customary to say that that is because no two great wars have ever been fought by the same generation. Perhaps in the case of the war just closed it may be different, since, nearly three quarters of a century from now, the great grandchildren of men who fought and died in this war will still be paying the cost – at least, this generation is condemning them to do so. Whether they will or not is another question, and that none of us will live to know.

Mildred talked about us today as if she could somehow see us way ahead in the future, a distant glimmer of hope that would enable the world to be a better, more fruitful place to live. She marvelled at how fast the telegraph system was being replaced with the telephone. It occurred to her that this development would eventually mean that a person sitting in New York would not only be able to 'talk to a friend in Paris or London', but also be 'able to see them at the same time'. Mildred's imagination foresaw technological advancements beyond her time:

> If the world of today were as intelligent as it proudly claims to be, it would not only know that of all the follies in life there is nothing so stupid as war; and nothing so silly as the dream of doing away with it so long as the generation that makes war does not itself pay the bills. Money is the root of all evil between governments as well as between individuals, and the generation which bequeaths its foreign debts to coming generations saddles its sons with resentment likely to lead to trouble. The order to 'cease firing' was given at eleven o'clock on the morning of November 11, 1918, and there has been war somewhere ever since.

Mildred found herself bemused and furious about the proclamations of money and its value and how the war debts were to be paid for and by whom. Money, one suspects was a perpetual mystery to Mildred, even with her own meagre finances, so anything greater than that only added to her bewilderment. Her real frustration was why huge debts had to be passed from pillar to political post to satisfy those in positions of power:

> I have felt obliged to acknowledge several times, with a sense of shame, that finance is a mystery to me. I never learned anything about it at school ... To be absolutely frank it seems to me that when finance becomes so complicated that the ordinary intelligence cannot grasp it, there is 'something rotten in Denmark', that when the finances of the world are so complex ... that only the financially expert and the stock gambler can play the game, to talk about a government for, of, and by the people seems absurd.
>
> What do the so called 'people' understand about exchange today? Simply no more than I do, which is nothing. It is useless for anyone to try to explain to me that, in the money-market, money is worth what those who want it are willing to pay for it. It means nothing to me, and if they are truthful I believe it means no more to many who try to explain it and take advantage of it.

The frustration felt by Mildred was perhaps exacerbated by the terrible poverty those who had fought in the war experienced in the years after its end. The money spent by governments to pay for the war had in fact brought many to the brink of bankruptcy; it was a bleak situation that caused more difficulty to those at the bottom of the social spectrum. Mildred explains her thoughts on the dollar and exchange processes as they affected her in France in the early 1920s:

> I take up my newspaper every morning, and the first thing I turn to is the financial page – to see what the dollar is worth. In one sense – the sense that interests most people – it makes no difference to me – I have no dollars to sell, and no money with which to buy them. All I know is that my daily living expenses will go up in the exact ratio that the franc goes down. Whatever else I may not know, I do know that, no matter where new taxes fall or how money depreciates, it is we – the people, and small consumers – who pay the cost always.
>
> I have a fanciful idea, when I read the exchange values every morning. I seem to see the little American gold dollar – I have not seen one for many years, but I remember the tiny little yellow thing – getting up very early in the morning, holding itself up in the air somewhere – I have no idea where – and shouting so as to be heard

all over the world – by radio 'This morning I am worth 26 francs', and all the world without a moment's hesitation, takes its word for it. The dollar rules.

That may sound very silly, but if anyone imagines the majority of women in the ordinary world think any differently about it, it is because they have never taken the trouble to find out. Most women never trouble to think about it at all. What they do think about over here is watching the exchange, and drawing on their letters of credit when they can get the biggest number of francs on the dollar, and bothering the bank clerk to tell them what the chances are of the dollar going higher. I have known women to spend twenty-five francs in cab hire to get at three in the afternoon two sous more on the dollar than they could have got at ten in the morning – a matter of ten francs on a hundred dollars.

Mildred's biggest frustration was why war debts had to be passed on, becoming a burden not only for those who had survived but also for those of generations yet to be born. It made no sense to her, and never could be explained to her in a way that she could fully understand:

I suppose I can give no better proof of how absolutely stupid I am in regard to finance than by frankly confessing that it seems to me a matter of no importance whose money paid for the ammunitions, or the ships, or the food which enabled the Allied countries to lick Germany. If it was necessary to overcome Germany, and it surely was, the resources of the countries allied against it should have been pooled, and the slate wiped clean at the end. Some of the nations united in the struggle – like England and France – lost an appalling proportion of the best of their young men. What was money compared to that.

I am convinced that if a sponge had been passed over the war debts the world would be happier today. It would not have taken so many years to have arrived at a state of confidence and prosperity as it has by treating the whole struggle as a business affair. The money that has been spent since 1919 in interminable conferences by governments that can't balance their budgets, impresses one as a bit farco-comical, not to mention the constantly recurring and fruitless night sessions in the French Chamber, each one of which costs tens of thousands of francs – and achieves nothing. I never enjoy a farce – but that is a matter of taste.

One hears a great deal about 'France is a rich country' – Lloyd George [Prime Minister] is eternally crying it in the ears of England. In a sense it is true – for its needs and its way of living. Yet its wealth per capita – that is to say, its visible wealth – is less than that of the other ... great powers.

I know of course that these small transactions are unimportant, but it is the principle of the thing that impresses me, and in all matters of principle the world does not progress – it changes. It changes its ways. It lights up with electricity instead of with candles. It rides in automobiles instead of in sedan chairs. It heats itself by hot air instead of wood in fireplaces. It travels by steam and electricity instead of sails. It can fly in the air and travel under the sea. It conquers space with the telephone, telegraph and radio. It has made photographic pictures move. It wears its hair short instead of long – and its skirts likewise. It shaves instead of growing beards. BUT it is the same old world – as much a world of slaves as ever it was in the days when Joseph went to Egypt.

As Mildred had been attempting to rationalise and correct the world's problems, her friends, organised by the ever-present Gertrude Stein, had been busily working away in the background to try and get France to acknowledge the great efforts Mildred had made on behalf of her adopted country by staying during the war and helping throughout. It was also noted with some admiration among her friends that, in spite of her own precarious financial position, with just a small pension to live on, Mildred had donated the royalties she had earned from her books to the charities offering relief to the wounded, the orphaned and those who had lost everything as a result of the war.

By 1922 they were becoming successful in their efforts and were able to submit a statement to the French government as to why they felt Mildred deserved to be considered for the Chevalier de la Légion d'Honneur Nationale de la République Française – France's highest award. The award was also championed by the artist Mira Edgerly, a famed portrait painter, and miniature artist of the time, and one of Mildred's many Parisian friends. Unbeknown to Mildred, it was Edgerly who had organised her pension, and also for the purchase of La Creste, so Mildred could afford to rent it out of her pension funds. Stein would reveal this, and her part in providing for Mildred, in the 1930s some years after Mildred's death. Mildred never knew the identity of her benefactors.

On the official papers the reasons why the ward was approved are stated clearly in the citation held in the archive of the Légion d'Honneur in Paris:

> Miss Aldrich has lived in France for the last 25 years, the first 18 years in Paris where she worked as an agent, journalist and a French modern theatre translator, helping to promote the plays in her country. In March 1914, she retired to the small village of Huiry at Couilly (Seine & Marne) having only just moved in when war started.
>
> When the first refugees, escaping the invasion, started to come to her village, she went to Paris and with all her available resources purchased supplies for them. By the end of August most of the villagers had left but she decided, despite being on her own, to stay in the village and kept on helping refugees and French and English soldiers who were passing by Huiry. The following winter, after the Marne victory, she carried on providing help to the families of soldiers still on duty.
>
> In 1915 the collection of letters she had written to her American friends describing what she had seen at Huiry, and moreover flatly defending the righteousness of the French cause, was published in America. Its truthful intent, contained emotion and high literary quality brought *Hilltop on the Marne* a wide-ranging fame and helped spread knowledge of the French cause's justness and the heroic behaviour of the French people. Because of this book full of humanity and eloquent in its simplicity, people who lived away from the Atlantic coast and who knew little of the terrible experience of the République began to realise what the French Ideal stood for and to appreciate the heroic courage of its civilian population as well as the military.
>
> Since then, Miss Aldrich, kept on writing and three more of her books were published to explain and defend the French cause. Their influence in America was enormous and the royalties were exclusively devoted to provide relief to the victims of the war.

Mildred was surprised to receive a notice from the mayor that she was being considered for the Légion d'Honneur. Knowing the pace at which most French government offices worked, she decided it was best not to hold her breath. That said, she was rather astounded, not to mention moved, that such an application for her had been submitted and, according to the mayor, supported by many of her neighbours.

That fact alone made her feel more proud than any medal, however high the official honour, because it proved she was an accepted part of the community. She loved her house on the hilltop, and had no intention of leaving. She was determined to end her days at La Creste.

The Treaty of Versailles had been signed on 28 June 1919 and it did not please the French at all. They felt that Germany should be crushed to a point where it could never again pose a threat to the peace of Europe. The French were angered that the other Allies would not support their suggestion that German territory should be confiscated up to the Rhine, thus giving the French some protection other than a land border with the defeated Germans. The French felt betrayed that the British, Americans and others failed to support them in this demand. Their bitterness and anger were exacerbated by the fact that their country had suffered such destruction while the British had the Channel and the Americans the Atlantic to shield them. The compromise was the demilitarisation of the Rhineland, but it did nothing to ease the sense of betrayal felt by many of the French.

The treaty did demand that Germany accept full responsibility for causing the war. Germany also had to disarm completely, and lose territories including the Alsace and Lorraine regions, which reverted to France. Germany also had to pay war reparations totalling 132 billion marks – the equivalent of about £284 billion today. The treaty did nothing but cause discontent on all fronts and would actually be a contributing factor to the Second World War twenty years later. It allowed for the rise of fascism as a result of the economic turmoil and collapse by the end of the 1920s.

Mildred had her own thoughts on the matter. She also considered what might have happened had the Germans won. The Germans might cry hardship at their treatment, but what sympathy had they ever shown any nation that stood in the way of their ambitions?

'Germany's aims in making the war deliberately were for conquest,' Mildred quoted from an American politician's statement on the situation. She continued with her own thoughts:

> That being true, we, who are to live in the half century of the world's convalescence, must console ourselves by realising how much worse it might have been. Had Germany won, as she so nearly did, while shortsighted people, wishing to stop bloodshed at any price, nagged at the heels of the countries who were pluckily bleeding to death,

with their foolish cry 'stop the war', it would have meant long ages of struggle. Not for more than a breathing spell would France have remained a vassal of Germany, and it would have taken as brief a time for the British Lion to have licked his bloody paws and be ready again to head the race who would rise up from the ground stronger than ever. How long would the Low Countries, who had fought so valiantly for independence, have submitted to the yoke of Germany? How long would the United States, even if they had kept out of the war, have put up with the natural insolence of a victorious Germany? The hoggish mouthful that Germany prepared to swallow would have eventually choked her to death, even after she had imposed her terms and collected her spoils. So in the face of what all the world is suffering it becomes us to realise that it might have been worse. If Germany had won, the horrors of 'the hundred years war' would not have been a patch on the fate of the 20th century.

Even as it is, the worst result of the war is the Hate it has engendered. Some of us cannot – alas – forget. I know that by my own case. It unbecomes one to make such a confession. I know that. Hatred is most distasteful and unnatural to me. Until this war came I cannot recall that I ever hated anything. But during the four years of active war I found myself developing an active hatred of everything German. It was a most unpleasant and demoralising experience, and still is, since I have to struggle against a resentment against those who seem to have forgotten, and a feeling that the Germans in power despise us for every concession they secure.

Mildred's feelings were universal in France. They naturally distrusted the aims of the Germans still. They felt betrayed by those governments that had fought so hard at their side. It created a feeling of betrayal among those close to Mildred. A young French doctor, aged 29, who was treating Mildred, and lived locally, told her his feelings on the situation, having abandoned his career to fight in the war:

I wish all your compatriots could know, just how Frenchmen of my class feel – we are profoundly wounded to the very depths of our souls, by the attitude of our late Allies to us since that abominable Armistice. If the world thinks that we, on whose soil the worst of the war was fought, our nation, which lost in four years one fourth of its valid young generation – ten of whose most prosperous departments

were largely destroyed – is less worth saving than Germany – of less
value to the development of the world – they are free to their opinion
– we have no right to protest their judgement, but, nevertheless, it
wounds every Frenchman, especially those who fought and survived,
and we resent, as we have the right to, every fresh sacrifice that is
demanded of us, who have sacrificed so much.

Mildred's heart broke. She recorded that all she could say to this young
man was, 'Wait. The end is not yet.' To feel so desolate and so enraged
could only lead to more of the same. That is what Mildred feared more
than anything.

The news that she had been formally accepted to become a Chevalier de la Légion d'Honneur Nationale de la République française
arrived at the hilltop. It seemed unreal to Mildred, who never felt
more proud but less worthy of the recognition. She felt she had done
nothing remarkable, and would have done the same whatever the circumstances, as would anyone else in her position. But her friends and
neighbours disagreed. She would wear the medal with pride for the
remainder of her days – which were few.

By 1926 Mildred had completed her journal, which would form what
she supposed would be her autobiography. But it never happened. The
younger generation were enjoying the economic boom years of the mid-
1920s and they wanted to forget about the war, not keep talking about
it. No publisher would consider it. Somehow in this fast, ever-changing,
and exciting decade Mildred slipped into the shadows and became old-
fashioned and slowly forgotten. She would live at La Creste until her
death in February 1928. She was buried in the local churchyard and
became a legend in that little corner of France, remembered even today
by a few villagers whose ancestors lived with Mildred. She didn't live to
see the great economic crash on Wall Street that reverberated through
the west and plunged the world into recession. She never saw the rise
of Hitler's Nazi Germany and the horrors that it would inflict on the
world. She would never have believed it possible that the world would
allow Germany to again cause such misery – but perhaps she knew that
it would come again if the world allowed it. It is a pity she never met
Winston Churchill, although she knew who he was; they would have
learnt a lot from each other.

One of the last things Mildred wrote at La Creste seems prophetic.
I will let Mildred have the last word. After all, she thought of us here

in the future, a future she knew she would never see. The world may have forgotten Mildred because the Second World War relegated her to a dusty corner of the archive, but, a century on, she has not forgotten us, and her experiences are even more enlightening as a result of that obscurity:

What the world lacks today is leaders. It is an epoch of a rather high grade of the mediocre. The world awaits the coming of a great leader as they once awaited the Messiah. He is nowhere in sight yet – or if he is he has not been recognised – or he may have been rejected already, to be crowned by future generations – just as the future is to benefit by our war.

APPENDIX 1

MINI BIOGRAPHIES

I have compiled brief biographies on some of the main characters mentioned in Mildred's narrative for those who would like a little more information about them.

CAPTAIN JOHN EDMUND SIMPSON (1873–1914)

2nd Battalion, King's Own Yorkshire Light Infantry.
[First British officer of BEF to meet Mildred at La Creste, Huiry]

John Edmund Simpson was born on 9 July 1873, at Bayswater, London, and was the eldest son of the Rev. John Curwen Simpson and Mrs Frances Maria Simpson of Thurcoe, Yorkshire. He was educated at Southleigh and St Paul's School, Stony Stratford, and later joined the 2nd (Volunteer) Battalion Yorkshire Regiment. On 5 May 1900, he was gazetted to the rank of Second Lieutenant with the 1st Battalion, King's Own Yorkshire Light Infantry, and later promoted to Lieutenant on 26 April 1901. He was promoted to Captain on 8 January 1907 and obtained his company with the 2nd Battalion King's Own Yorkshire Light Infantry. From October 1910 until September 1913, he was adjutant of the 3rd Reserve Battalion of his regiment at Pontefract and served in Gibraltar and South Africa. Captain John Simpson was in Carrickfergus, Ireland, when war broke out and left for France with the first contingent of the British Expeditionary Force on 10 August 1914. He was mentioned in Sir John French's dispatch of 8 October

1914 for gallant and distinguished service in the field. Captain John Simpson was shot through the chest and killed instantaneously, whilst leading his men in an attack on a farmhouse at Messines, Flanders on the 31 October 1914, aged 41. He was buried in a field near where he fell but his body was never found. He is commemorated on the Ypres (Menin Gate) Memorial, Ypres, Belgium (Addenda Panel 57). *Courtesy of Michael Lawson.*

LIEUTENANT EDWIN ALLEN JAMES EDWARDS (1895–1914)

1st Battalion Bedfordshire Regiment
[Met Mildred at La Creste]

Edwin Allen James Edwards was born on 13 March 1895 at 22 Loughborough Road, Lambeth, London, the youngest of four children born to Herbert Edwards (born 1857), a bank clerk, and his wife, Louisa Mary Edwards (nee Ounstead, born 1858). He had two elder brothers, Herbert (born 1882) and Gerald (born 1883), and an elder sister Mary (born 1886). In 1911 the family were living at 14 Lorn Road, Brixton, where Edwin attended St John's College, Brixton, and Dulwich College, before matriculating in June 1911. Whilst at Dulwich, he joined the OTC and in the army qualifying examination passed top of the list, being gazetted to the rank of Second Lieutenant to the 3rd Battalion Bedfordshire Regiment on 1 October 1912. Edwin was a good left-handed tennis player and was fond of boating. In June 1914, he was promoted to Lieutenant and was sent to France with the 1st Battalion Bedfordshire Regiment, British Expeditionary Force, on 16 August 1914, where he later fought at the battles of the Marne and the Aisne, during August and September. On 15 October 1914, Edwin was wounded whilst gallantly leading his men at Givenchy and was sent home later for treatment at the Fishmonger's Hall Hospital, London Bridge, where he died from his wounds on 31 December 1914, aged 19. He is buried in Long Ditton (St Mary) Churchyard, Long Ditton, Surrey. *Courtesy of Michael Lawson.*

FIELD MARSHAL SIR JOHN FRENCH (1852–1925)

Born in 1852, French joined the Royal Navy at an early age before switching to the army in 1874. He quickly rose through the ranks during service in the Sudan, and South Africa during the Boer Wars. By 1912 he was serving as the Chief of the Imperial General Staff and he was then promoted to Field Marshall by the end of 1913. French was then chosen, in spite of grave doubts voiced to King George V by Douglas Haig, as commander of the British Expeditionary Force at the outbreak of World War I in 1914. He quickly found himself at odds with Lord Kitchener and Haig, and he also found it difficult to get along with the French commander, Joffre. The lack of organisation and ammunition was the subject of much criticism in the London press. It became an intolerable situation, not aided by his highly erratic behaviour and volatile temper. French was replaced by Haig as commander of the BEF in the December of 1915. French was given command of the home front for the rest of the war – his leadership was required to suppress the Easter Rising in Ireland in 1916. He retired and died in London in 1925. His legacy has been tainted and brought into question many times since World War I, most notably by the eventual release of Sir Douglas Haig's diaries and letters from the period of his command of the BEF in 1914–15.

SIR DOUGLAS HAIG (1861–1928)

Douglas Haig was born in 1861. He was the son of a wealthy whisky distiller and as a result was educated at Oxford and then Sandhurst. His early career in the army saw him taking part in the Omdurman Campaign and then the Boer War. He then became Inspector General of Cavalry in India until 1906, when he became Director of Military Training at the War Office. By 1909 he was Chief of Staff of the Indian Army. When the First World War broke out he commanded, under Sir John French, the 1st Army Corps. By December 1915 questions were being raised about the leadership of Sir John French and how badly the war was going. French was replaced by Douglas Haig, who had himself criticised French's leadership, on 10 December 1915. He was 54 years old. Haig led British troops into the disastrous battle at the Somme River. The Battle of the Somme was the most bloody of the

First World War, and earned Haig the title 'Butcher of the Somme' after he sent thousands to an unnecessary death. Haig died in London on 28 January 1928. His diaries, papers and letters were eventually released and caused much controversy – and still do. Haig has been accused of tampering with his diary entries prior to their eventual publication. This has never been proven. However, there is no doubt that he had a fractious relationship with French and others in the military high command during the war.

LORD KITCHENER (1850–1916)

Horatio Herbert, Earl Kitchener of Khartoum, was born in County Kerry, Ireland, in 1850. He was commissioned in 1871 and by 1882 was with the Egyptian Army and promoted to Commander-in-Chief by 1892. He was largely responsible for the defeat of the Sudanese dervishes at Omdurman in 1898 and reoccupied Khartoum. During the Boer War he was chief of staff from 1900 to 1902. From 1902 he commanded the forces in India and was made Secretary of State for War at the outbreak of the First World War. He had a fractious relationship with Sir John French and the French, creating confusion as to who was in charge of the British Expeditionary Forces overall. He was drowned in 1916 when his ship sank, after hitting a German mine, on its way to Russia to meet the Tsar and his generals. He is largely remembered for modernising the British army. His reputation was questioned by Lloyd George who criticised Kitchener for some of his decisions during the first two years of the First World War. However, contemporary historians have rehabilitated his reputation and skills as a military strategist and administrator.

GENERAL JOSEPH JOFFRE (1852–1931)

Joffre was born in Roussillon in 1852 and went on to attend the École Polytechnique, graduating as a career army officer. He served in the Franco-Prussian War and later in conflicts in China. In spite of his limited leadership experience, he was made Commander-in-Chief of the French Army. The outbreak of war in 1914 took him by surprise but his determined stand at the Battle of the Marne, preventing German forces from capturing Paris, resulted in his promotion to Supreme Commander of French Armies by 1915. However, his star soon waned in the face of disaster at Verdun and the Somme – he was replaced in 1916 by Nivelle. He was appointed head of the French Military Mission and leader of the War Council in the USA. He passed away in 1931. Mount Joffre in Canada was named after him.

MARSHAL FERDINAND FOCH (1851–1929)

Foch was born in Tarbes, Southern France, and enlisted during the Franco-Prussian War as an infantry soldier; he eventually became an infantry officer. At the outbreak of the First World War he was the Marshal of France and was largely responsible for the success of the first Battle of the Marne in September 1914. He continued to command troops on the front from 1914 to September 1916. He became Chief-of-Staff in 1918 and Commander of the Allied Armies. Under his leadership the final Allied offensive was launched and resulted in the Armistice negotiations. As a result of this he was made an Honorary Field Marshal of the British army and in 1923 a Marshal of Poland. He died in France in 1929.

GENERAL ALEXANDER VON KLUCK (1846–1934)

General von Kluck was born in Prussia in 1846 and initially joined the Prussian Army and served in the short Austro-Prussian War of 1866 and then the Franco-Prussian War, where he was wounded in battle and awarded the Iron Cross. For World War I he was in charge of the German 1st Army in its objective to quickly sweep through Belgium into France and capture Paris – hoping for a swift capitulation. His army fought at Mons and the Marne but was eventually pushed back beyond the Aisne. Kluck was criticised for pushing ahead and ignoring direct orders from his superiors; this exposed his troops to attacks from the French and the BEF Many blamed him for the failure of the Schlieffen plan to capture Paris. The war continued in the trenches. Kluck died in Germany in 1934.

GENERAL HELMUTH VON MOLTKE (1848–1916)

General Moltke was born in Mecklenburg-Schwerin, Germany, in 1848. During the Franco-Prussian War he served with the 7th Grenadier Regiment and was mentioned for his bravery. He attended the War Academy 1875–78, going on to join the General Military Staff in 1880. By 1891 he had become aide-de-camp to Kaiser Wilhelm II, and an influential member of the Kaiser's court. At the outbreak of World War I he became Commander of the German Army but he had a hostile relationship with generals like von Kluck, who considered him too old for the post. After the disaster of the first Battle of the Marne he argued with the Kaiser and as a result his health broke down. The failure of the Marne and his tampering and weakening of the Schlieffen plan is subject to much discussion. He died in 1916 of a massive heart attack and did not live to see the terrible outcome of the war for Germany.

KAISER WILHELM II (1859–1941)

The last German Emperor and King of Prussia, Wilhelm was born in Berlin on 27 January 1859. He was the first child of Frederic of Prussia and Victoria, Queen Victoria's eldest daughter. Problems at his birth resulted in a withered arm that many say affected him throughout his life; it was a time when any kind of illness or disability was hidden and was regarded as something to be ashamed of. In 1890, after his succession on the death of his father Wilhelm I, he forced Bismarck to resign and took over control of foreign policy, with disastrous results for the unified Germany. Always jealous of his English and Russian cousins – King George V and Tsar Nicholas – he was determined to build German armed forces and the navy to match their power. In 1914 he supported Austria's ultimatum to Serbia and then, realising war was inevitable, tried to prevent it. It has been widely acknowledged that his actions and aggressive policies caused the First World War. In 1918 he was forced to abdicate and lived in exile in House Doorn, near Utrecht, Holland. He died in 1941 during the Second World War, having seen the initial success of Hitler's aggressive Germany. He is buried there and the house contains his Imperial possessions to this day.

EMPEROR FRANZ JOSEF (1830–1916)

Last Emperor of Austria (1848–1916) and King of Hungary (1867–1916). Franz Josef was born on 18 August 1830 at Schloss Schönbrunn near Vienna. He became emperor during the 1848 revolution after the abdication of Ferdinand I, his uncle. His rule was harsh and dictatorial but did produce strong government within Austria – however, this resulted in riots and assassination attempts. Following Austria's defeat by Prussia in 1886, and Hungarian unrest, he formed an alliance in 1882 (the Triple Alliance) with the Prussian-led German government. He was no stranger to personal tragedy. His wife was assassinated in 1898, and this was followed by his son Rudolf's suicide after a forbidden love affair. In 1914 he gave Serbia an ultimatum, after his heir Franz Ferdinand was assassinated in Sarajevo, which ultimately led Austria and Germany into the First World War. He died at Schloss Schönbrunn on 21 November 1916. His empire was dismantled and redistributed after the First World War.

TSAR NICHOLAS II (1868–1918)

Nicholas Romanov was born on 6 May 1868 in Tsarkoye Selo, the Imperial summer palace near St Petersburg, Russia. Unlike the rest of the Romanov men, Nicholas was not very big – under 5ft 8in – and naturally slight of frame. He compensated for this by using weights and other equipment. In spite of this he had a regal appearance and was an attractive man with lively blue eyes. He was well educated and intelligent and knew full well the difficulties facing him as the next Russian tsar. He fell in love with Alex of Hess, even though she was not considered a good match; he insisted and they married. Their wedding day was marked by tragedy when crowds were trampled to death – it was seen as a bad omen for their future and marriage. When he became tsar his rule was absolute and his country so vast as to make it almost impossible to relate to the people. Nicholas took charge of the Russian army by 1915. He made a mistake in leaving the Russian government in the hands of his unpopular wife. Discontent spread fast through Russia as a result of the terrible loss of life and military disorganisation. The country fell into disarray and the anti-tsarist factions took full advantage of the situation. By March 1917 Nicholas was forced to abdicate. He was arrested, along with his wife, daughters and only son. They were murdered at Ekaterinburg on 16 July 1918. The Romanov dynasty died with them.

GERTRUDE STEIN (1874–1946)

Stein was born in Allegheny, Pennsylvania, in 1874. He father was a wealthy executive who made his money from real estate and the spread of railroads and streetcars. After a brief spell living in Vienna, the family returned to live in California in 1878. Stein made her name as a writer and poet, and after completing her studies in America she moved to Paris in 1903, living with her brother Leo Stein. She began to hold her famous salons for the artistic and literary set along with her partner and lifelong friend Alice B. Toklas. She met Mildred Aldrich within weeks of her arrival and they quickly established a firm friendship. Aldrich also introduced Stein to artist Mira Edgerly, and another firm friendship was formed. Picasso, James Stephens, F. Scott Fitzgerald and later Ernest Hemingway, who were influenced by her cinematic technique, were all associated with this Paris set. Many experimental thinkers, writers and artists have admired Stein's works but she failed to be embraced by the mainstream literary world. Her book *The Autobiography of Alice B. Toklas* was released in 1933 to great success. However, in spite of doubts, she remains a prominent voice of American literature. She died in Paris in 1946 with Alice B. Toklas at her side.

ALICE B. TOKLAS (1877–1967)

Alice Babette Toklas was born to a middle-class Jewish family in San Francisco. She originally wanted to study music, and attended Washington University but it wasn't to last. The day she arrived in Paris changed her life – it was also the day she met Gertrude Stein, who became her lifelong partner. Their salons attracted the great and good of the literary and artistic elite of the time, including Picasso, Hemingway, Wilder, Matisse *et al.* She was also a friend to Mildred Aldrich, who introduced artist Mira Edgerly to the salon set in Paris. She acted as secretary and confidante to Stein and preferred to remain in the background. They remained a devoted couple until Stein's death in 1946.

MIRA EDGERLY (1872–1954)

Mira Edgerly was born in Illinois in 1872. Her father was a wealthy director of the Michigan Central Railroad. She was a self-taught artist and started working with portrait photographer Arnold Genthe, and went on to study in Paris. She married Frederick Burt in 1914, but it lasted a matter of months. In Paris she was encouraged to continue her painting on ivory by John Singer Sargent. At a time when miniature portraits were palm sized, she specialised in using large ivory pieces. She befriended Mildred Aldrich, who in turn introduced her to Gertrude Stein and Alice B. Toklas, and she became an established member of Stein's artistic and literary salons in Paris. It was Edgerly who, along with some help from Stein, organised the pension for Aldrich and also helped her find and lease La Creste at Huiry. Aldrich never knew that her main benefactor was Edgerly. Mira Edgerly went on to meet and marry, in 1919, the Polish count, Alfred Korzybski, a well-known Polish-American linguist, author and pioneer of semantics. The marriage lasted until her death in 1954.

JAMES STEPHENS (1882–1950)

Stephens, an Irish novelist and poet, was born in Dublin in 1882 and lived in the home of the Collins family. They eventually adopted him. He attended school with his adopted brothers, Thomas and Richard, before graduating as a solicitor's clerk. He was small and slight – he stood less than 5ft in his stocking feet. He was an avid socialist and a dedicated Irish Republican, and he enjoyed a friendship with James Joyce. He produced many retellings of Irish myths and fairy tales – with a rare combination of humour and lyricism – including *Deirde* and *Irish Fairy Tales*, and also several original novels, *Crock of Gold*, *Etched in Moonlight* and *Demi-Gods. Crock of Gold* influenced Mildred Aldrich and she was delighted to make a friend of Stephens and his family. Stephens visited Aldrich several times at La Creste before, during and after the First World War. He died in Ireland in 1950.

APPENDIX 2

FOREVER NINETEEN: CAST DETAILS AND REVIEWS

A play in two acts by David Slattery-Christy
Includes the song 'The Green Fields of France' by Eric Bogle

My stage play received its first performance in Manchester in 1993 after some development workshops at the Actors' Centre. After a couple of try-outs and inevitable cast changes it opened at the Green Room in March 1993. I thank all of those dedicated people for helping me bring the play to life.

It received an award for 'Best Play' and 'Best New Theatre Company' alongside the Manchester production of *Les Misérables* in June 1993. It went on to receive 'Best Play' at the Buxton Festival in July of the same year

I would like to give special thanks to Eric Bogle, who wrote 'No Man's Land', later recorded famously by The Furey's as 'The Green Fields of France', for allowing me to use the song within the play.

> The ghosts of soldiers and the very characters the writer is researching play out scenes while she sleeps, until the two worlds meet in a powerful confrontation and solution.
>
> Omer Ali – *The Scotsman*

> This new play, telling the story of Mildred Aldrich an American veteran of the Great War, has earned praise for its skilful crafting.
>
> *The Guardian*

David Christy's new play is a wholly enthralling piece of drama ... with the playwright's own sensitive direction ensuring its special atmosphere is both created and sustained. Based on the true story of Mildred Aldrich, an American living in France during the First World War, who witnessed the horrors of the Battle of the Marne and devoted herself to helping British soldiers, the play uses both flashback and the ghosts of the dead warriors to create an intense, deeply atmospheric drama.

A novelist, Jenny, arrives at the house where Mildred lived to research a book about the First World War. She hears someone whistling 'It's a Long Way to Tipperary' catches the thunder of guns and in her sleep is visited by Mildred, her maid, and three soldiers. The Tommies do more than recall the horror and camaraderie of the war. The bitterness at the slaughter endured by a whole generation persists at still being tied to the house, for their spirits await heavenly freedom. They remain Forever Nineteen, until they reveal themselves to Jenny, who sets them free and discovers the truth surrounding the mysterious house.

Brian G. Cooper – The Stage

Cast:
William McBride: Tim Bohannon
Johnny Holbrook: Scott Kentell (played by Gary Talbot at initial performances)
Ted Pratley: Lee Wolstenholme
Madame/Mildred: Mary Drake (played by Joanna Glover at initial performances and later by Caroline Woodruff)
Jenny Slattery: Christine Brennan (played by Helen Wingrave at initial performances)
German Soldier/Vocals/Understudy: Steve Evets
Vocals: 'Silent Night' – David Christy. 'The Green Fields of France', written by Eric Bogle – Ensemble.

Directed by David Christy (initial workshop directed by Paul Jaynes)
Produced by Maiden Theatre Company
Stage/Company Manager: Meryl Bruen
Costumes: Mitchell's Theatre Hire
Sound Design: Riverside Recording Studios, Huddersfield
Supported by: *City Life Magazine*, Contact Theatre & North West Arts Board

FURTHER READING AND SOURCES

Aldrich, Mildred. *Hilltop on the Marne*. Small, Maynard & Co. Publishers, Boston, 1915.

Aldrich, Mildred. *Told in a French Garden*. Small, Maynard & Co. Publishers, Boston, 1917.

Aldrich, Mildred. *On the Edge of the War Zone*. Small, Maynard & Co. Publishers, Boston, 1917.

Aldrich, Mildred. *When Johnny Comes Marching Home*. Small Maynard & Co. Publishers, Boston, 1919.

Aldrich, Mildred. *The Peak of the Load*. Constable & Company, London, 1919.

Arthur, Max. *Forgotten Voices of the Great War*. Ebury Press, London, 2003.

Carless-Davis, H.W., Hilditch, Neville. *1914: the Marne and the Aisne*. Oakpast Publishers, 2011.

Clark, Christopher. *The Sleepwalkers*. Penguin, London, 2012.

Herwig, Holger H. *The Marne, 1914*. Random House, 2009.

Holmes, Richard. *The Little Field Marshal: The Life of Sir John French*. Weidenfeld & Nicolson Publishers, London, 1981.

Macdonald, Lyn. *1914*. Penguin, London, 1987.

Scott Chessman, Harriet. *The Public is Invited to Dance. Representation, the Body, and Dialogue in Gertrude Stein*. Stanford University Press, California, 1989.

Sheffield, Gary & Bourne, John. *Douglas Haig. War Diaries and Letters 1914–1918*. Weidenfeld & Nicolson Publishers, London, 2005.

Stein, Gertrude. *The Autobiography of Alice B. Toklas.* John Lane Publishers, London, 1933.

Sumner, Ian. *The First Battle of the Marne 1914.* Osprey Publishing, 2010.

UNIVERSITY SOURCES

Schlesinger Library – http://www.radcliffe.harvard.edu/schlesinger-library
History of Women in America
Harvard University

Mildred Aldrich Papers
Aldrich, Mildred. *Confessions of a Breadwinner.* Unpublished, 1922.

Beinecke Library – http://beinecke.library.yale.edu/
Yale University

Letters to Gertrude Stein from Mildred Aldrich 1914–28

These letters were those used by Mildred to create the book *Hilltop on the Marne,* published in 1915. Mildred copied these and others in her journal for future use. Thankfully Mildred typed up, for her own records, the contents of these letters, as her handwriting is hard to transpose due to the age of the original letters. It also saved an awful amount of time – for that I appreciate her forethought and love of using her small typewriter!

MILITARY STRATEGY AND DETAILS FOR THE BEF, FRENCH ARMY AND GERMAN ARMY

I made the decision not to explain too deeply the military strategies and finer details of the BEF, French army or German army lest it detract from Mildred's story. I have included the general details of troop movements that are relevant to what Mildred experienced at Huiry. Please look at the 'Further Reading' section for books that have detailed military information, troop movements and statistics for the period.

INDEX